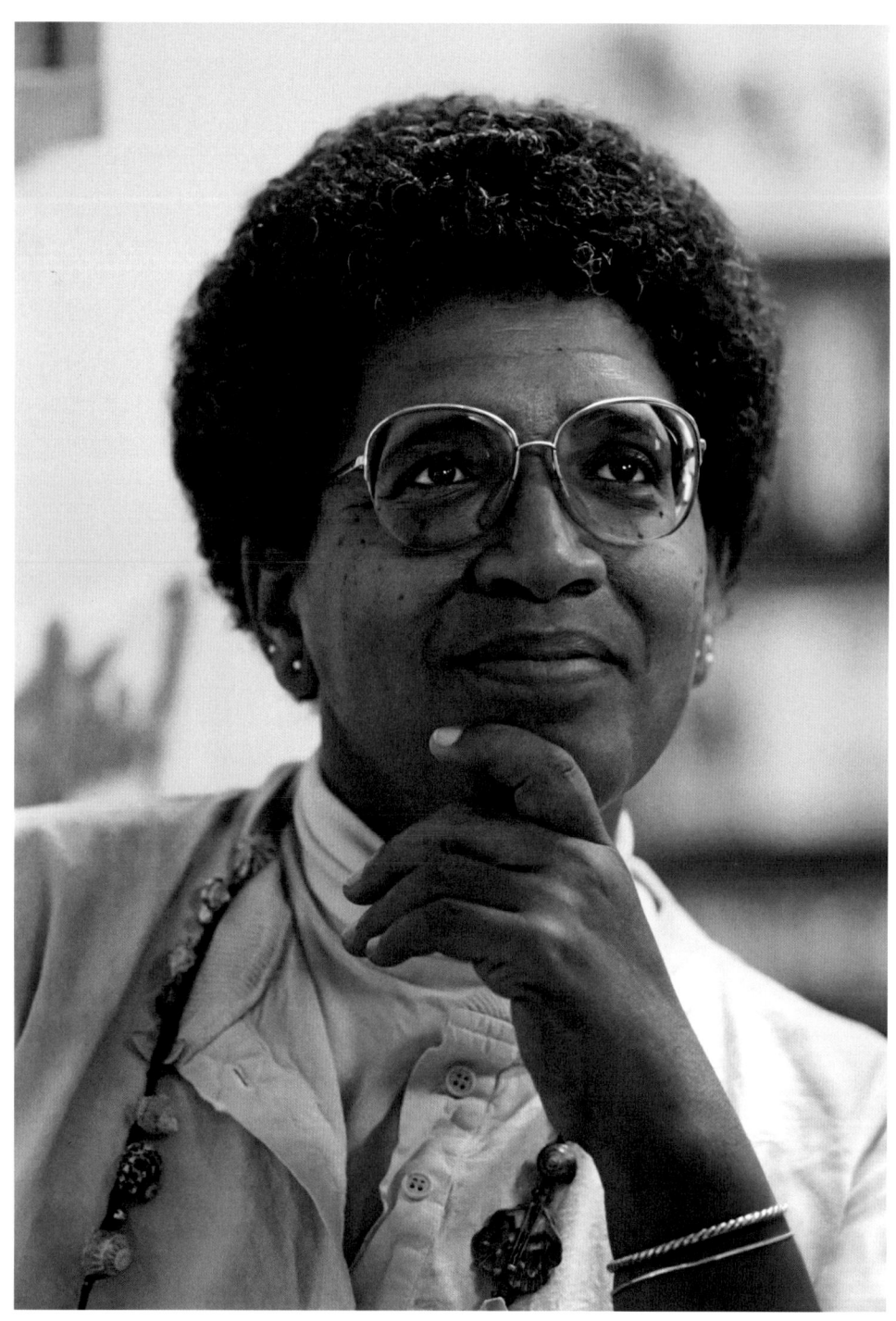

This book is for Audre Lorde who has taught me.

"We fear the visibility without which we cannot truly live. ... And that visibility which makes us most vulnerable is that which is also the source of our greatest strength ...

For us all, it is necessary to teach by living and speaking those truths which we believe and know beyond understanding. Because in this way alone we can survive."

From "The Transformation of Silence into Language and Action" in *Sister Outsider* by Audre Lorde

JEB (Joan E. Biren)
Making A Way: Lesbians Out Front

Originally published in 1987 by Glad Hag Books
This edition published by Anthology Editions, 2025
With thanks to the Sophia Smith Collection of Women's History, Special Collections Department, Smith College

Publication © 2025 Anthology Editions, LLC
Images © 2025 JEB (Joan E. Biren)

Editor: JEB
Editorial Assistants: Mark Iosifescu, Donna Allen, Mavis Simpson-Ernst
First Edition Text Editing: Lauren Taylor
Designer: Martha Ormiston
First Edition Design: Sarna Marcus, Page Designs Unlimited
Design Contributions: Studio Elana Schlenker, Bryan Cipolla
Image Editing: JEB, Maura Murnane
Creative Direction: Jesse Pollock

First Edition

Printed in Singapore on FSC-certified paper
Library of Congress Catalog Card Number: 2024944551
ISBN: 978-1-944860-66-0

anthologyeditions.com
87 Guernsey Street
Brooklyn, NY 11222

Publication of the original edition of this book was made possible through the generosity of many people, including

Evelyn Torton Beck
Simone and Jack Biren
Barbara Bue
Capital City NOW
Patricia Carlton
Robin Ching
Chloe Fessler
Marianne Follingstad
Nanette Gartrell
Dianne Haber
Barbara Herbert
Nancy Rogers Iacullo
Anne M. Kempe

L. Lee Knefelkamp
Barbara R. Lewis
Eleanor Lord
Mary-Helen Mautner
Money for Women Fund
Dee Mosbacher
Nancy Polikoff
Margaret Randall
Sue Sasser
Judith E. Schaeffer
M. Sandra Scurria
Sari Staver
Pam Wax

Also by JEB
Eye To Eye: Portraits Of Lesbians (Anthology Editions)

PHOTOGRAPHS BY JEB
(JOAN E. BIREN)

MAKING A WAY:
LESBIANS OUT FRONT

ESSAYS CONTRIBUTED BY:
MINNIE BRUCE PRATT • CHERYL CLARKE
JD SAMSON

Anthology Editions • New York • 2025

Photographer's Notes

This book is the result of my efforts to document lesbian life in the U.S. during the eight years between the First and Second National Marches on Washington for Lesbian and Gay Rights. These years—the 1980s—were years of increasing repression and then increasing resistance; years in which I held my camera and felt it to be a barometer measuring the pressure against us. When more and more lesbians chose to step in front of my lens, I knew the atmosphere had changed and that we had changed it. I consider each of the lesbians in this book a fighter for our freedom. By courageously choosing to have their photographs and their names in print, these lesbians are definitely out for good, for the good of all of us who need to see ourselves as real people with daily lives and work to do. The women in this book move me because I know how fiercely they have struggled to love themselves in spite of the hatred that surrounds us all. To love each other and ourselves, to allow our love to overcome our fears—I believe that this is the way we begin to change the world. So my heartfelt acknowledgment and thanks go to each lesbian who agreed to be photographed, whether or not her photograph appears here. I would also like to thank the lesbians who are in the book for responding to my invitation to write about themselves. Their statements are collected in the "Speak Out" section, which is toward the end of the book.

During the past year, many energetic women worked to bring *Out of Bounds: A Lesbian Journey*, my multi-image presentation, to their hometowns and their campuses. They made it possible for me to travel around the country making photographs and to pay my rent at the same time. I am indebted to them all; and send extra hugs to Michelle Crone for her special efforts. I would also like to thank all the women who helped me to meet lesbians I otherwise would not have known, so that we could make these photographs together. The money necessary for publishing this book has come, almost exclusively, from within the lesbian community. I appreciate the financial and moral support of all those who contributed.

I discovered the title for *Making A Way: Lesbians Out Front* during a wonderful conversation with Rose Gladney. The women of my home community, especially Nancy Polikoff, have helped in many ways, from giving opinions on the photographs to proofreading. For guiding me through the intricacies of the production process, I am especially grateful to Lauren Taylor on the text, Sarna Marcus on the design, and Karen Bowie on the printing. Barbara Herbert assisted with the computer and Jennifer Murphy with layout and paste-up. For many years, Sherry Thomas of Spinsters/Aunt Lute has offered encouragement and good advice as a friend and as a distributor.

I want to thank my lover Minnie Bruce Pratt and my dear friends Dee Mosbacher and Nanette Gartrell for their sustaining belief in my work, for all they have done materially to help in the publication of this book, and for their love. Dee and Nanette have repeatedly restored my confidence that I really could get this work done. Being with Minnie Bruce has increased my understanding of the creative process and of the importance of all of us being able to live in creative ways. And I'm glad she loves the outrageous queer parts of me. I'm grateful, too, for the beautiful foreword she wrote.

Two final notes: The women whose names appear in the captions to the photographs are identifying themselves as lesbians. Please do not make any assumptions about the sexuality of people who appear in these photographs, but who are not identified by name. Unless otherwise noted, all identifications in the captions are made from left to right. I hope you will enjoy my new book.

JEB (Joan E. Biren)
July, 1987
Washington, D.C.

Notes on the 2025 Edition

I grieve Minnie Bruce's death in 2023 and hold her memory as a blessing. During the 11 years we were lovers, Minnie Bruce and I intentionally shared our relationship through our art in a dynamic collaboration that I treasured. Among other projects, our works from this period included Minnie Bruce's poetry books *We Say We Love Each Other* and *Crime Against Nature*, my slide show about the Seneca Peace Camp, and the first edition of this book. We were building a new culture together with many of the people who are part of *Making A Way: Lesbians Out Front*. I miss all those who have passed on and cried many times as I revisited their images for this new edition. I hope the work honors every person pictured here and helps you to know at least some of what they gave us. Huge radical love and gratitude to my queer family for holding me always.

JEB
August, 2024

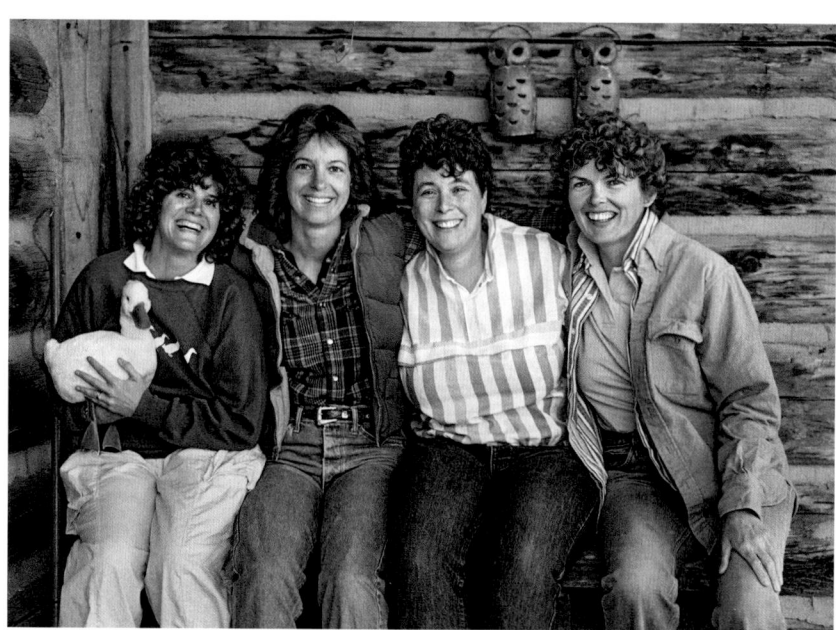

Dee Mosbacher,
Nanette Gartrell, JEB
(Joan E. Biren) and
Minnie Bruce Pratt,
1984.

Foreword

Here we are, the other women and I, in these photographs made by Joan (my lover who you may know as JEB). We are looking at the photographer, the lesbian, who is looking at us, the lesbians; and all of you are looking at us, too.

And we know what it has meant to be looked at, as lesbians, by the world. Most of us, perhaps all of us at some time, have hidden. From names used in an ugly way, and from the real losses that have come with that naming: loss of belief in ourselves; loss of children, family, friends; yes, and the loss of liberty itself as we have been arrested for who we love or how we dress, or have been locked up in mental institutions. We can all name our losses, what we may lose if we are seen.

But we know there is another way of looking, of being looked at, as lesbians. The way we see each other, the way our eyes say "I know you" and the recognition of how we need each other. The power of this to give us joy, to bring us forward toward each other out of isolation; the power of knowing that we see what others do not. The possibility we have of seeing a new kind of beauty, a new way to live. That we see from the edge, and what we know about exclusion, oppression, and loss because of this; and what we know about risk, bravery, imagination, and survival, because we stand and look from the edge.

This book of photographs was made by Joan from that visionary edge, a lesbian perspective. The photographs are of women who are carrying forward what we have learned as lesbians, each in her own way, taking this knowledge into hoped-for, open spaces where no one will have to deny who she is. The women and the pictures take us to a place where we can be ourselves and be proud, be more powerful in order to create a just world. The photographs signify the creation of this space; they reveal, through a visual sequence of moments, what we have made.

We see lesbians at play, and as we invent new ways of having family, community, lovers; we see ourselves healing through spiritual work, through work in health care, through work against violence against women and homophobia. There are pictures of us at our jobs and in the community; of us creating a literature and a communications network that connect and inspire us. We see the physical spaces that we have made, where we can gather openly as lesbians; we see the variety of cultural work that we do, from music and comedy to filmmaking and sound engineering. The book closes with a look at us shaping a politics with lesbian visibility, through national gay and lesbian rights groups, a lesbian presence in electoral politics, and a mass lesbian and gay movement. The pictures reveal a culture that we are making, one that can have room for all our differences, moods, realities; for our complicated daily lives; for the necessity of our particular strengths and of our steadfastness to other women.

When I look at the pictures Joan has made, I think of myself as a girl, and how different my life might have been if I had known, then, one openly lesbian woman. Her life might have suggested to me the possibilities within my life, and her gaze might have asked me to look at myself. But for me this shift in perspective came later, when I met women active in women's liberation. Joan's photographs document that change and expansion during the past decade, out of our confinement as women, beyond our limitation as lesbians to the one or two private places of home or gay bar. The pictures reveal that now we are speaking as ourselves, working for ourselves, in the most public forums, as well as within the most individual circumstances. The photographs disclose the vital work of lesbians as we invent our lives, and the passionate, committed work of lesbians within many political movements, including women's organizations, civil rights groups and organizations by peoples of color, as well as anti-intervention and peace movements.

When I look at these pictures, I remember when I first saw a photograph of myself published with words that explicitly named me as *lesbian*. I had agreed to the appearance of the picture, which Joan had taken, in a gay newspaper. Yet when I unfolded the pages, I felt a shiver of fear. Even after many years of publishing my writing as a lesbian under my own name, I felt afraid at the finality of my face being seen. This book could not have been made if women had not pushed past fear and been willing to claim their lesbian identity, to be seen and named so; but this has been a difficult process for many. Some hesitated over their pictures, not liking how they looked; how many years we have had of the critical eye that saw us as ugly women, that also feared to see the lesbian in us. Some, wanting to be photographed, in the end refused because of losses they feared, perhaps a lover who did not want the connection to so known a lesbian, perhaps a job. Some women, eager to affirm lesbian existence, were photographed, but had to withdraw their pictures, painfully, because suddenly loss threatened, the danger of their children being taken, other dangers. Nevertheless, many of us are here, beautiful and various in the light of these photographs, convinced of the importance of seeing each other, knowing that to claim our selves openly and fully is to lay claim to survival and to joy.

I think of the first photograph of lesbians I ever saw: two women in bed together under rumpled covers, on a poster that said *Sisterhood Is Powerful*. The photograph mirrored the lives of lesbians I'd begun to meet; it made me see lesbian existence as a reality that stretched beyond the small town we lived in; it offered me a possibility of daily life and love.

Now, over ten years later, looking at Joan's pictures, I am challenged again to see lesbian lives, to admit the reality that we have made. When, for instance, I see her picture of Jean in the classroom, so passionately teaching, I see more of what it means for me to be out as a lesbian when I teach or speak. I reconnect to my life; I see the solidity of what we do beyond, but connected to, the intimacies of our individual lives. I have looked at the photographs many times, trying to look carefully, not with the eye of a tv watcher, a shopper, a consumer; not with the eye that averts from the queer, the different; but with an eye that gives a full gaze, an eye that sees the profundity of our struggles, the beauty, usefulness, inventiveness of our lives. The pictures are a moment in each woman's life; the possibility of connection is there if we look.

Through mainstream media many images have been burned into our retinas, images of death, war, violence against women, images that float behind our closed eyes if we ask, "What photographs do I recall? Which do I remember?" But the images in Joan's book urge us to life, to live toward the future, toward each other. In your looking I hope you will watch for the image that imprints powerfully upon your eye, an image that you can use to summon hidden strength, a reminder of yourself. These pictures urge us to see our selves, our fire of life, to imagine and create a future where we see each other, distinctly, in all our differences, and honor each other there.

Minnie Bruce Pratt
1987

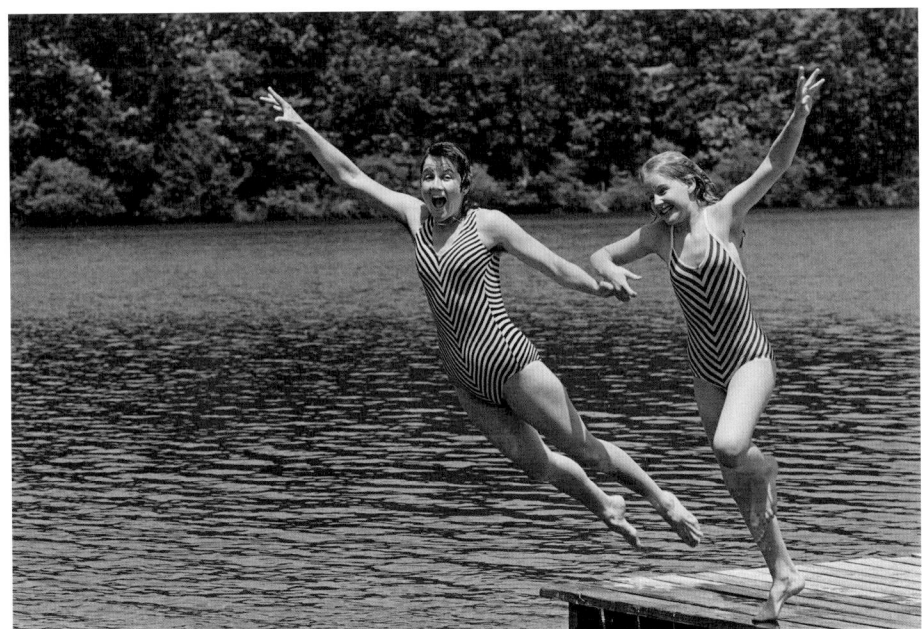

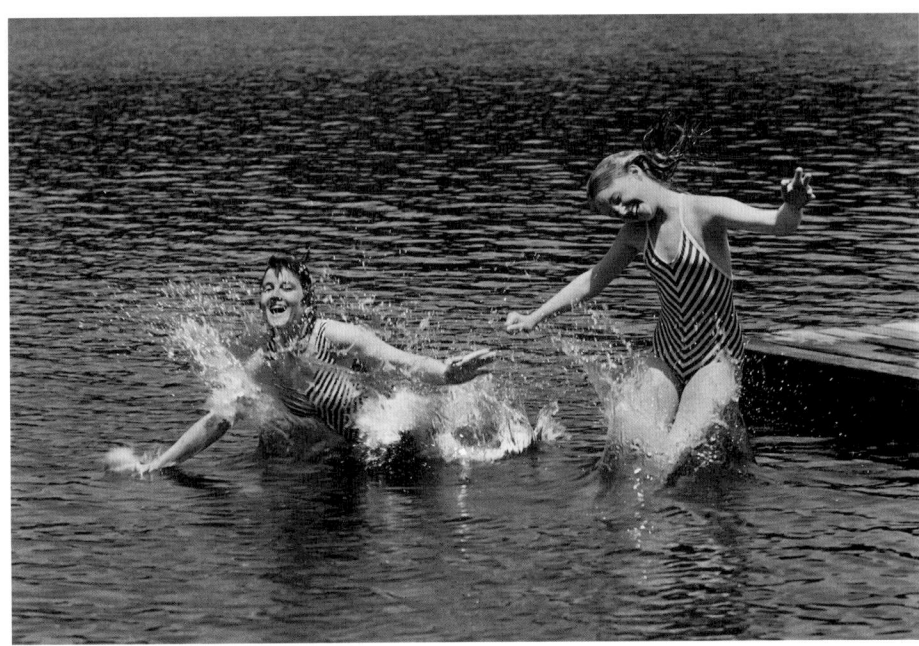

Sarah Thorson and her daughter Song jump up and splash down into the lake at Indian Springs, Georgia, at Womonwrites, an annual conference of lesbian writers. 1983.

Looking/Seeing from the Edge

> When more and more lesbians chose to step in front of my lens, I knew the atmosphere had changed and that we had changed it. (JEB, Photographer's Notes, 1987)

The moniker "JEB" taunts the masculine. And we can just as well hear "Joanie" in the teasing sound of the literal/legal name, Joan *E.* Biren. She takes very good pictures–of women, of women who are lesbians. In her Foreword to the original *Making A Way: Lesbians Out Front* in 1987, Minnie Bruce Pratt lays before us ways of "looking" and "seeing." The photographer must do both, and JEB does. Minnie Bruce reminds us what the *looking* and *seeing* mean to lesbians who must still be careful–even in 2024–of how we present ourselves to those who *look* at and *see* us–even friends.

Reading the Photographer's Notes, the Foreword, and leafing through the rest of this 37-year-old classic photographic work summons an intentional hypnosis–purposely calling up memories of early lesbian communities. I hear the lineation, the metric knowledge, and the literariness of Minnie Bruce's tribute. We are *looking at/seeing* these images from what Minnie Bruce calls JEB's "visionary edge," abutting the righteous imaginary. I go back with them–JEB and Minnie Bruce and *Making A Way*.

JEB's photograph of Audre Lorde, in large spectacles, beguiling smile, forefinger grazing chin, greets my gaze. "This book is for Audre Lorde who has taught me," says JEB's dedication. She taught all our generation (and beyond). We come to understand how much of a feminist project *Making A Way* was as we read the names listed in JEB's acknowledgment: "The money necessary for publishing this book has come almost exclusively from within the lesbian community." *Making A Way* is evidence of how lesbians "make a way"–out of "no way," as Black people say.

There are 112 pages with 108 photographs *leafing* through our consciousness. Who saw the photographs? And what did they say and think? I know what some of the audience thought, because I was *in* some of the audience and said, out loud, "Right On," which I declare every day for lesbians.

> *I am a black lesbian and loving it.* (Lynn Walker, Speak Out #4)

Most of JEB's images reveal white women in the U.S. There is more reticence among women of color about "coming out" as a lesbian or queer. But JEB's lens has emboldened women of color and she has coaxed more of us in front of her camera in *Making A Way* than she did in her first book, *Eye to Eye*. Had *Making A Way* been produced this year, I daresay, there would be much more difference before JEB's lens.

The women in this book range in age from twenty-four (Brenda Crumley, #90) to seventy-five (May Sarton, #52). I was thirty-six when I stepped in front of JEB's camera (#56), wearing a tie and minding the Kitchen Table Women of Color Press book table at the 1983 National Women's Studies Association Conference; on the next page is thirty-four-year-old Elana Dykewomon, (#57), also wearing a tie, tonguing and taunting the seer.

JEB made a way for lesbians but made a way for non-lesbian and non-gay people to view lesbians as women (surprise), as workers, as teachers, as tradeswomen, as reproductive rights and anti-violence and rape crisis organizers, as lesbian rights advocates, as elected officials, as journalists, as multi-faceted/talented people and communities. Most of the women photographed have nine-to-five jobs and do activist work in addition in all the aforementioned categories of endeavor. I remember all of it. Lesbians work hard, and JEB worked hard to show that in her photos of us.

JEB's photographs, beginning in 1979 with *Eye to Eye: Portraits of Lesbians*, have connected and inspired lesbians. *Eye to Eye* sits within a catalogue of 1970s watershed works of lesbian feminism, e.g., *Gynecology, Conditions: Five* (The Black Women's Issue), *Lesbian Woman, Movement in Black, Rubyfruit Jungle, Our Right to Love, Loving Her*, that *made a way* for *Making A Way* and enabled and mentored late twentieth century lesbian feminist culture—and our steadfastness to women.

JEB arouses seeing from her visionary edge. And as lesbians, queer women, trans people, and all the rest of us who claim the LGBTQ sobriquet, let's fly to the edge and shake the center up and out. And let's call "LESBIAN!" out loud and be "out front"—doing our work along with the rest of the feminist, progressive, and radical/revolutionary world.

> *I resist the idea that sexuality is private—after all, heterosexuality isn't the least bit private.* (Nancy Polikoff, Speak Out #13–14)

This time in revisiting *Making A Way*, I realize, from the captions and the subjects' biographical narratives in the brilliant Speak Out section, how much work lesbians have done to free us from heterosexual, patriarchal customs and systems: marriage, the family, motherhood, domestic violence, sexist employment practices, sexual harassment in the workplace, to name a few. Still, there are plenty more heterosexual conventions that keep women oppressed.

Yet, this is what draws me into these images in 2024: the lives that lesbians were living and the places and spaces we took up—with ordinary and valorous acts—out, in the street, and in front of JEB's lens: Kim Samsel and Robin Ching conversing in ASL (#3); Kris Kleindienst sprinting (#6); Hortense Conner being a Black lesbian grandmother (#15); Mona Bachmann patching a roof (#16); Michelle Parkerson being arrested at an anti-Apartheid demonstration (#83); Toni White [now Maya White Sparks] (#19) and lynda lou ease, beckie lee and Sandra Lambert (#20) enjoying our nudity; Rabbi Linda Holtzman conducting temple services (#22); Kathryn L. Edwards in a lab (#24); Eleanor N. Soto counseling survivors of domestic violence (#32); Shannon Morse on a forklift (#42); Patte Martin at her abortion clinic confronting an anti-abortion picketer (#25); Joyce Hunter counseling lesbian and gay youth (#36): the joyous photo of Del Martin and Phyllis Lyon (#12), founders in 1955 of Daughters of Bilitis—and most of all, bearing out JEB's claim that lesbians changed the atmosphere of invisibility to one of *look at/see* us as lesbians doing our work.

I think it is important for us to keep our history alive and that we celebrate our lesbian identity—for those of us who know, for those who want to know, and for those who need to know. (Kimberly Samsel, Speak Out #3)

Making A Way marks the days before the ascendancy of same-sex marriage—that time when lesbian, gay, bisexual people thought we were making a way from heterosexuality and marriage. The more deeply middle-class we become, the more we demand the protections we think straight conventions give us—the protections *and* the freedoms. Yet, we have even given *tired* marriage some flair.

My lesbianism is fundamental to my work and vision as an agent of change. (Billie Potts, Speak Out #23)

JEB's visionary edge confronts me with the somber expressiveness of Adrienne Rich (#53); the empathic eyes of Elvira Williams (#33); Audre Lorde in-office reviewing the final draft of *Zami: A New Spelling of My Name* (#50); the storied Stormé DeLarverié bouncing at the Cubby Hole in Manhattan's West Village (#81); twenty-five-year-old Wisconsin *out* lesbian Supervisor Tammy S. G. Baldwin (with a totally different 'do than the one she now sports) smiling broadly with *out* sister elected officials Kathleen Nichols and Karen Clark (#99); in rain and in raincoat indomitable organizer, Leslie Cagan (#94), leading a protest on the U.S. Capitol, which included Jesse Jackson, Eleanor Smeal, Ed Asner; dark, dapper, and lesbian-proud Colevia Carter, D.C. Human Rights Commissioner and AIDS educator (#38); artist Claire Olivia Moed and archivist Joan Nestle (#62) kissing in front of 1500 women at the tenth anniversary Lesbian Herstory Archives benefit in 1986—oh, so hot; the insistently compassionate face of Eleanor N. Soto (#32), domestic violence counselor, on the phone with her client; and Casselberry and Dupreé moving fast in sound and song in front of the dancing lens (#80). These are some of my favorite takes, if I may be so bold as to impose my views upon you, dear reader, *seer, looker.*

Is lesbianism yet a *way*, a very cogent *way*, to lead a self-determining woman's life, if a woman wants to live it? I know all my straight girlfriends will say, "I don't have to call myself a lesbian to be 'self-determining.'" I will say, why not? You call yourself Democrat, Republican, Independent, Feminist, Progressive, Radical, Socialist, Communist. Why not Lesbian?

Making A Way remains a radical celebration and confirmation—*out front*—of lesbians in all our astuteness, romanticism, grace, and waywardness. Then (1987) and now (2024), the lesbians photographed in *Making A Way* show us a way out of convention and stasis, if we want to take it. Heterosexuals are invited.

Cheryl Clarke
2024

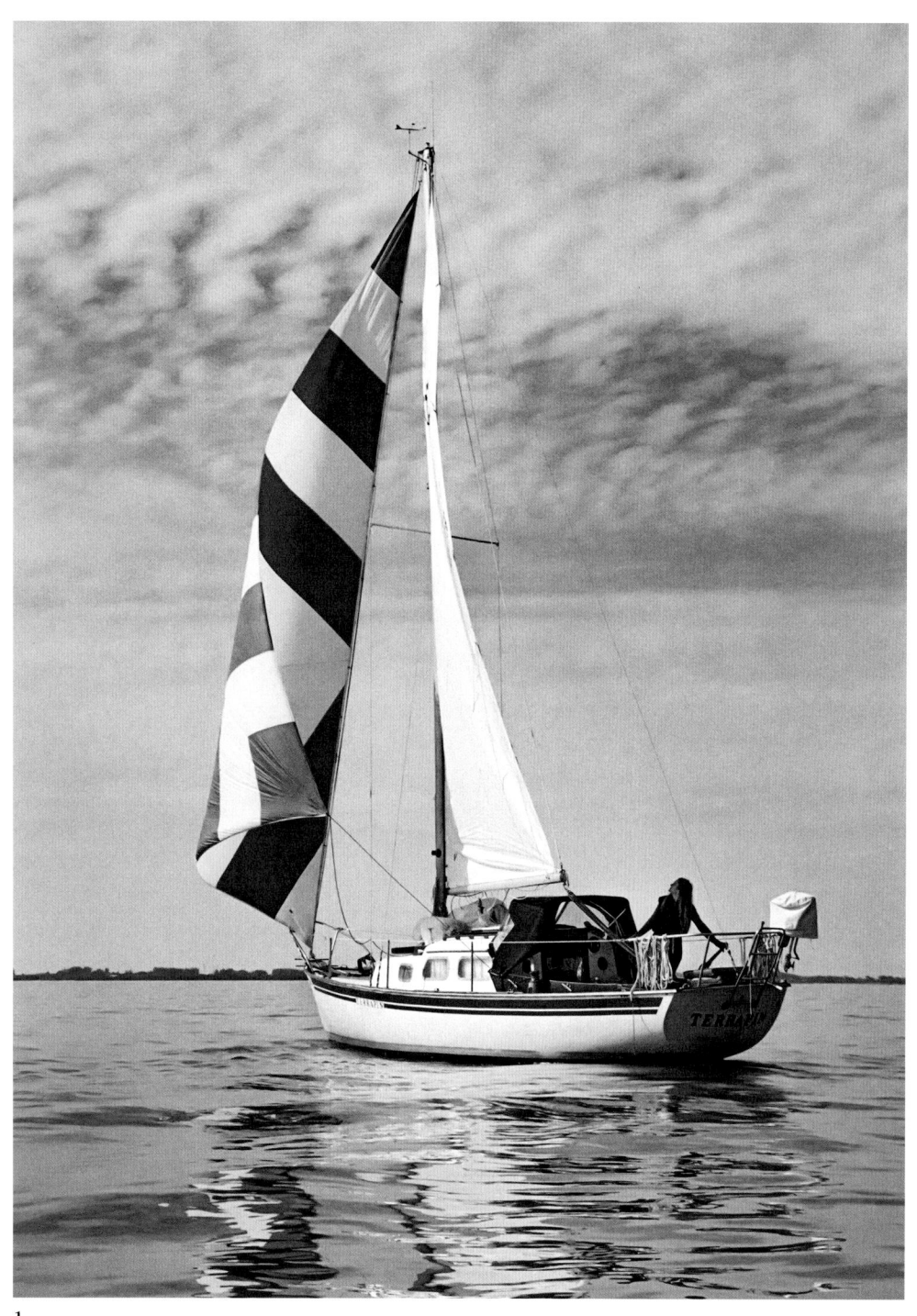

1

1. Captain Lynda Suzanne of
Whelk Women watches the sails as
she prepares to "come about" on
the Gulf of Mexico. Lynda is taking
a day off from her charter sailing
business to enjoy a solo sail in her
sloop *Terrapin*. Charlotte Harbor,
Florida, 1987.

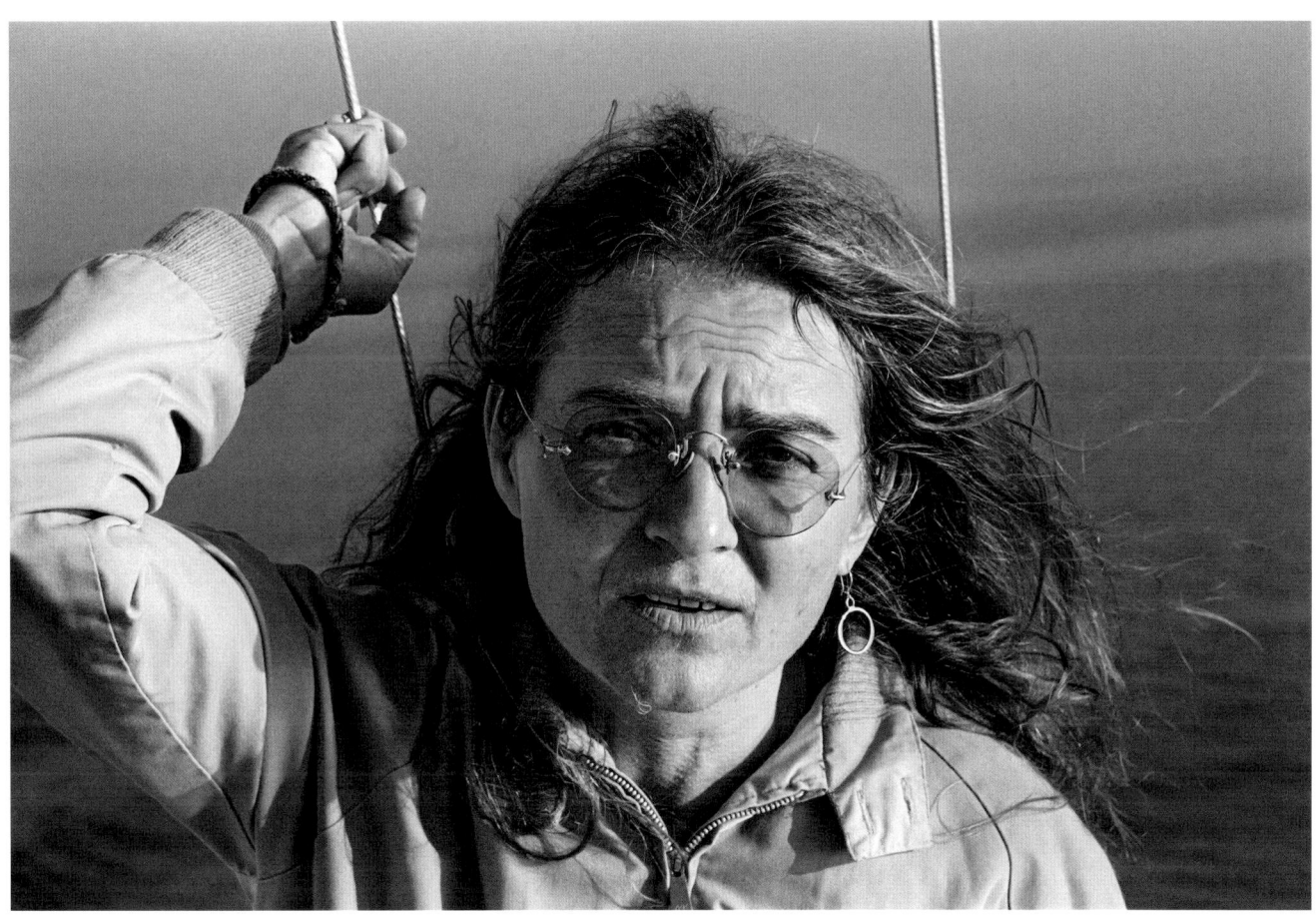

2

2. Lynda sails women among
dolphins to islands where wild
orchids bloom, and bald eagles
and sea turtles nest. Boca Grande,
Florida, 1987.

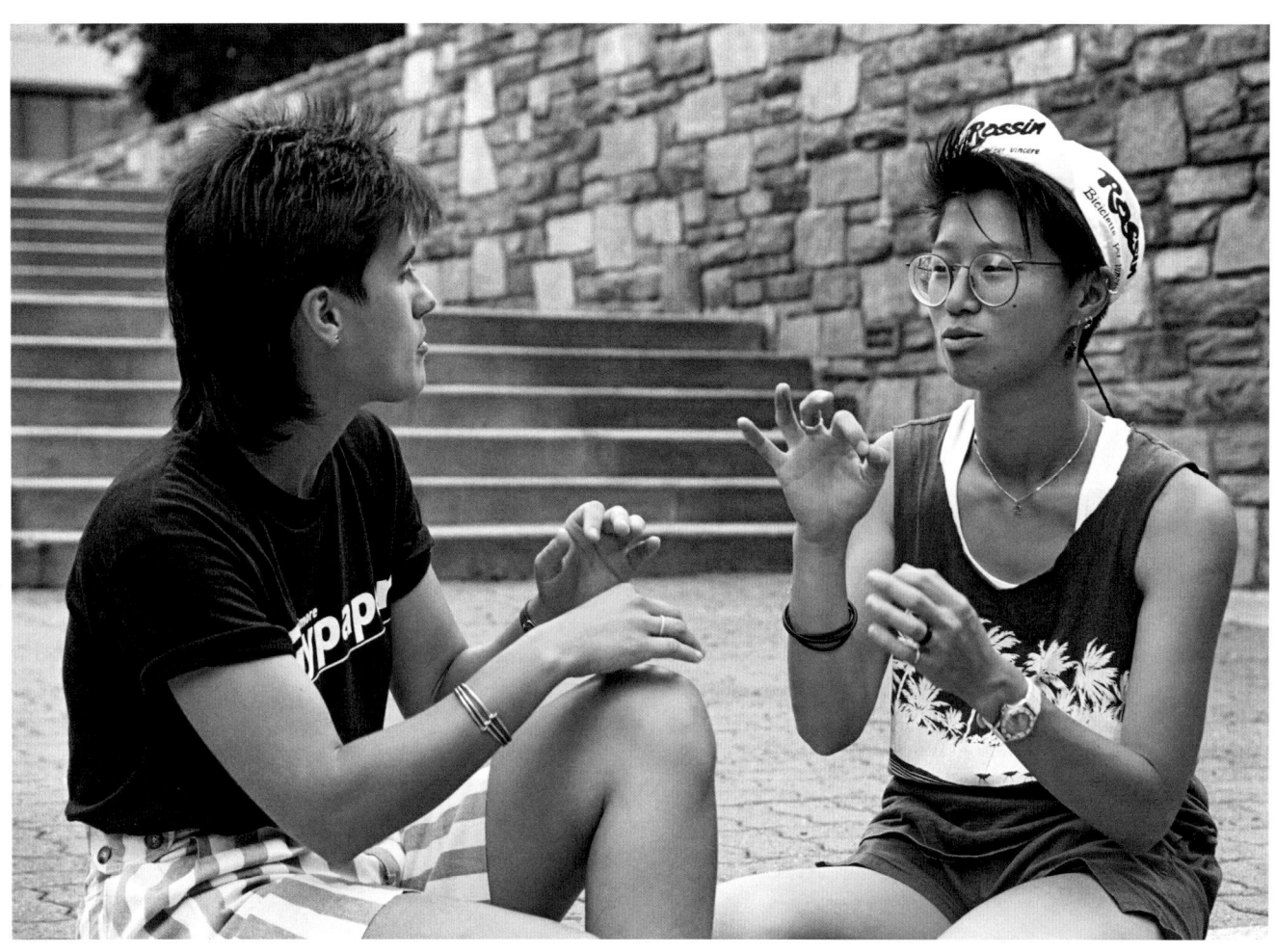

3

3. Friends Kim Samsel and Robin
Ching get together for conversation
in American Sign Language.
Baltimore, Maryland, 1987.

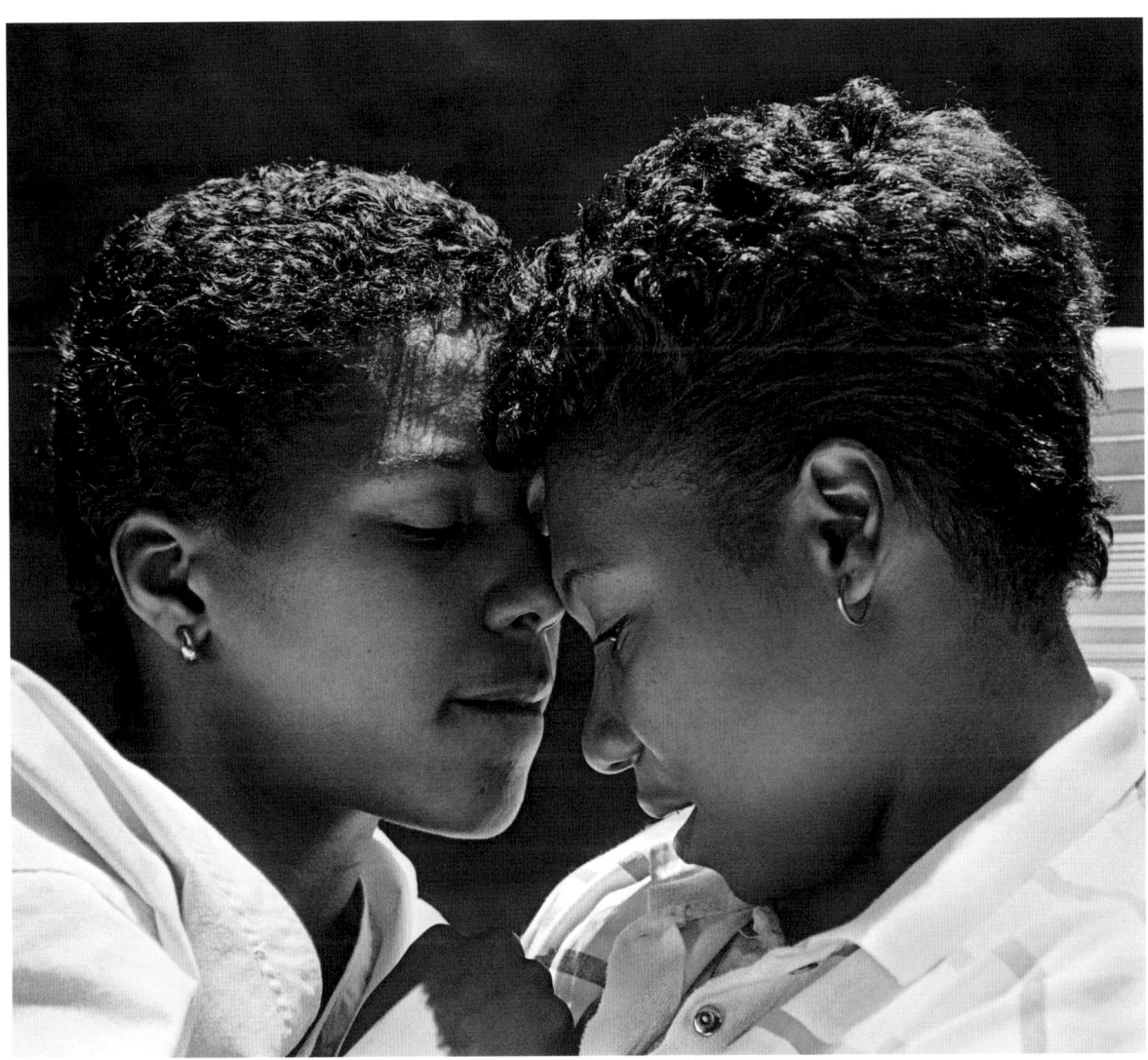

4

4. Archene Turner and Lynn Walker
share a sweet moment in the
backyard of their home in Atlanta,
Georgia, 1987.

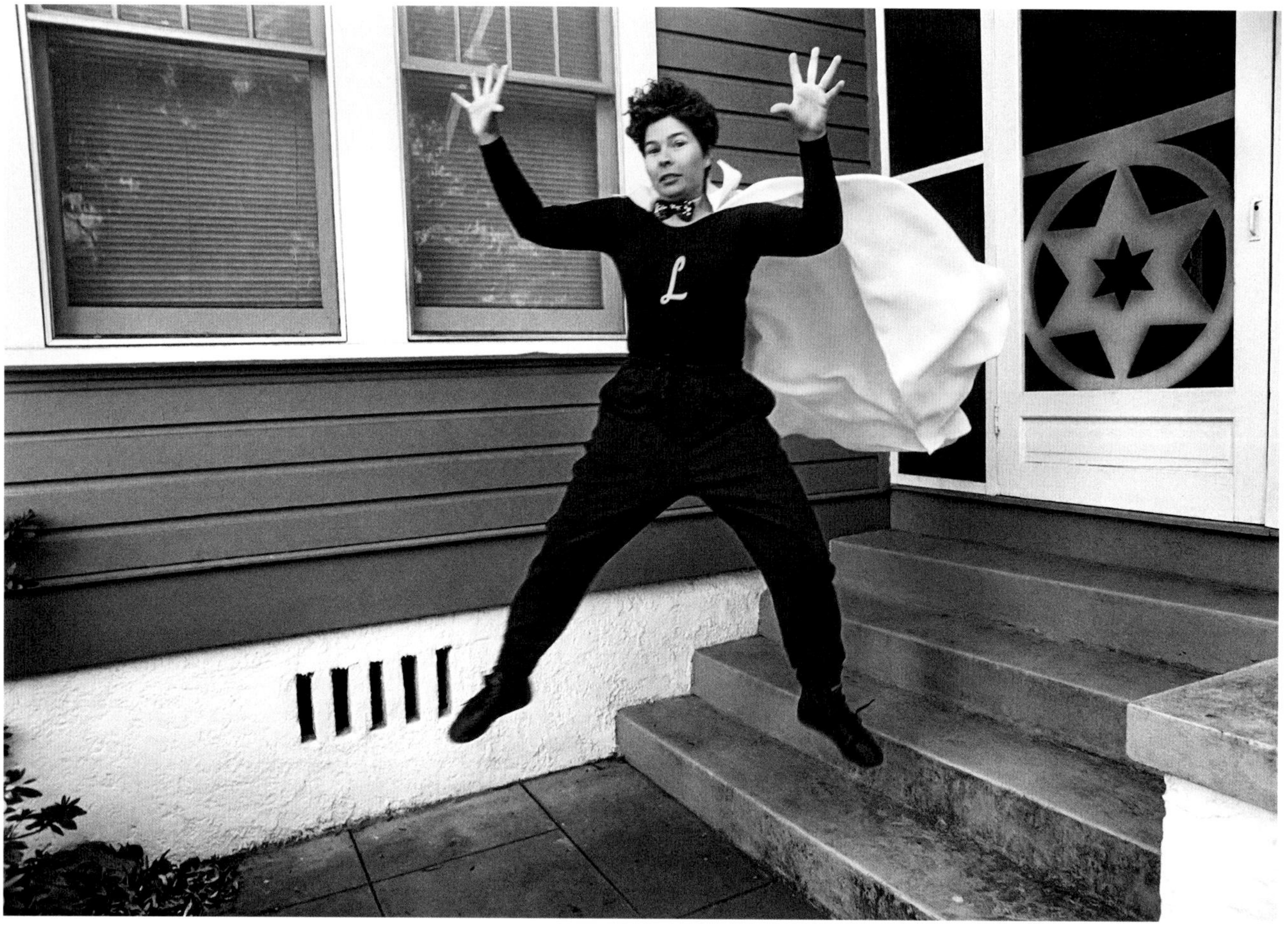

5

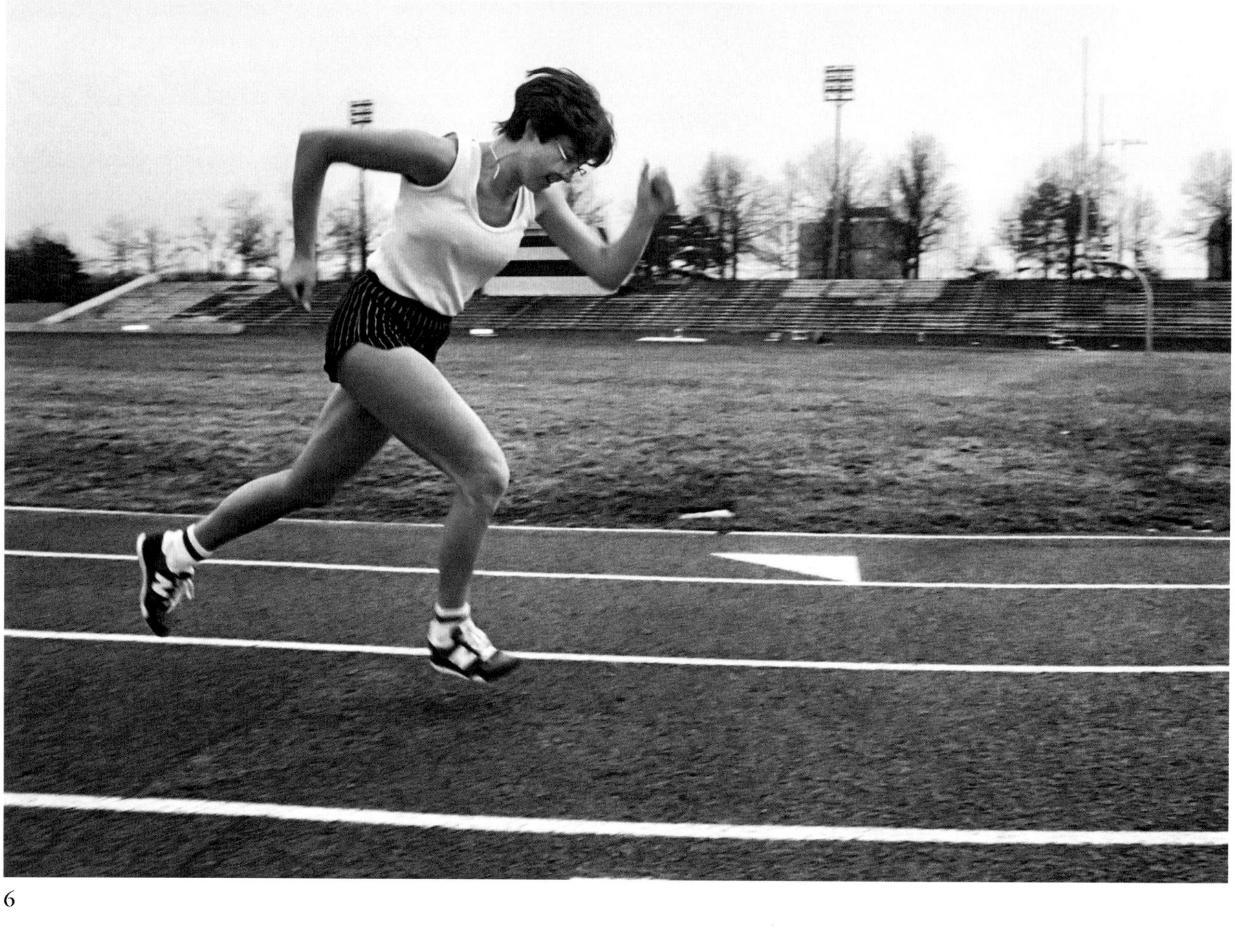

6

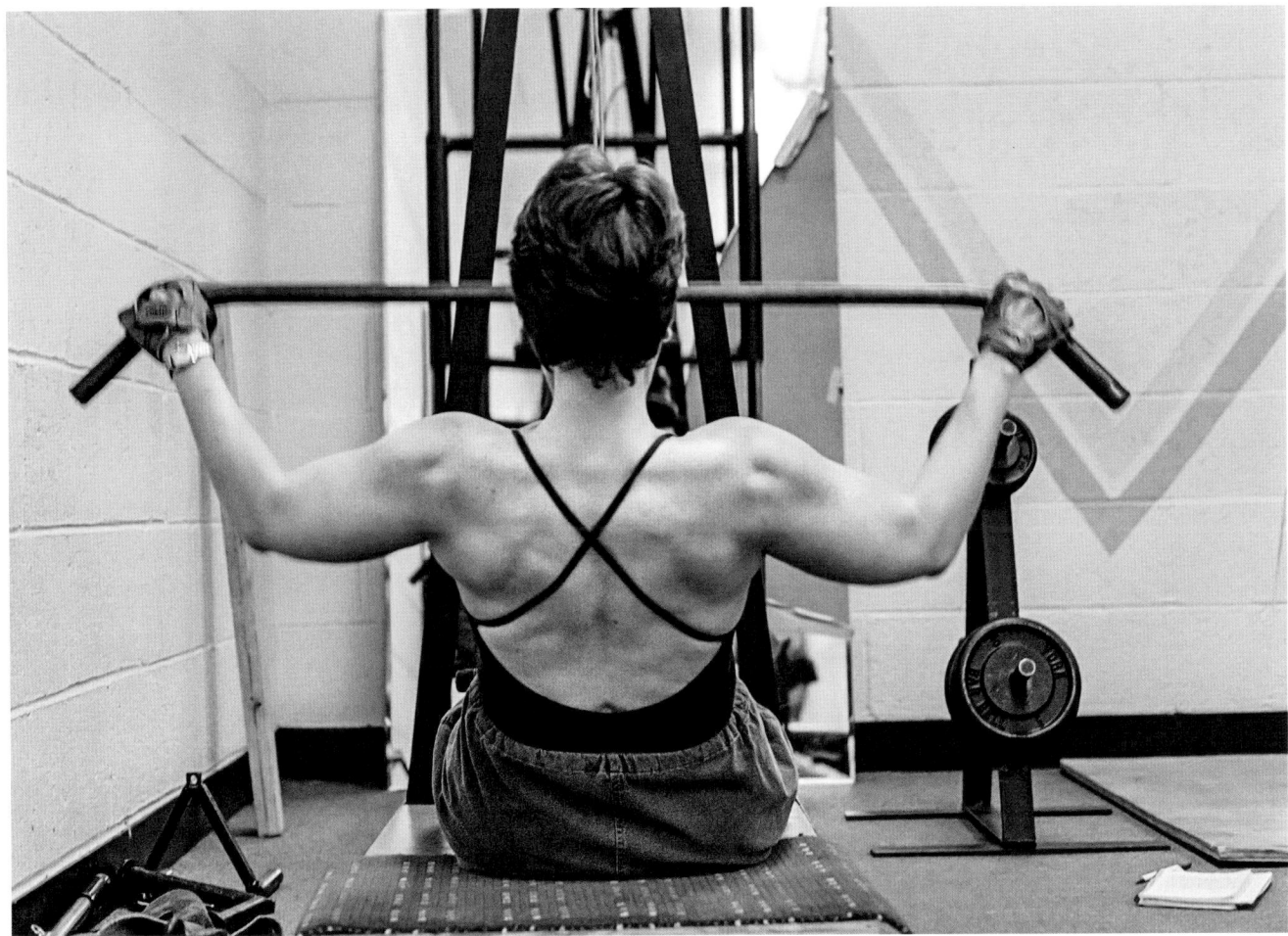

7

5. Faith Stayer, dressed for Halloween, leaps into the unknown. Tuscaloosa, Alabama, 1986.

6. Sprinter Kris Kleindienst, who won two silver medals at the Gay Games II in 1986, trains in her hometown of St. Louis, Missouri, 1987.

7. Jamie Hecker does the pull down at the Women's Fitness Center, the only women's gym in Cleveland, which opened in 1982 in the Women's Building Project. Ohio, 1986.

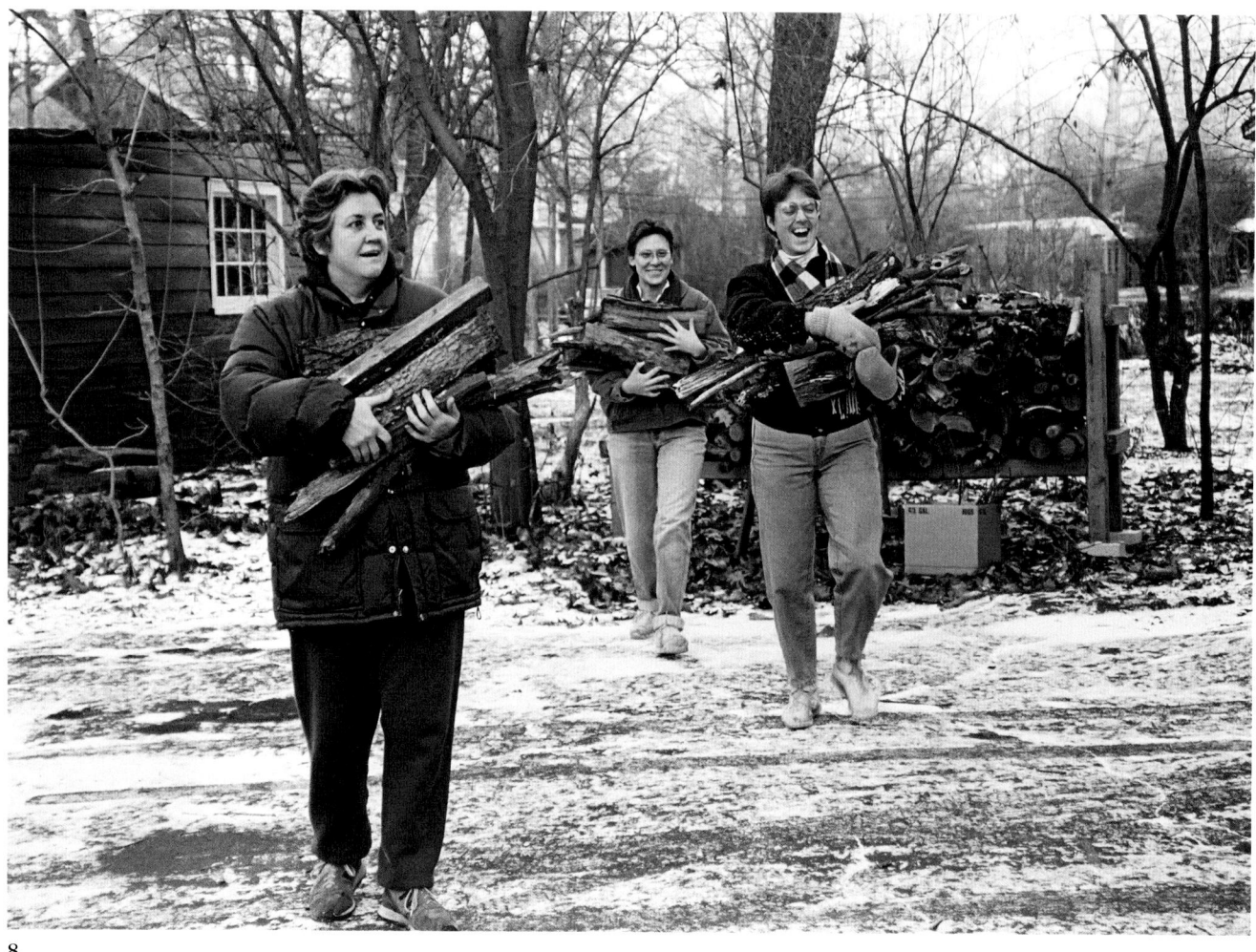

8

8. Hag House Collective members Sally Tatnall, Phyllis Balcerzak, and Jamie Hecker prepare for the sixth feminist winter celebration the household has created for women in their community. Collective member Debra Hirshberg is not pictured. Cleveland Heights, Ohio, 1986.

9. Lana Wall and Judith Carr share the snuggle of women who have loved each other a long time. Logan, Ohio, 1986.

10. Judith, Chris DeLamatre, and Lana live in a committed, open relationship. Floating on the pond in the middle of 46 acres of jointly-owned land is one of their favorite ways to spend time together. Logan, Ohio, 1986.

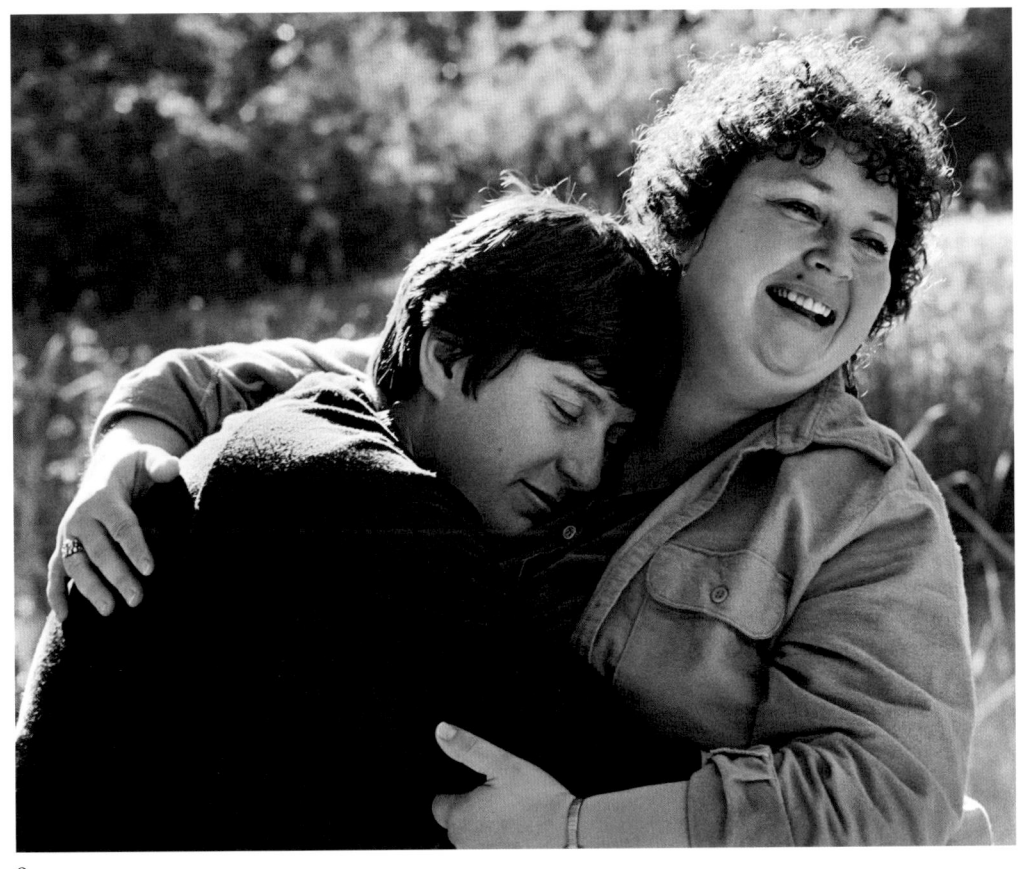

9

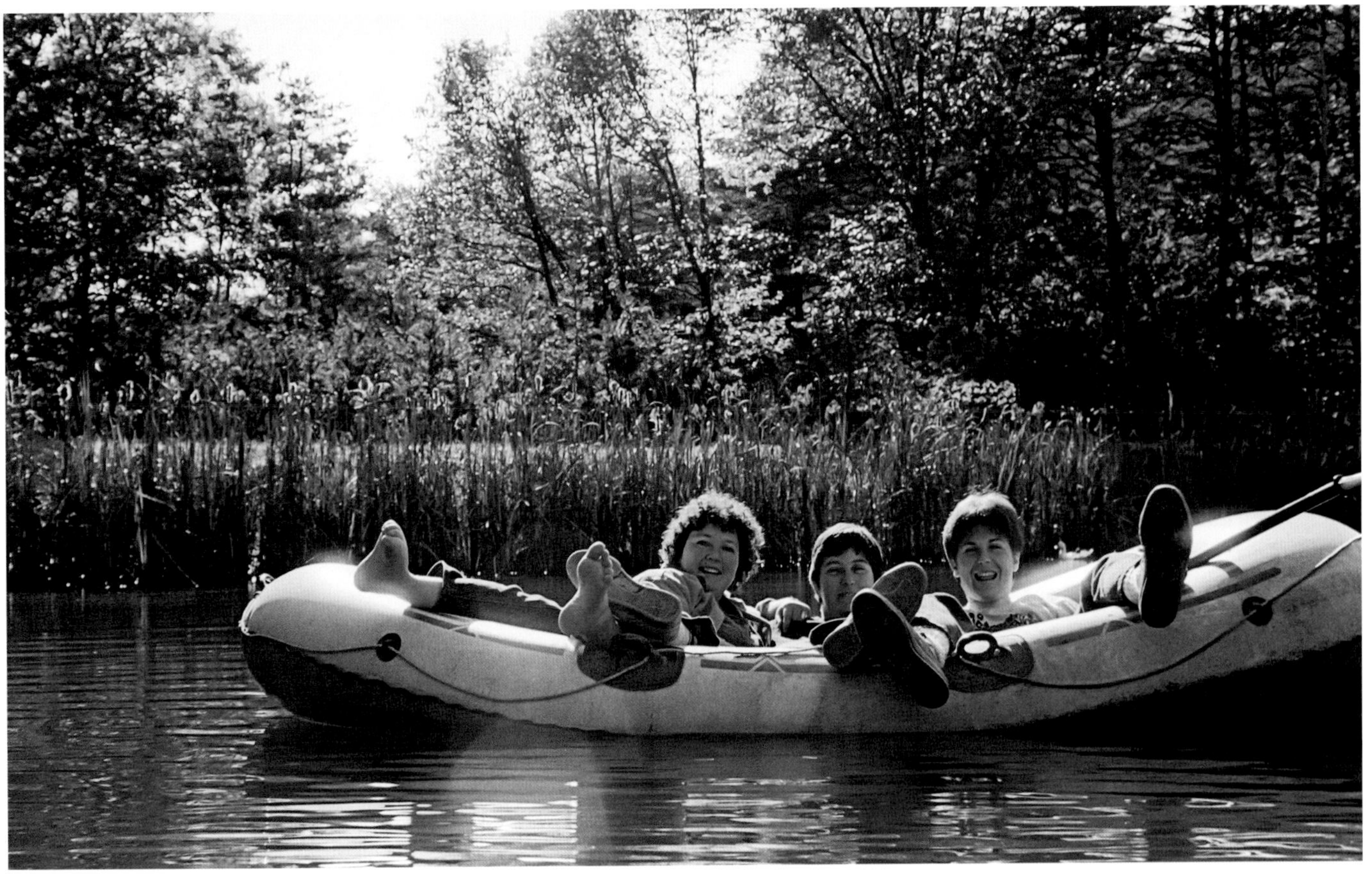

10

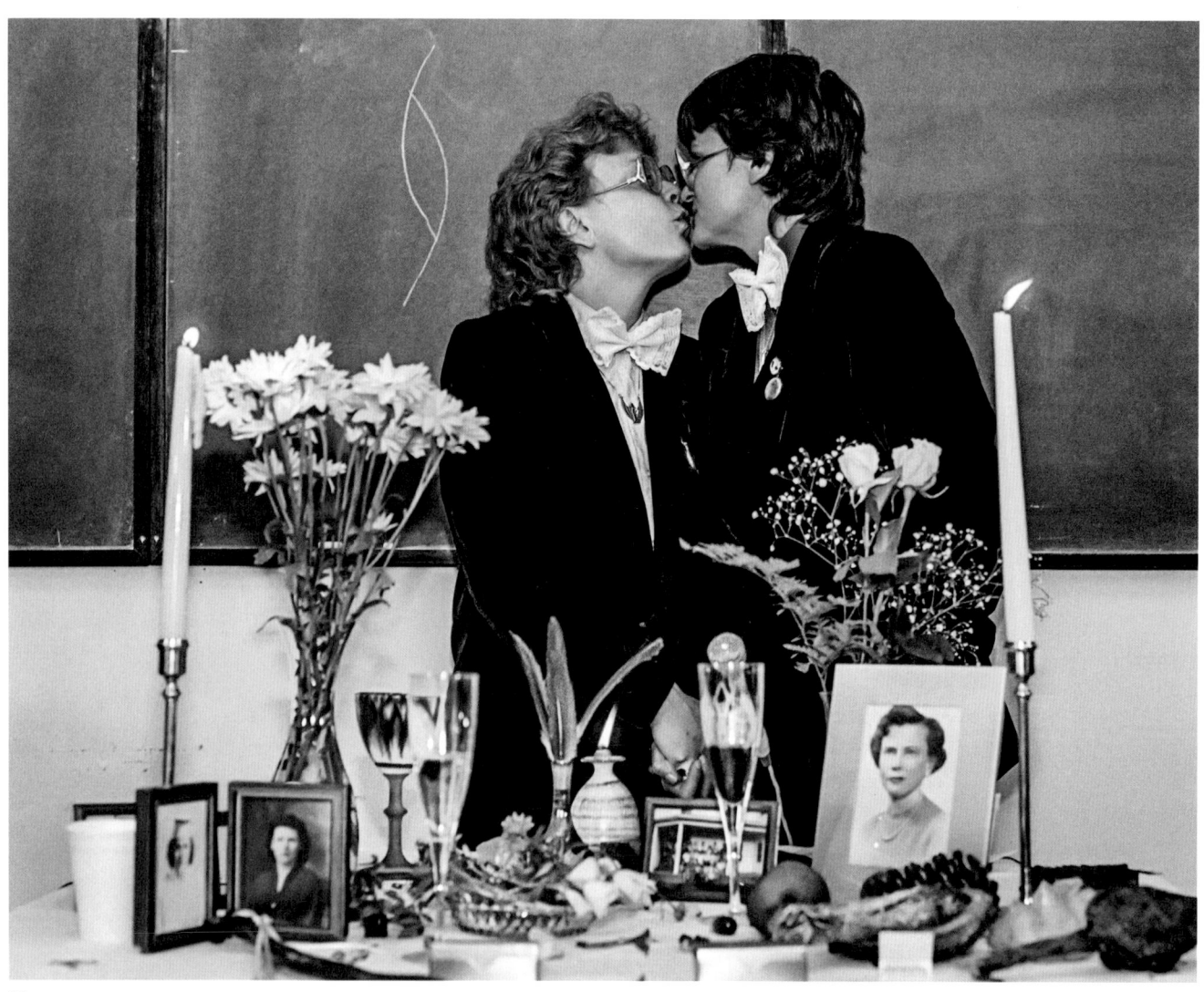

11

11. Cindy Miller and Bernadette Ryan seal their wedding vows at The Women's Group in Houston, Texas. On the table are photographs and other representations of family and friends who were unable to attend the wedding. 1987.

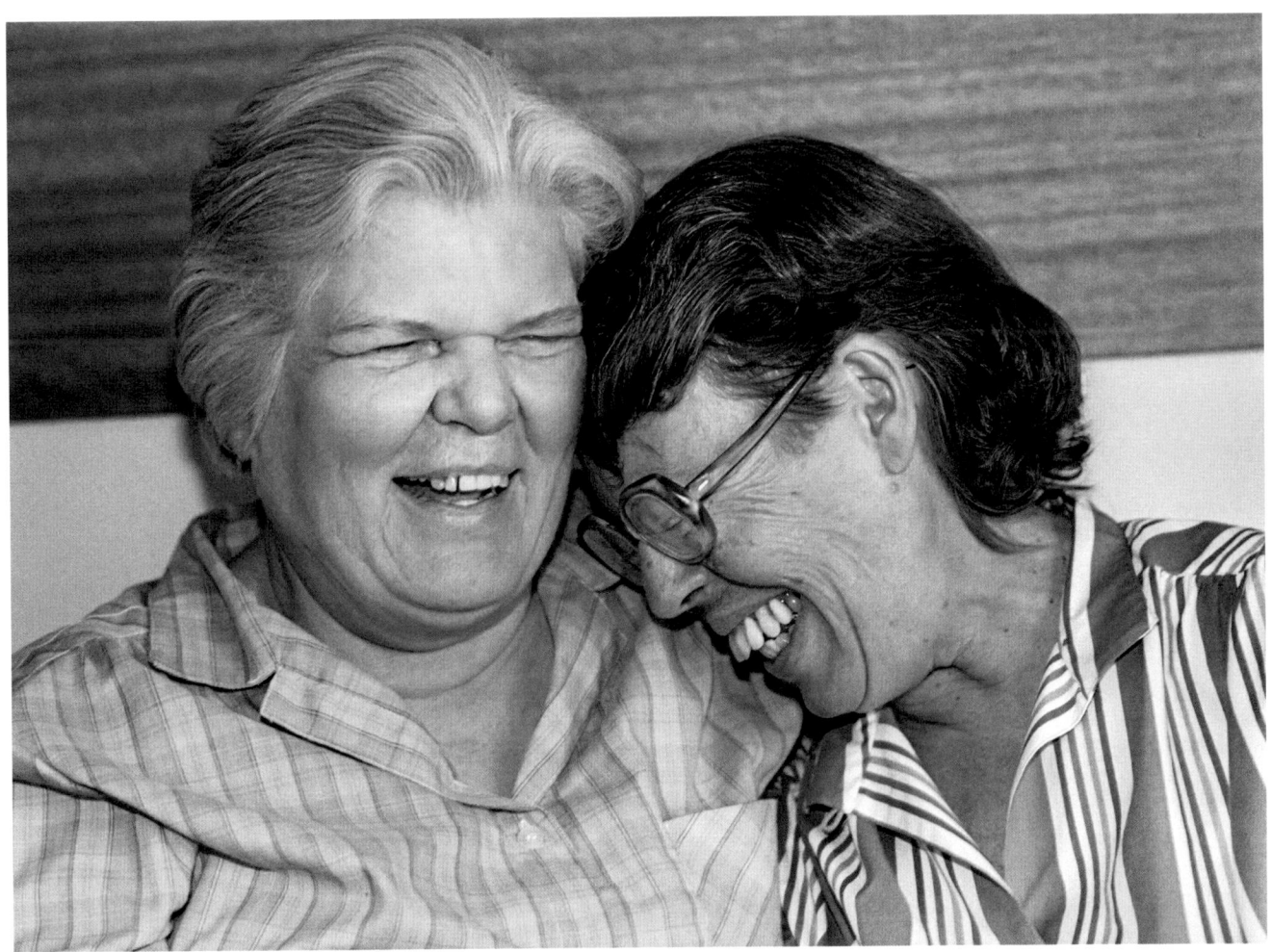

12

12. Del Martin and Phyllis Lyon
have been domestic partners since
Valentine's Day, 1953. In 1955,
they co-founded the Daughters of
Bilitis (DOB), the oldest lesbian
organization in the U.S. Here at
Habromania House (habromania:
having delusions of a pleasing
nature), their San Francisco home,
Del and Phyllis pause in the midst
of their many movement activities.
1984.

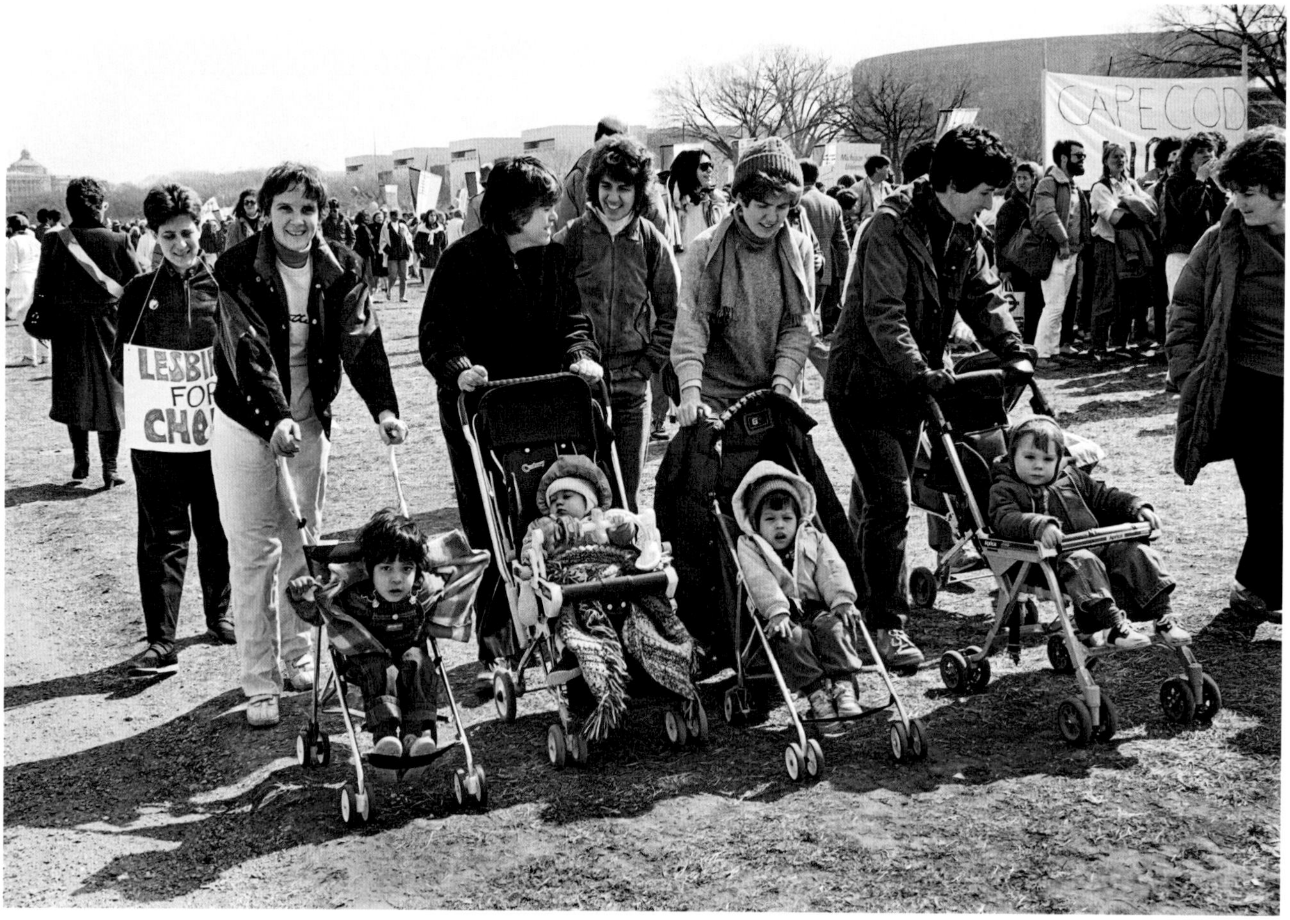

13

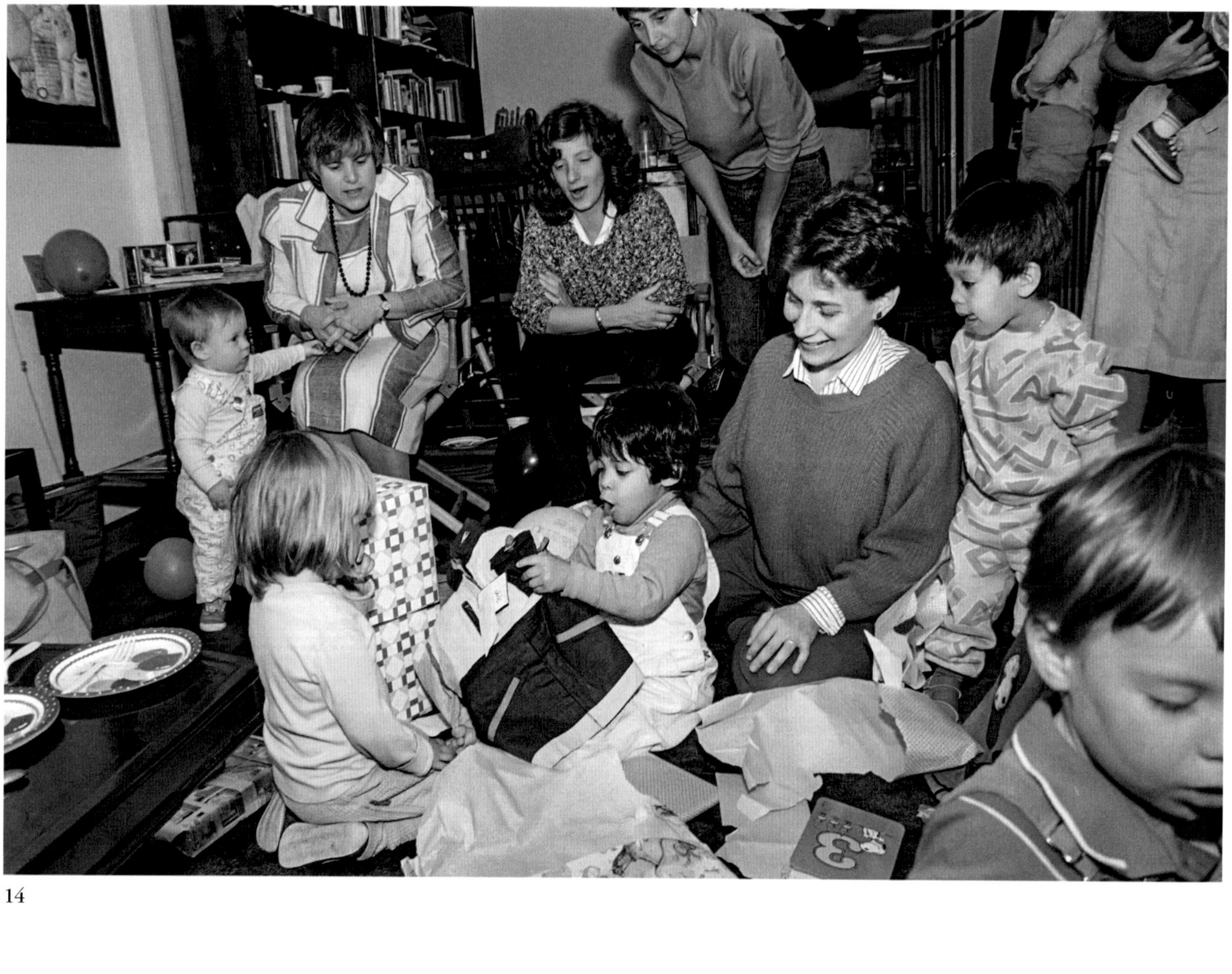

14

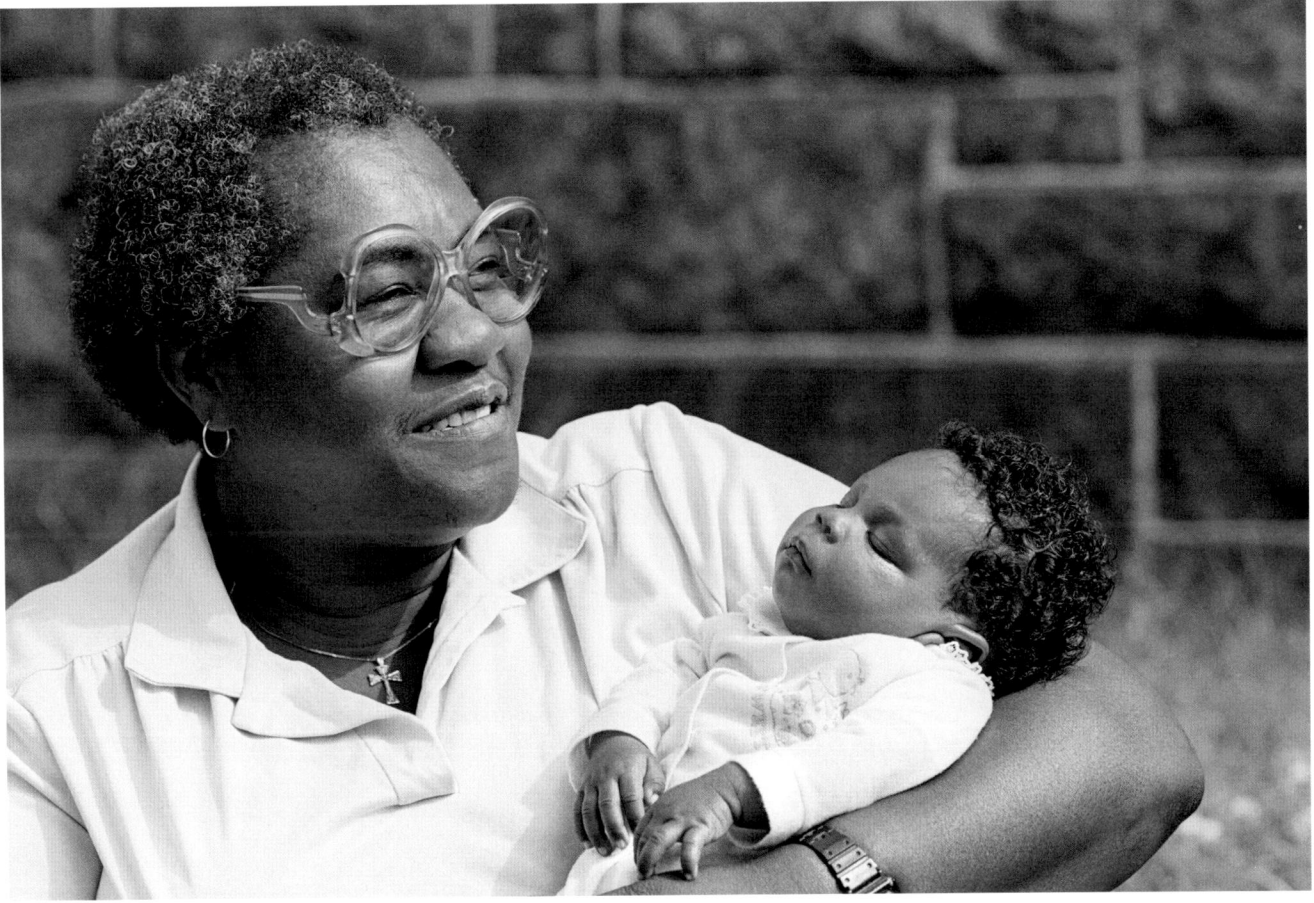

15

13. A Washington, D.C. mothers' group baby brigade strolls out at the pro-choice March for Women's Lives on March 9, 1986. Children Elena (Lainey) Herbert Polikoff, Anne (Addie) Miriam Leader-Zavos, Jordan Raphael Rolnick-Melechen, and Michael Noonan (front row) are backed up by some of their mothers: Nancy Polikoff, Barbara Herbert, Michele Zavos, Libby Leader, Wendy Melechen, and Eileen Harrington.

14. Lainey opens a present at her birthday party with (clockwise) Addie, Michele, Doris Indyke, a friend, Nancy, Jordan, and (foreground) Michael all taking part in the celebration. The Washington, D.C. mothers' group is five years old and now includes ten adults with seven children. 1986.

15. Hortense Conner is as proud as she can be of her six-week-old granddaughter Tyisha. Baltimore, Maryland, 1987.

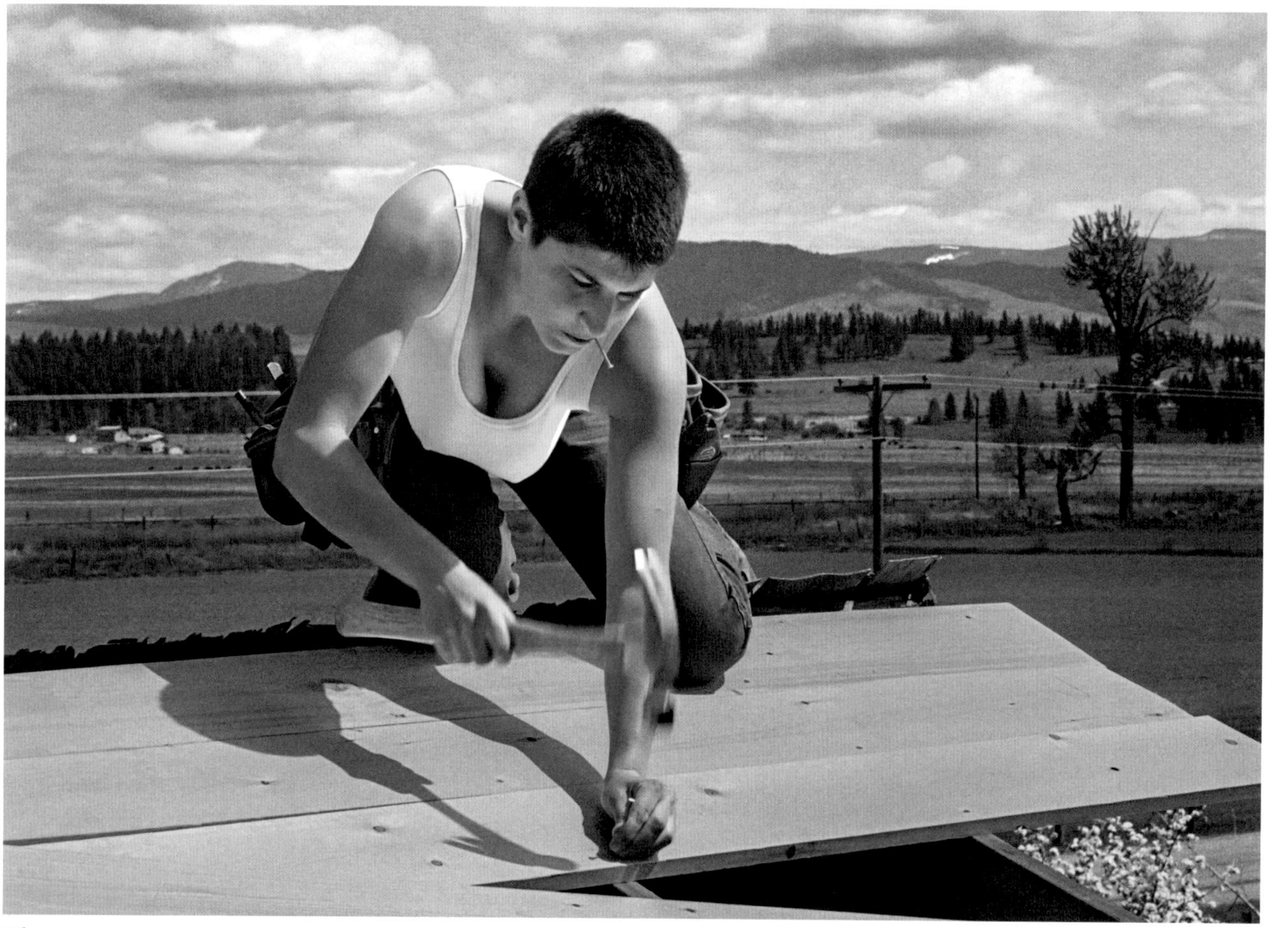

16

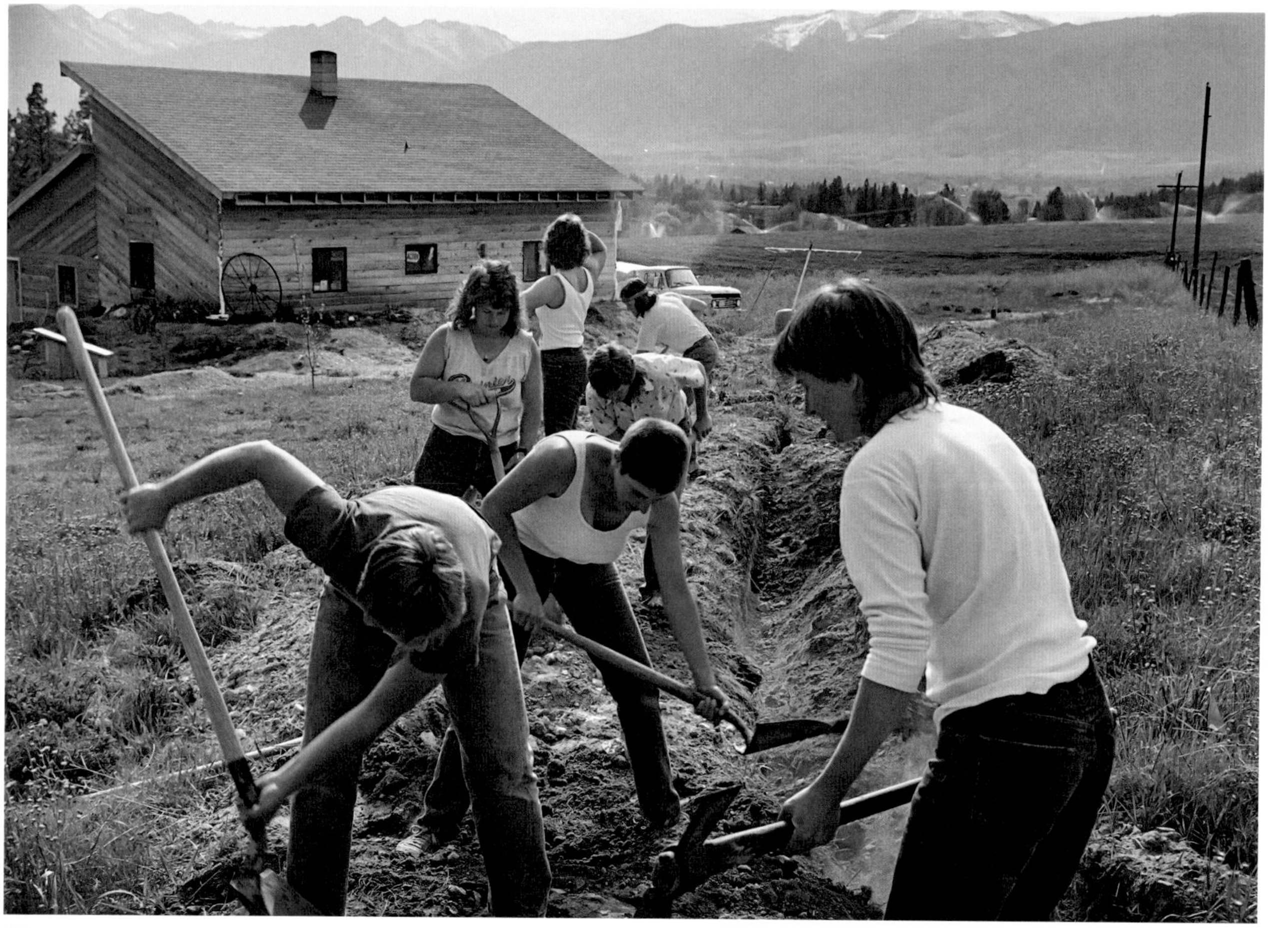

17

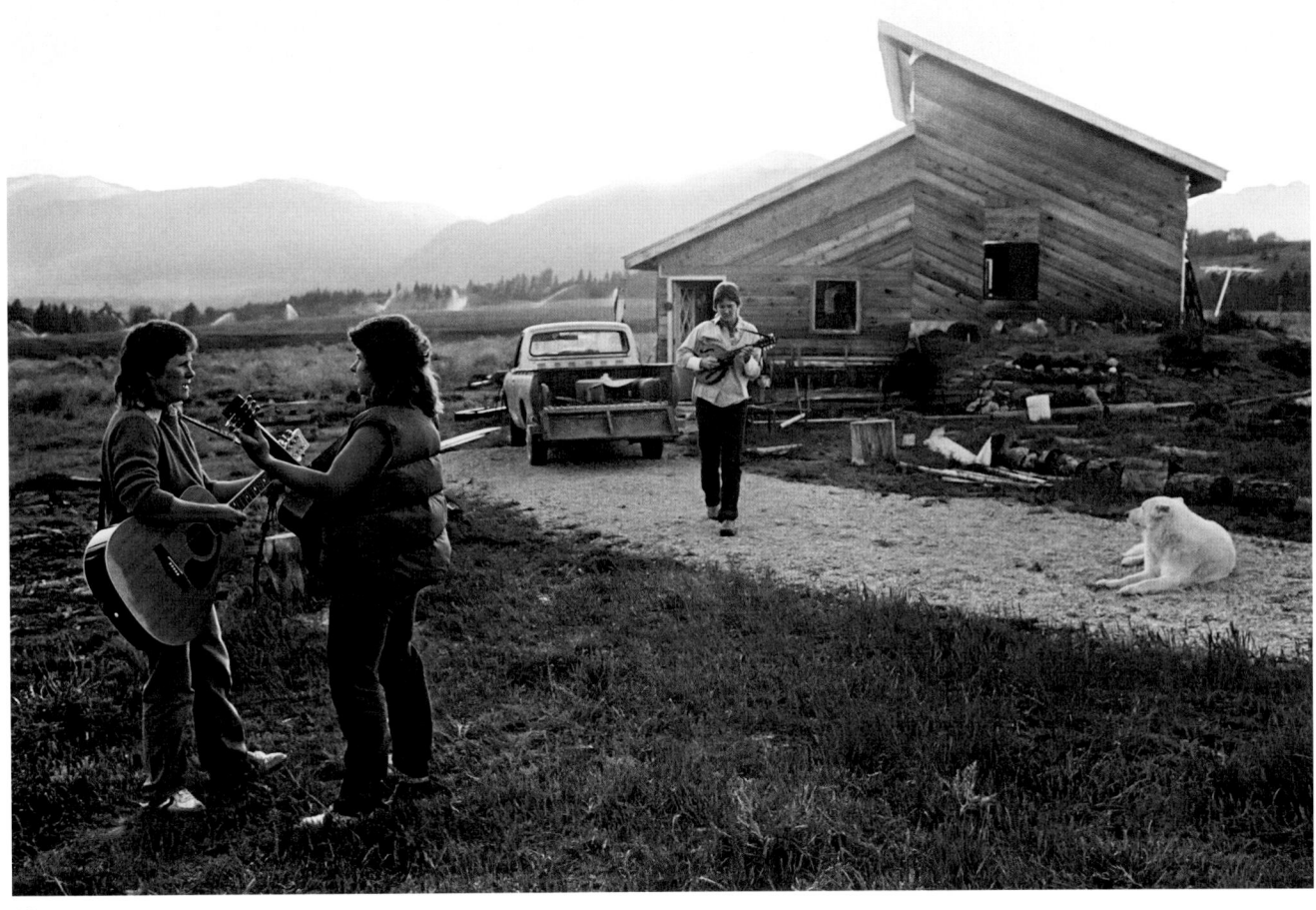

18

16. Mona Bachmann is part of a crew patching the roof of a friend's house in preparation for a community Fourth of July celebration in the Bitterroot Valley of Montana. 1987.

17. Boo Dawson, Pat Greytak, Mona, KD Dickinson, Mary Wildeman, and friends (front to back) backfill a ditch that runs a power line to Boo's house in the Bitterroot Valley. Like Boo, most of these women built their own homes with the help of family and friends. 1987.

18. Mary, KD, and Boo end a full day of work and play with music. These "valley girls" have been together, building a community of women, for ten years. Stevensville, Montana, 1987.

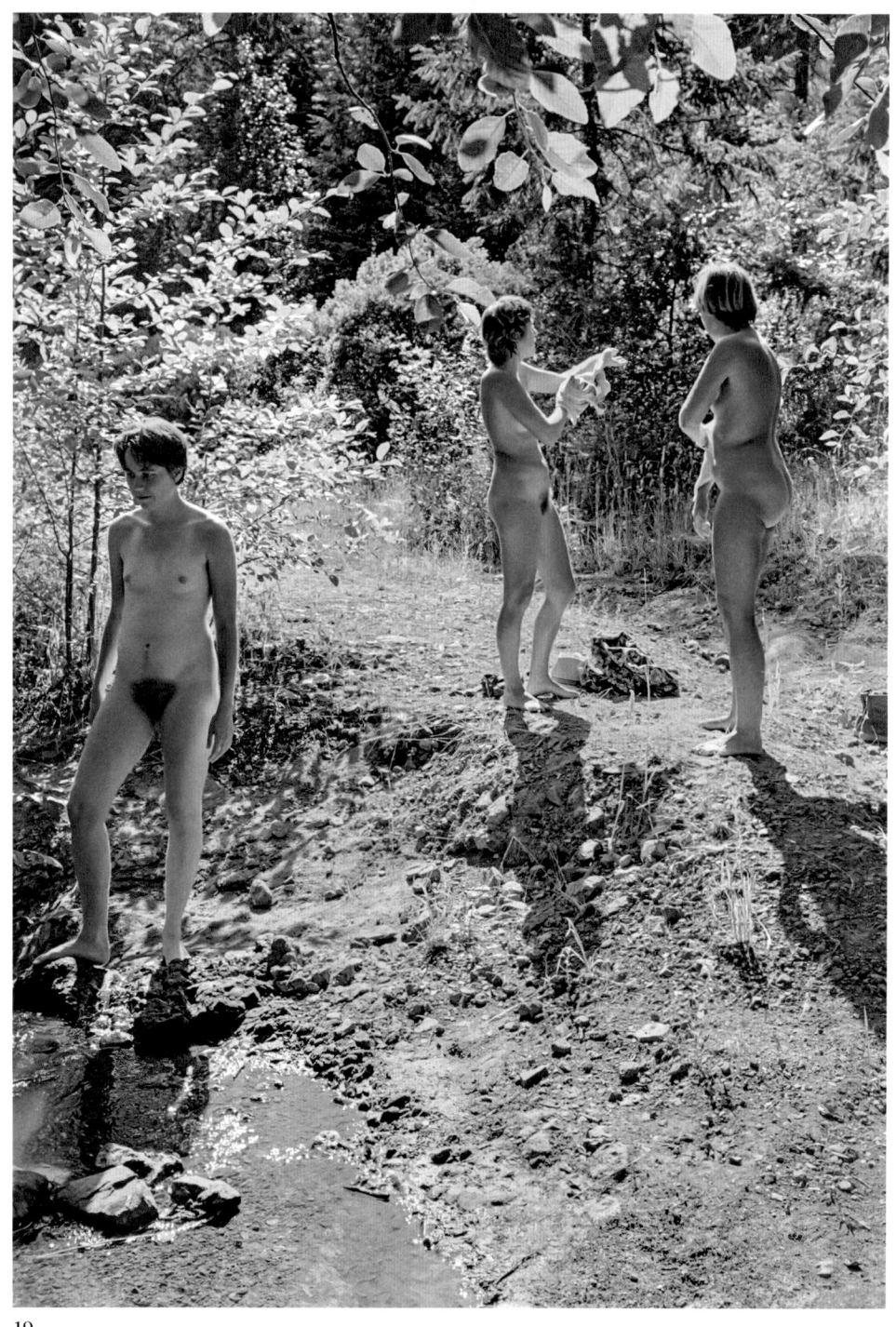

19

19. Toni White (now known as
Maya White Sparks) lingers by
the stream with two visitors from
Europe. On the photographer's
birthday, they splashed her in a
ritual of cleansing and rebirth.
Southern Oregon, 1980.

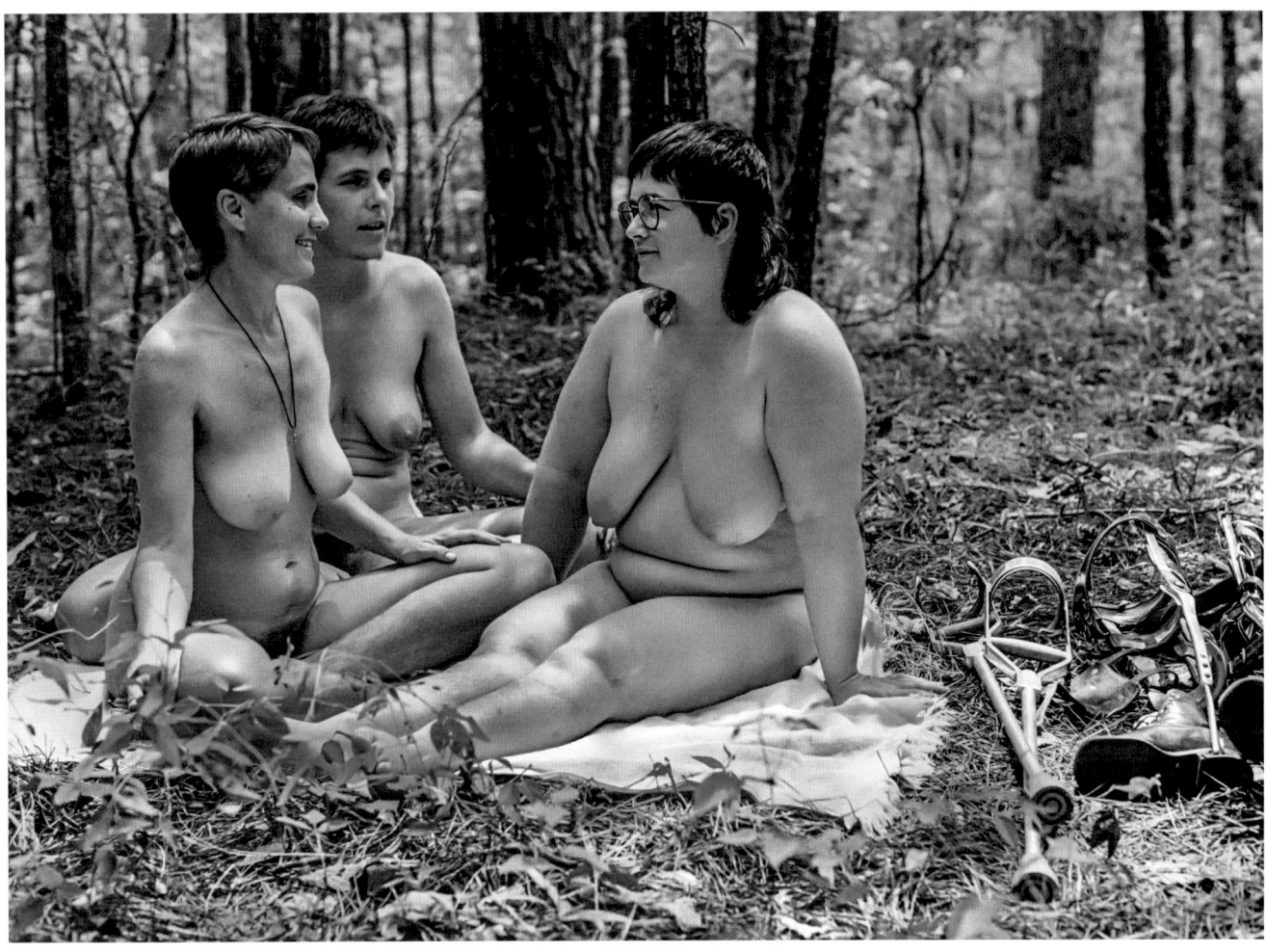

20

20. Longtime friends lynda lou
ease, beckie lee, and Sandra
Lambert relax together in the
Georgia woods. 1986.

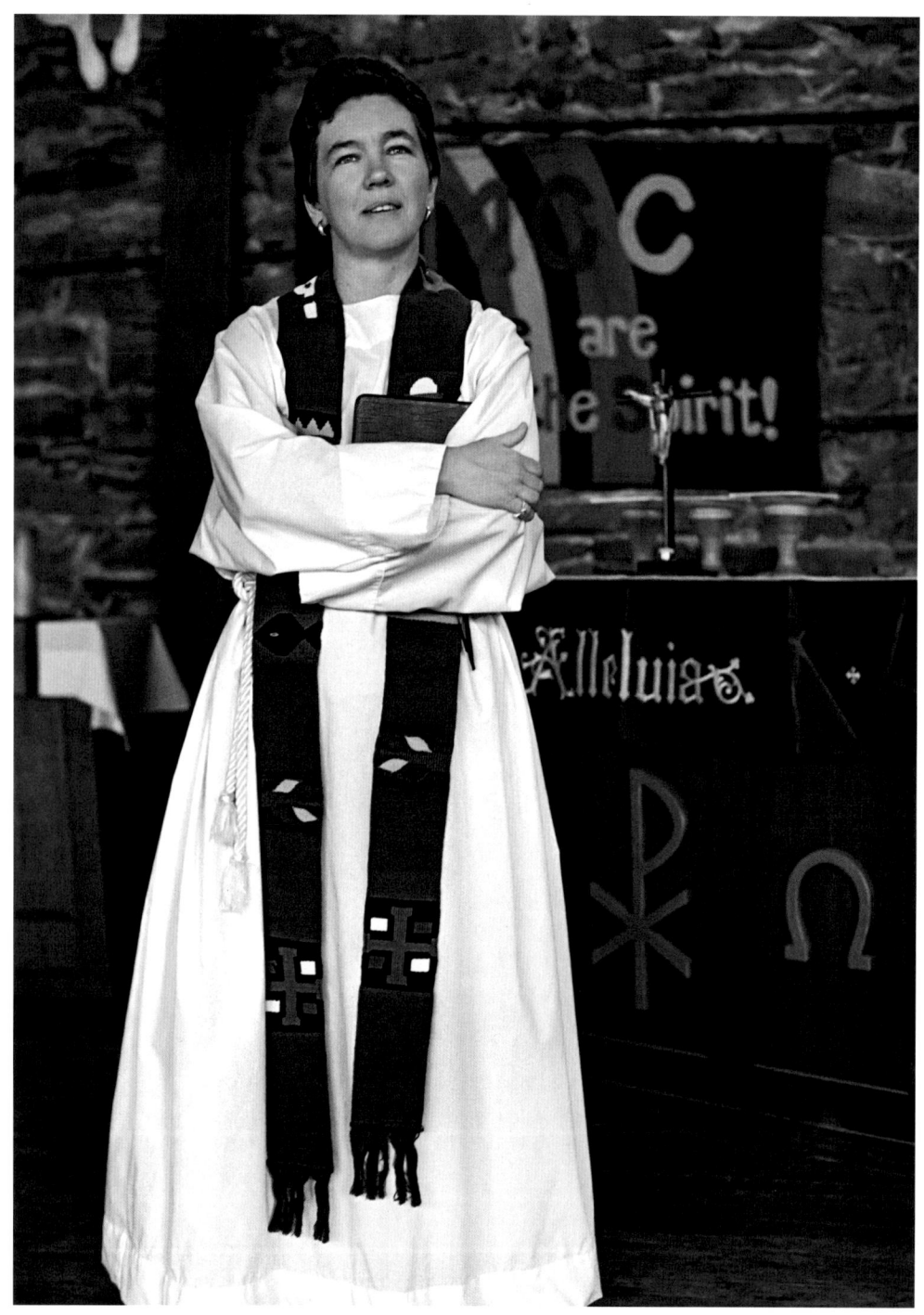

21

21. Rev. Jennie Boyd Bull enjoys pastoring the Metropolitan Community of Church (MCC) of Baltimore, Maryland, an ecumenical Christian church of the lesbian and gay communities. 1987.

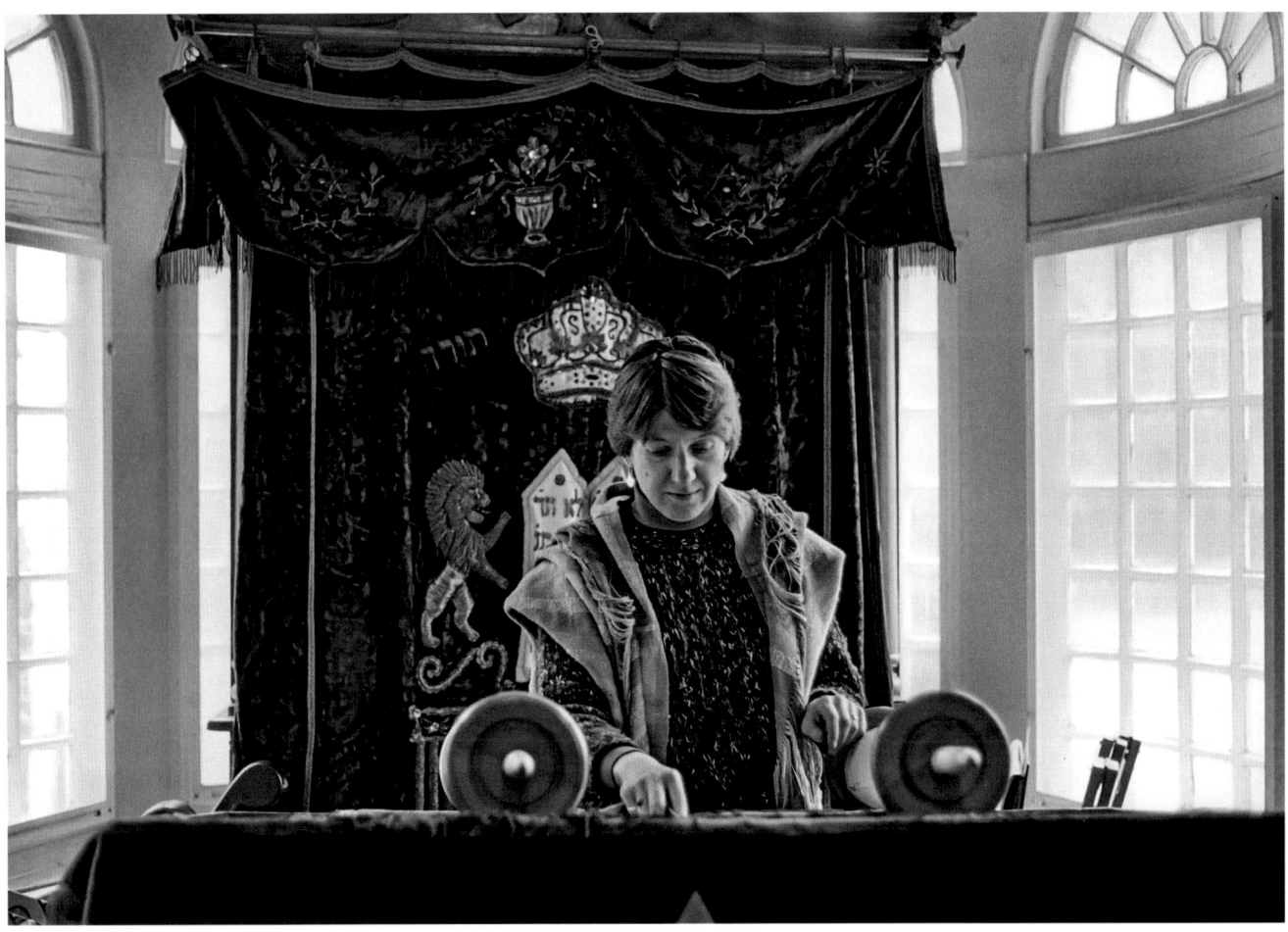

22

22. Rabbi Linda Holtzman reads
from the Torah, the Jewish
scriptures, at Beth Ahavah,
Philadelphia's gay and lesbian
synagogue. Pennsylvania, 1987.

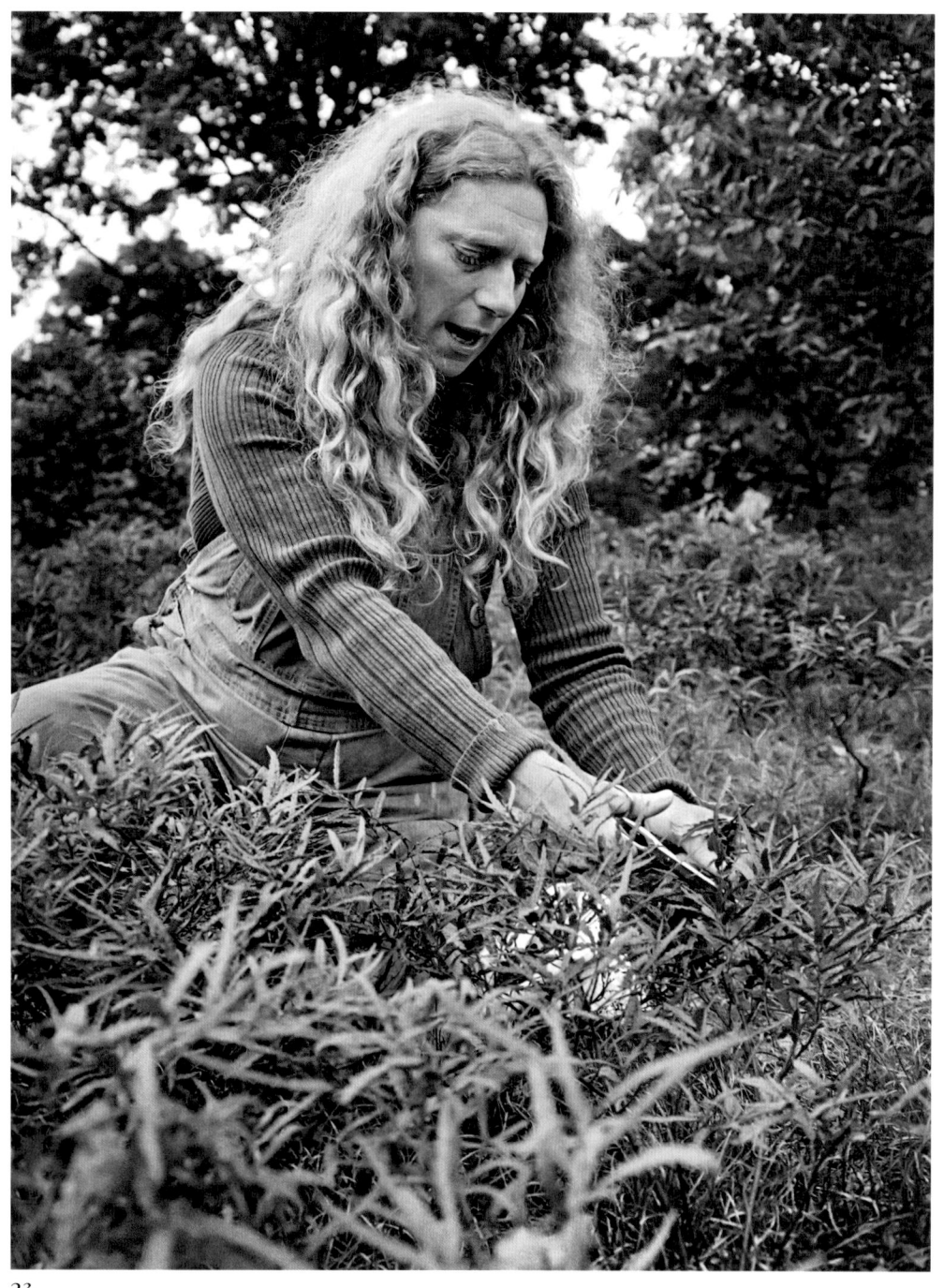

23

23. Billie Potts, author of *Witches Heal: Lesbian Herbal Self-Sufficiency*, gathers sweet fern, a medicinal herb. Michigan, 1983.

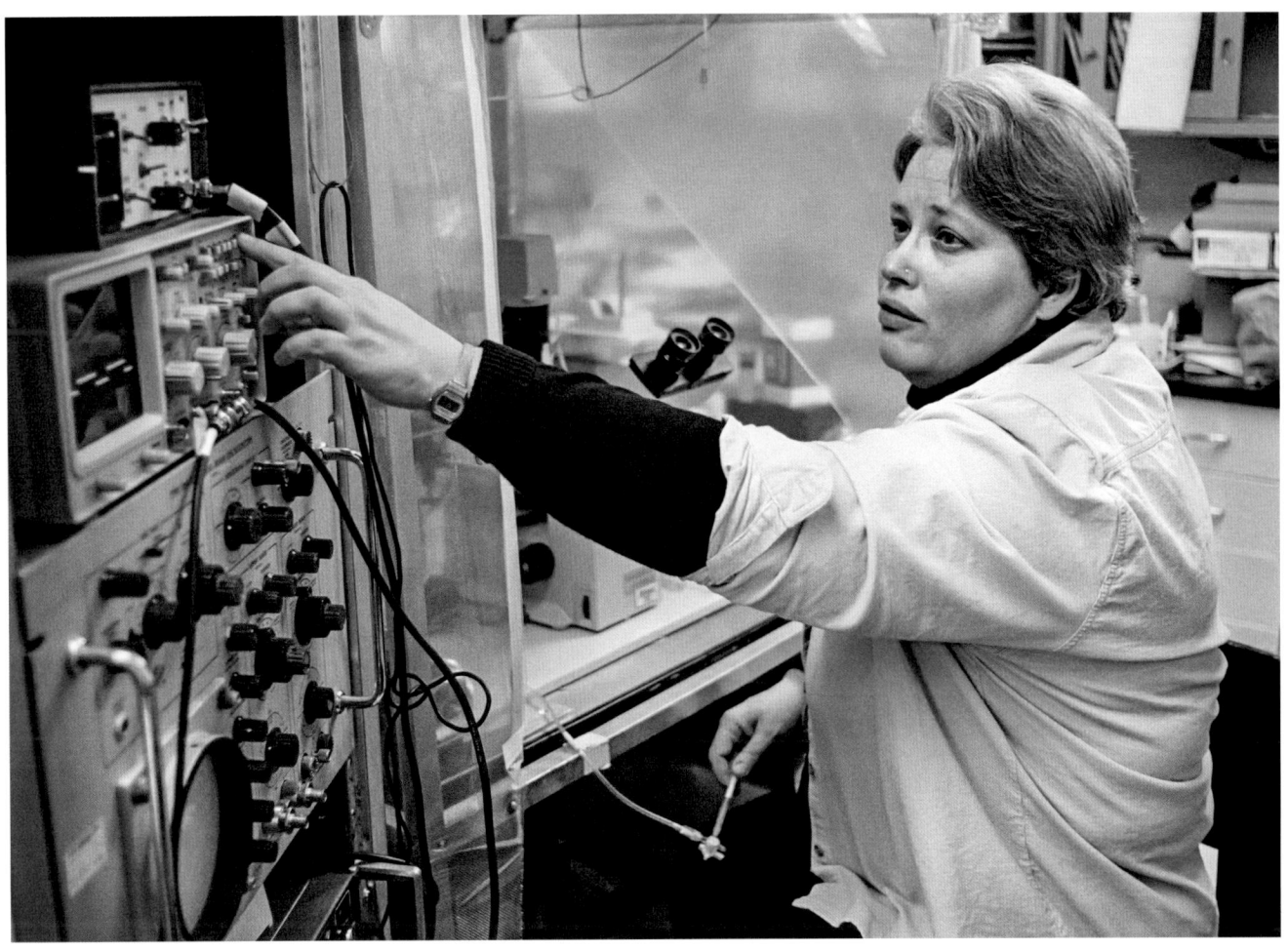

24

24. Associate professor Kathryn L. Edwards uses her patch clamp rig to investigate how single proteins in plant cell membranes respond to gravity. The study is revealing how insulin secretion is regulated in humans. St. Louis, Missouri, 1987.

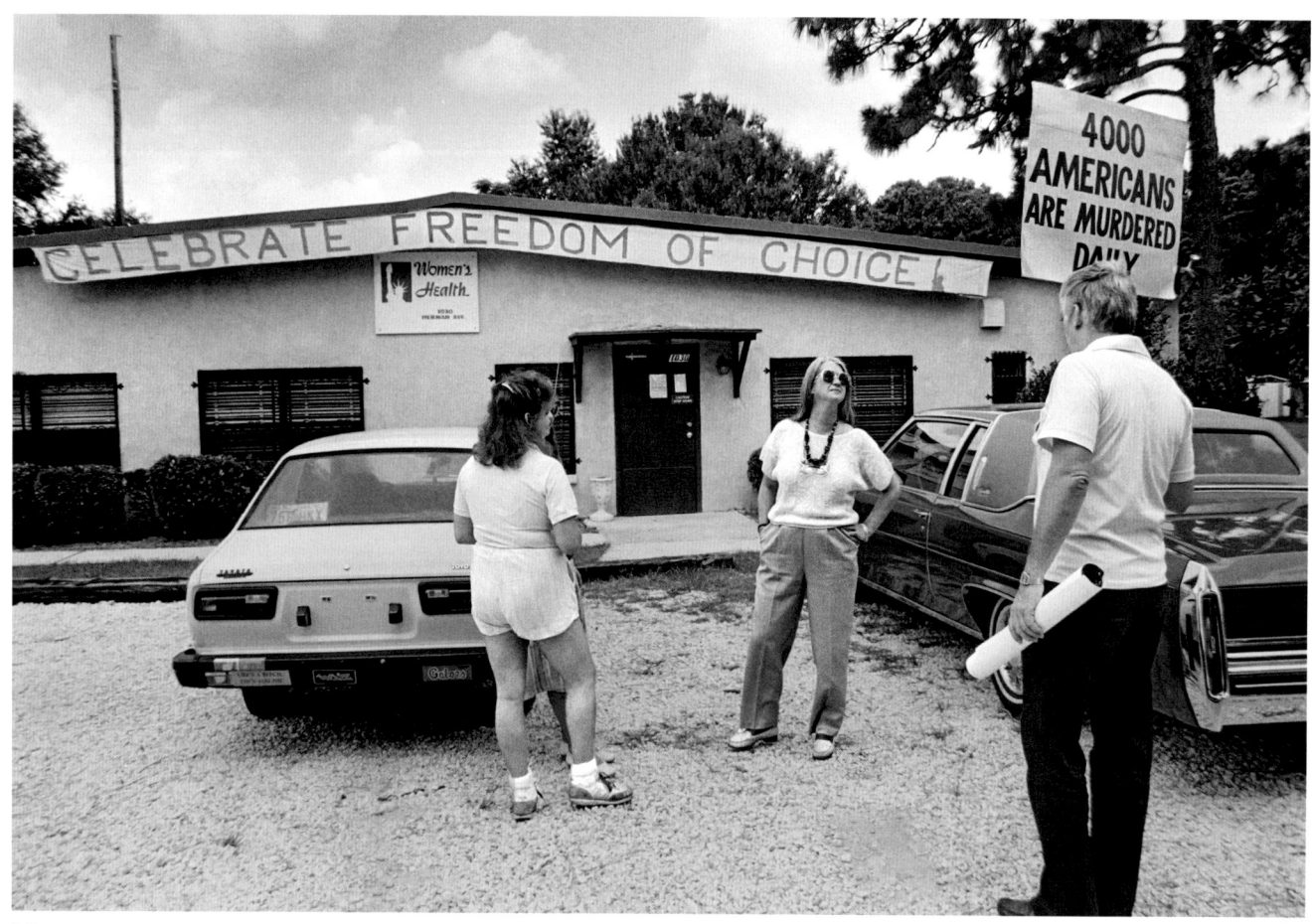

25

25. Patte Martin (center), owner/
director of the Women's Health
Center, an abortion clinic in
Orlando, Florida, confronts an anti-
abortion picketer who has come
to the clinic every week for the
past three years in an attempt to
intimidate the clients and the staff.
1986.

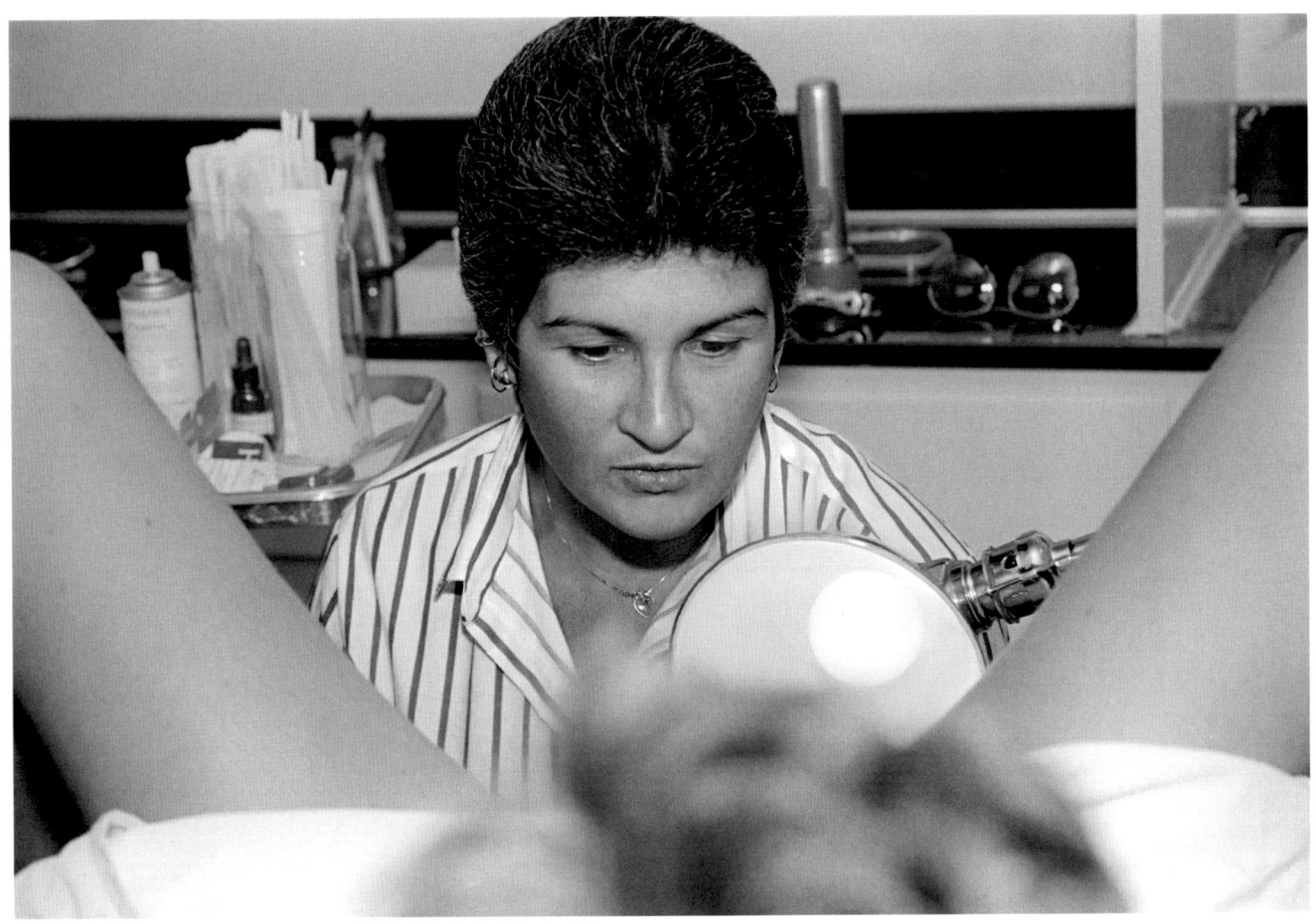

26

26. Ana Maldonado, physician associate and women's health care specialist, provides lesbian health services at the Santa Cruz Women's Health Center. Here she assists a client in seeing her cervix. California, 1986.

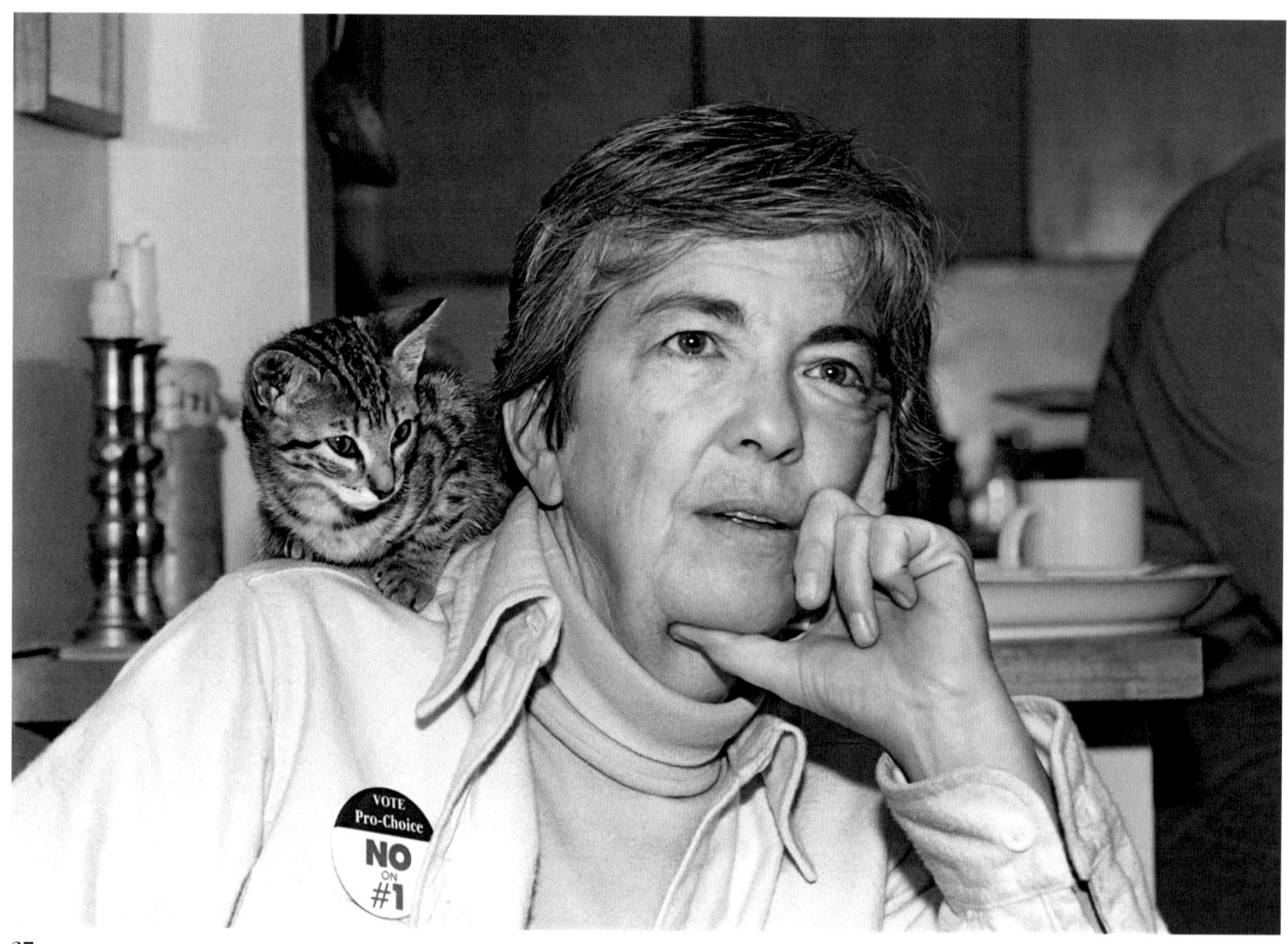

27

27. Eleanor Lord discusses politics over brunch while Billie Jean observes. Massachusetts Proposition #1, which would have restricted women's right to abortion, was defeated. Berkshire County, 1986.

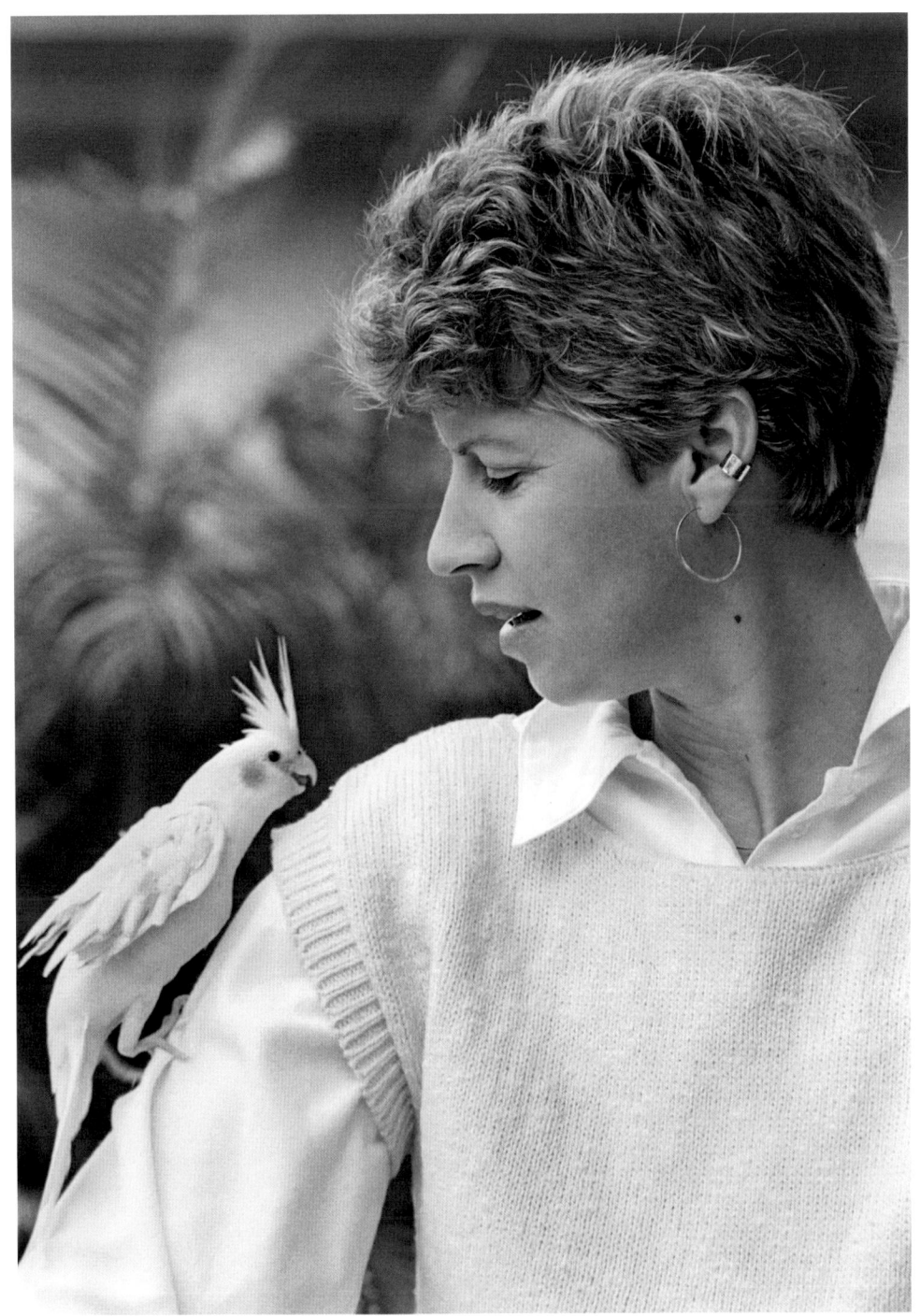

28

28. Nita O'Brien, who worked
for many years at a rape crisis
center, now has a counseling
practice specializing in sexual
assault recovery. Here she takes
time out with her friend Spike.
St. Petersburg, Florida, 1987.

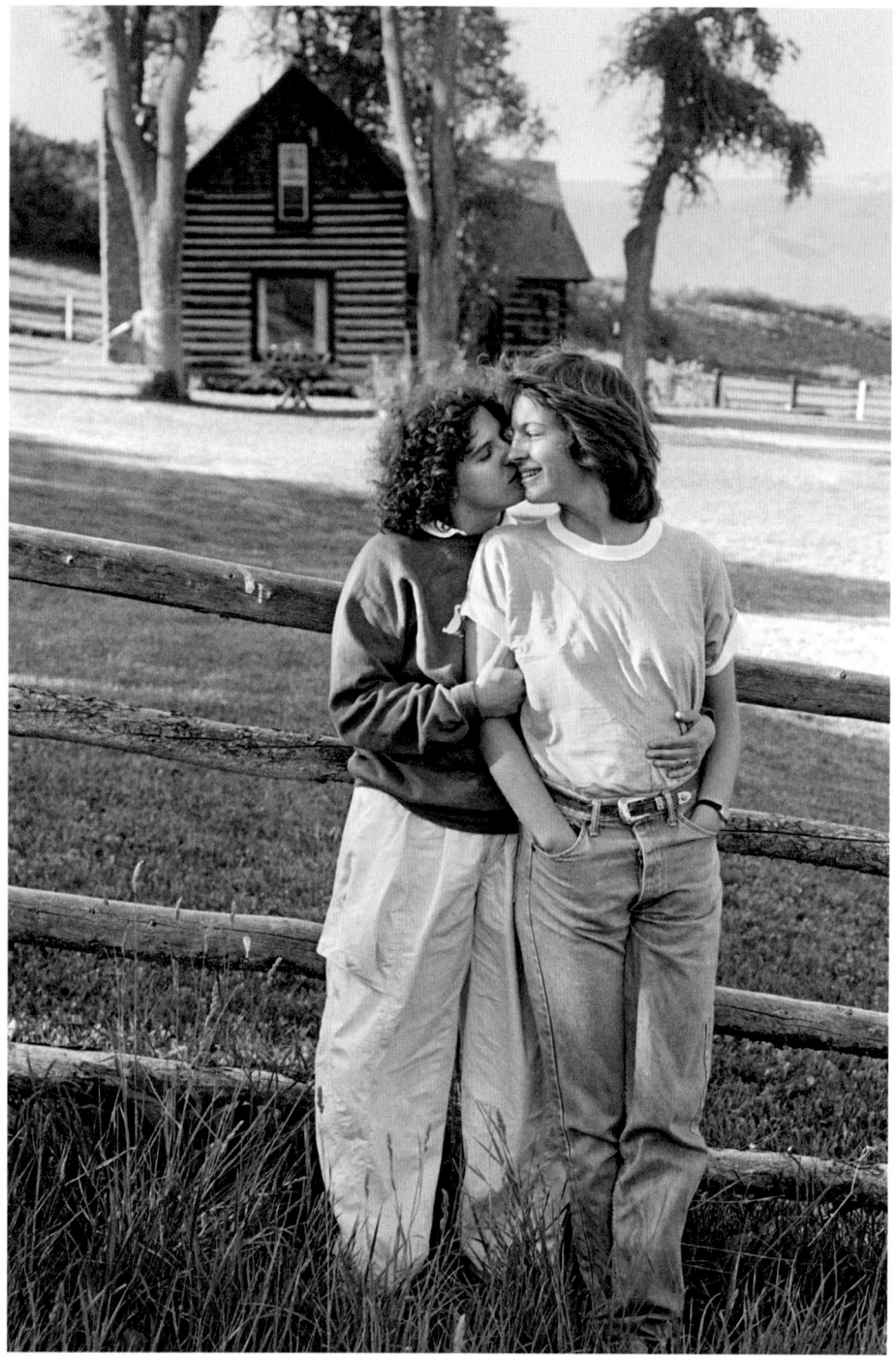

29

29. Dr. Dee Mosbacher and Dr. Nanette Gartrell relax while on vacation in Colorado. 1984.

30. Nanette, an assistant professor of psychiatry at Harvard University Medical School, works in her home office investigating sexual abuse of clients by psychiatrists. Cambridge, Massachusetts, 1986.

31. Dee smiles during a lighter moment in a consultation at Somerville Mental Health Clinic, where she is chief resident. Massachusetts, 1986.

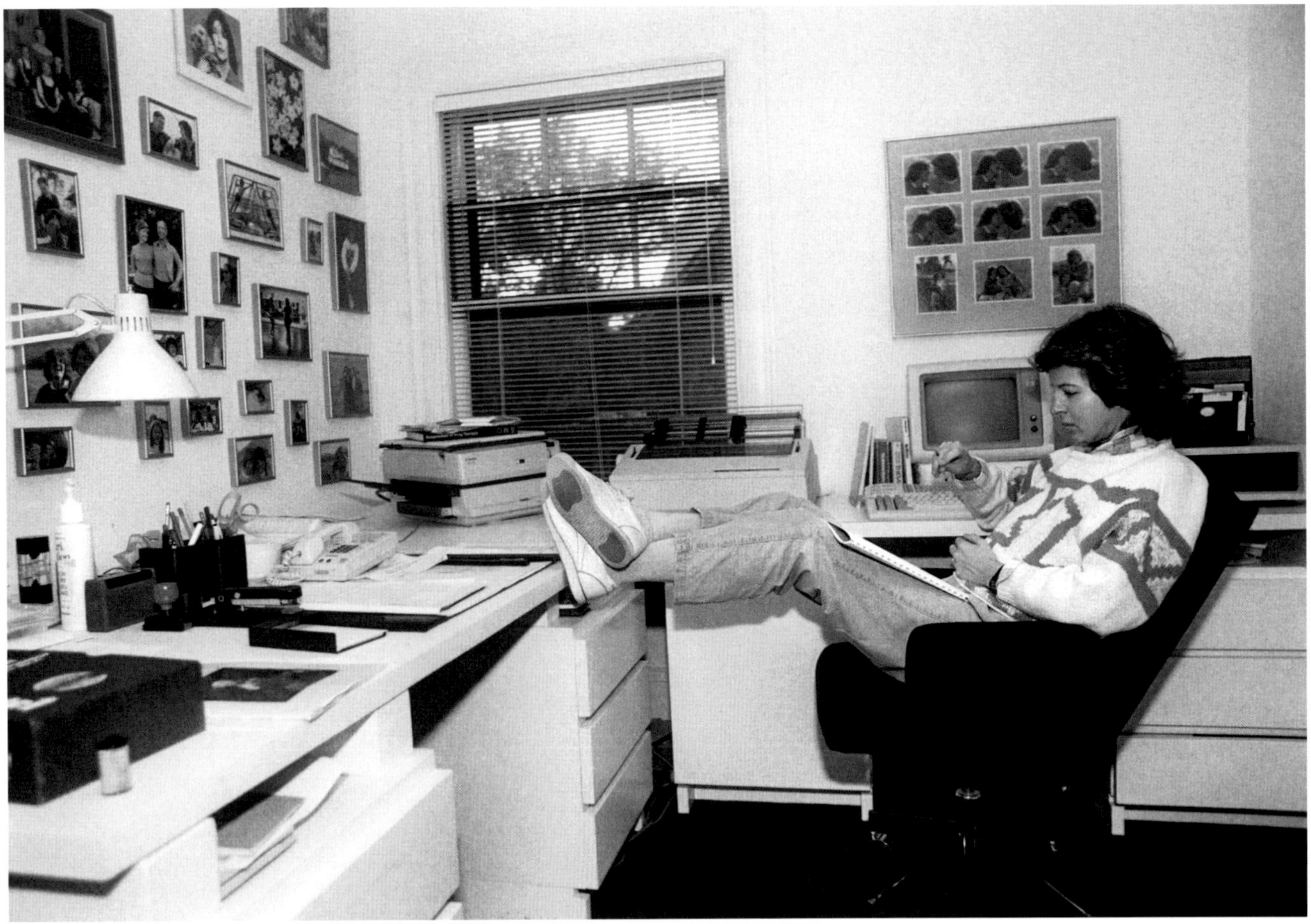

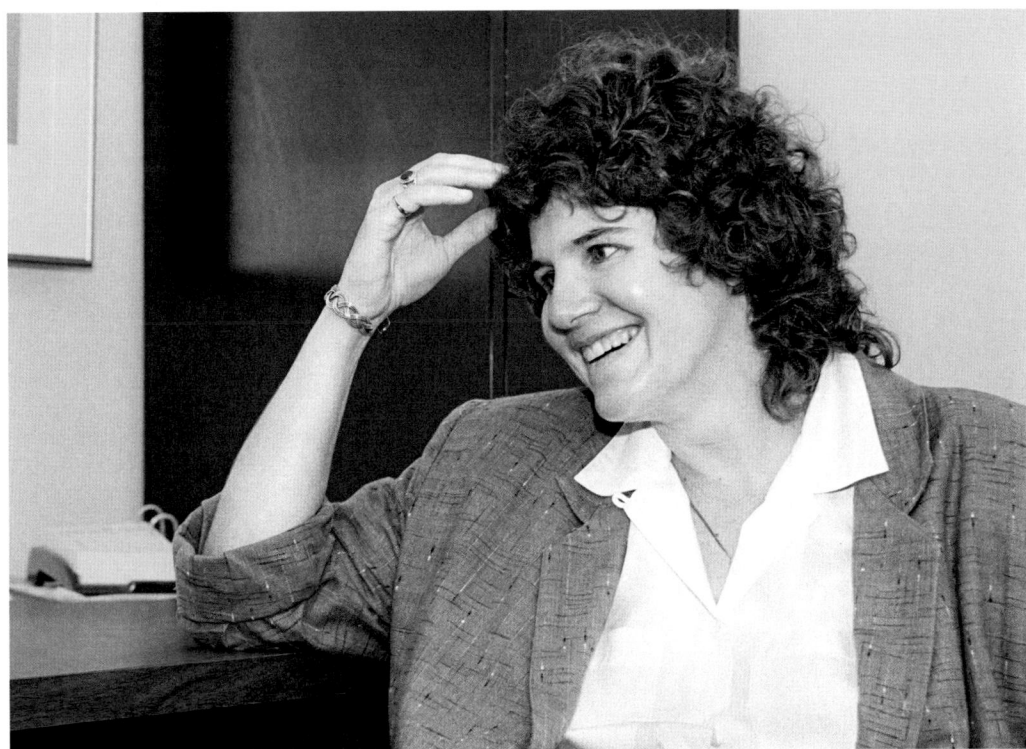

30

31

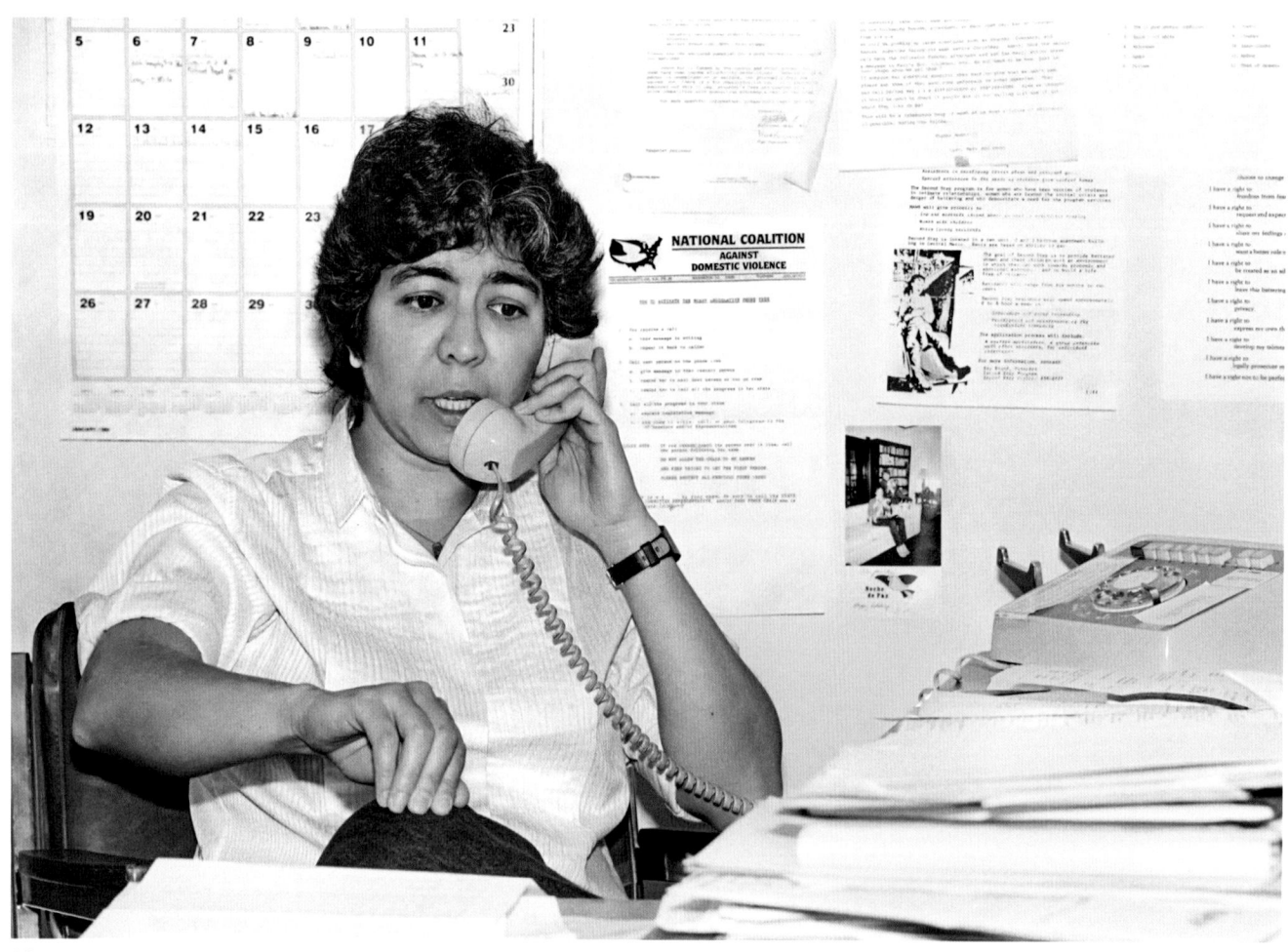

32

32. Eleanor N. Soto takes a turn
on the 24-hour crisis line at the
Mid-Peninsula Support Network in
Mountain View, California. Eleanor
was co-director of this agency,
which serves battered women and
their children. 1986.

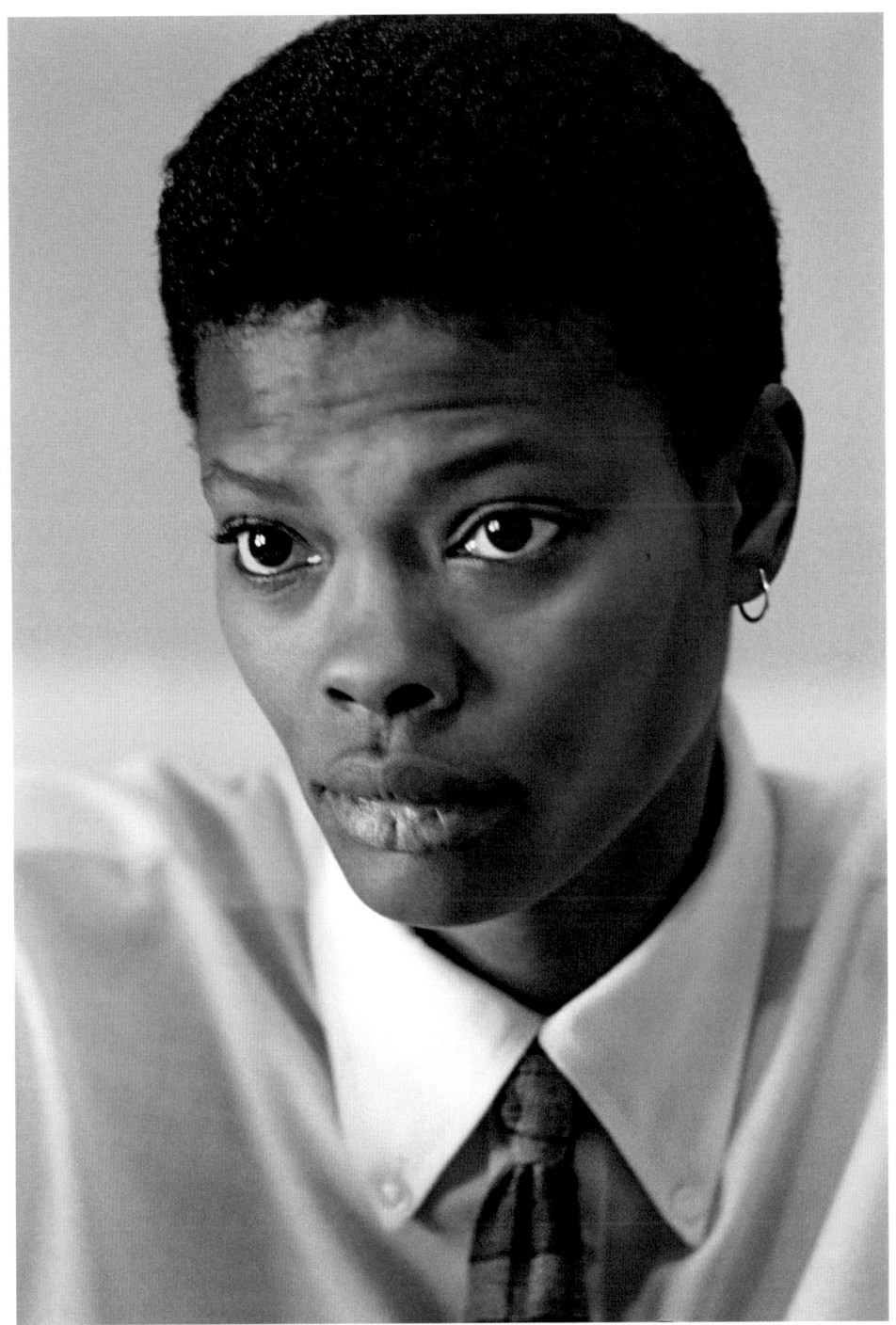

33

33. Elvira Williams counsels
battered women and abused youth
in Troy, New York. 1986.

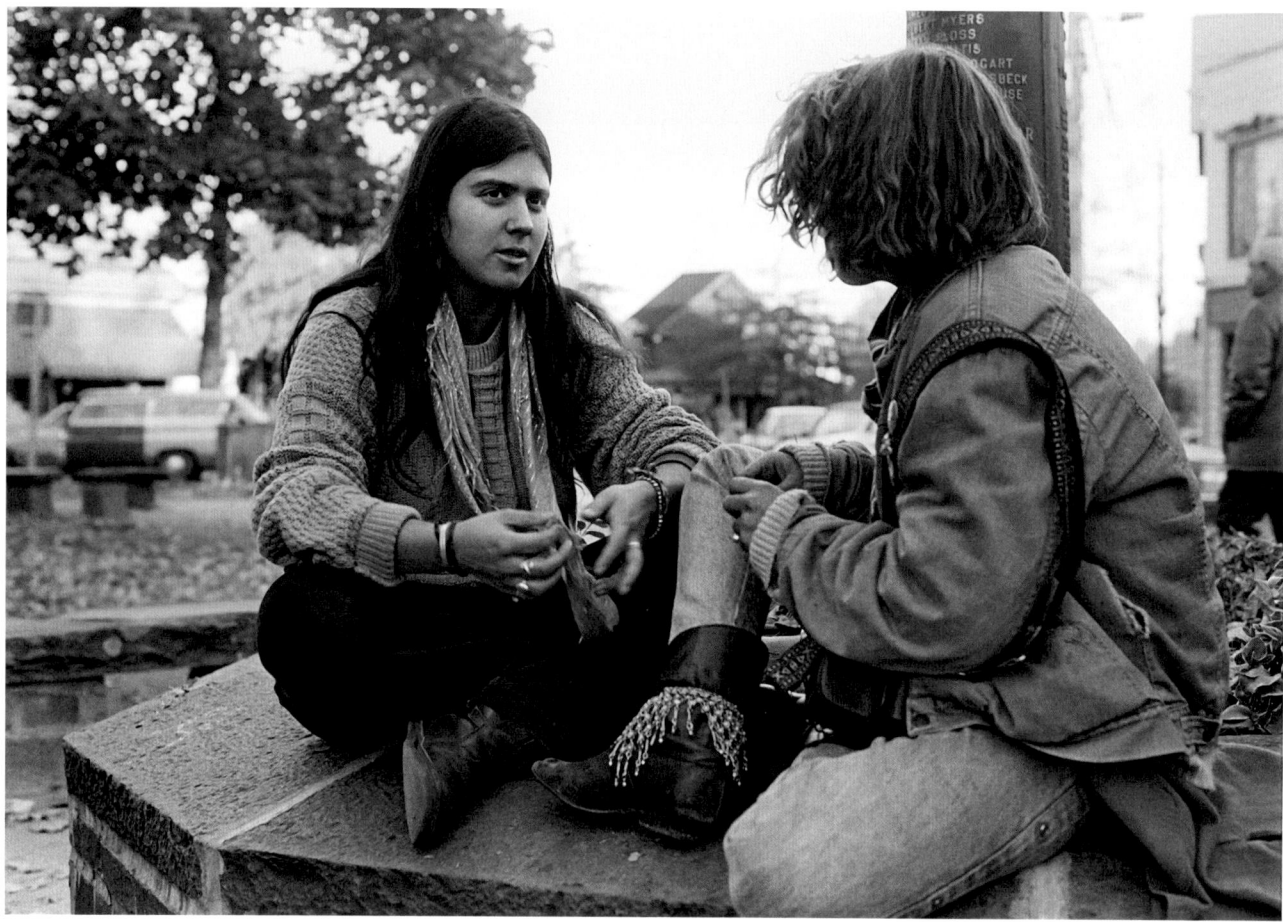

34

34. Ruthie Crone talks with a
runaway on the town green in
Woodstock, New York. Ruthie
is the senior counselor and case
manager at Family House, a
runaway and homeless youth
crisis intervention shelter. 1986.

35. Joyce Hunter, director of social
services at the Hetrick/Martin
Institute for the Protection of
Lesbian and Gay Youth, discusses
the Harvey Milk School, a
program of the Institute, with two
prospective students. New York
City, 1986.

36. Joyce talks with lesbian and
gay youth on the streets of New
York, and hands them cards, so
that when they are ready or if they
need help, they can come to the
institute. 1986.

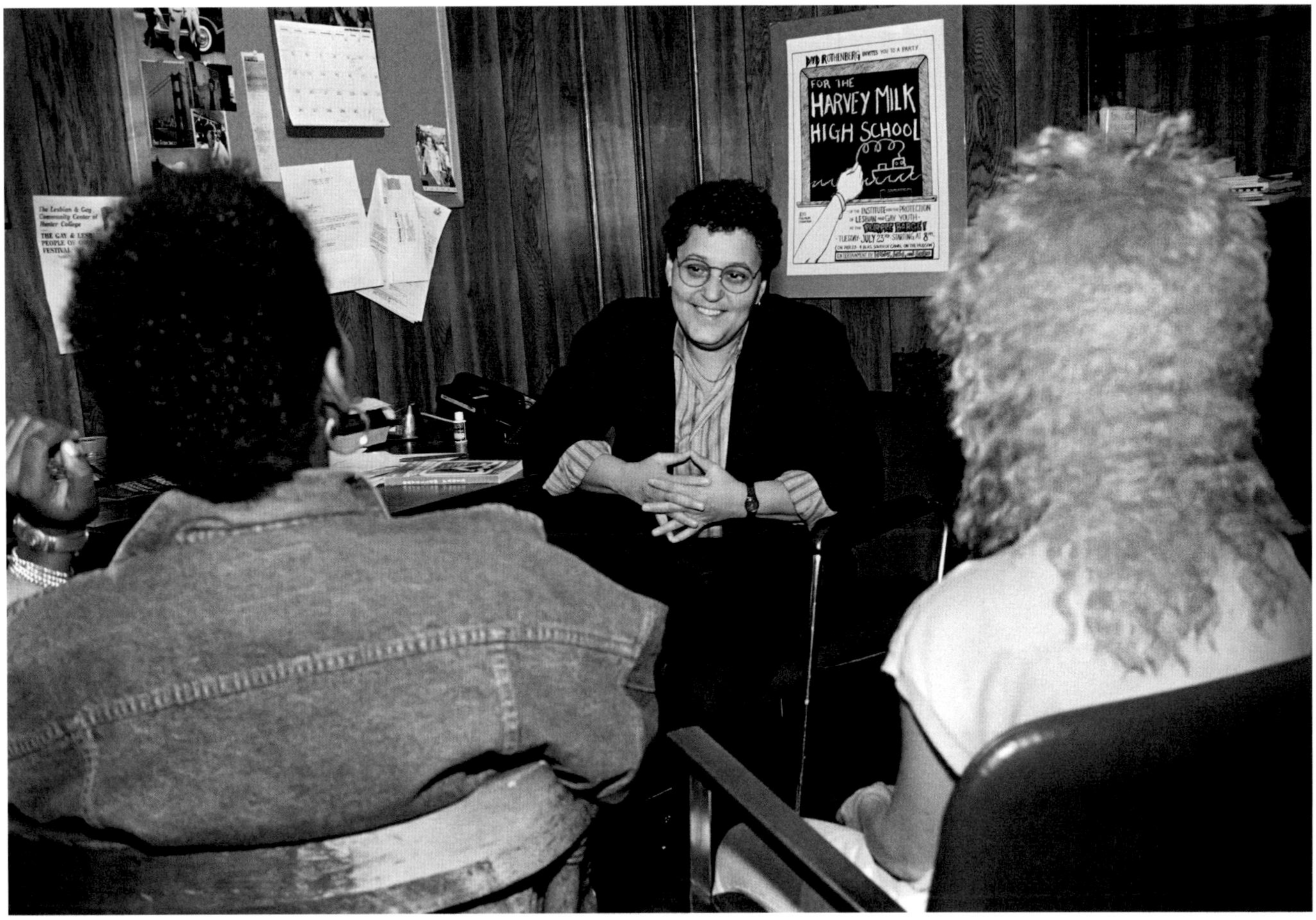

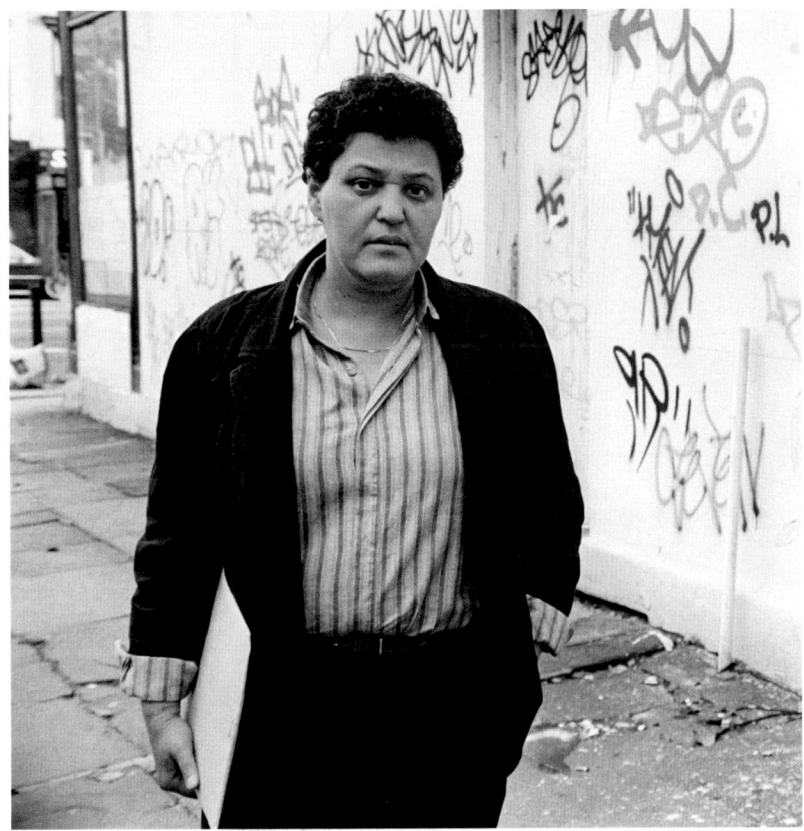

35

36

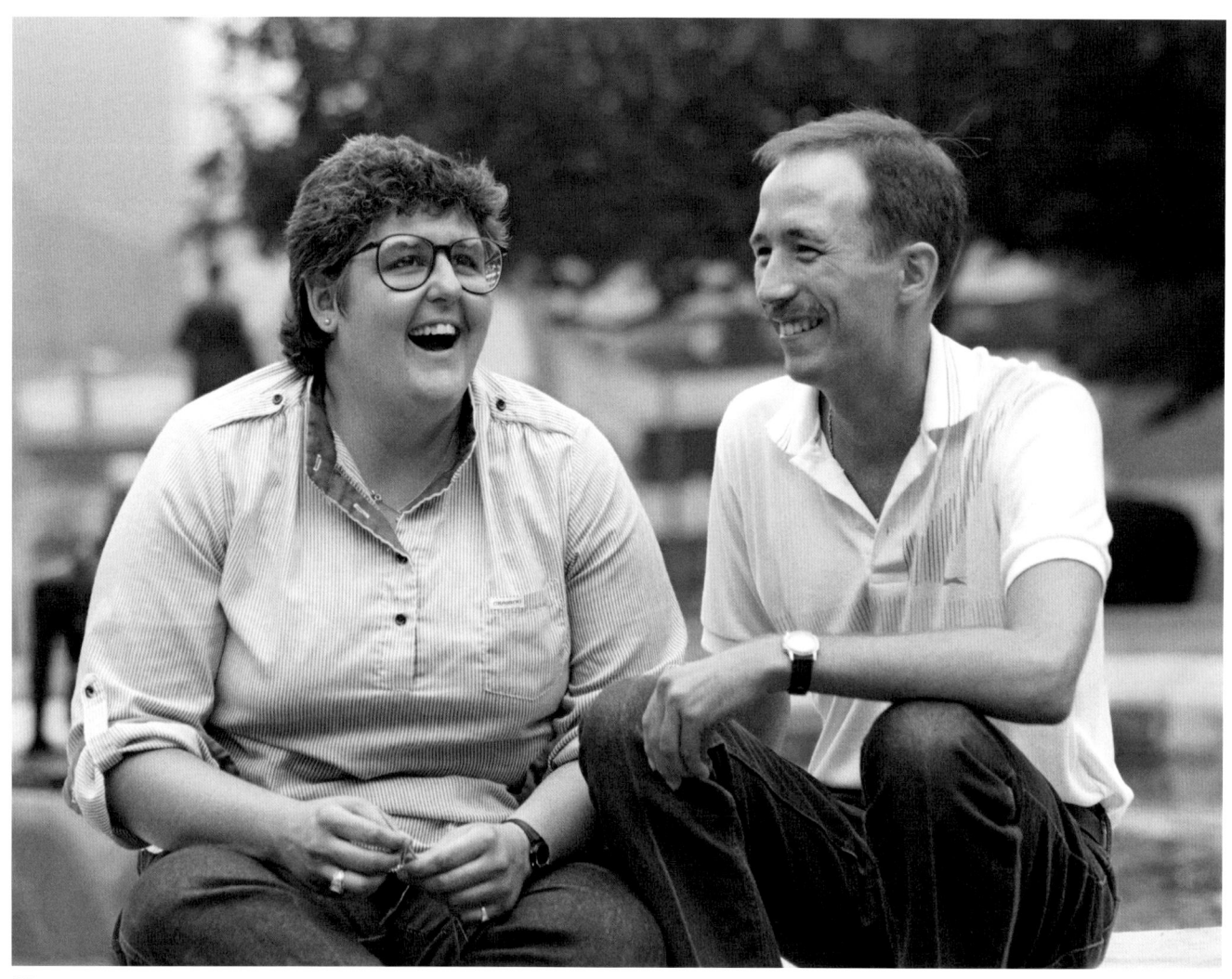

37

37. Maureen Schorr trains and coordinates buddies for people with AIDS for the Health Education Resource Organization (HERO) in Baltimore, Maryland. Fred, who has AIDS, is a volunteer trainer who works with Maureen. 1987.

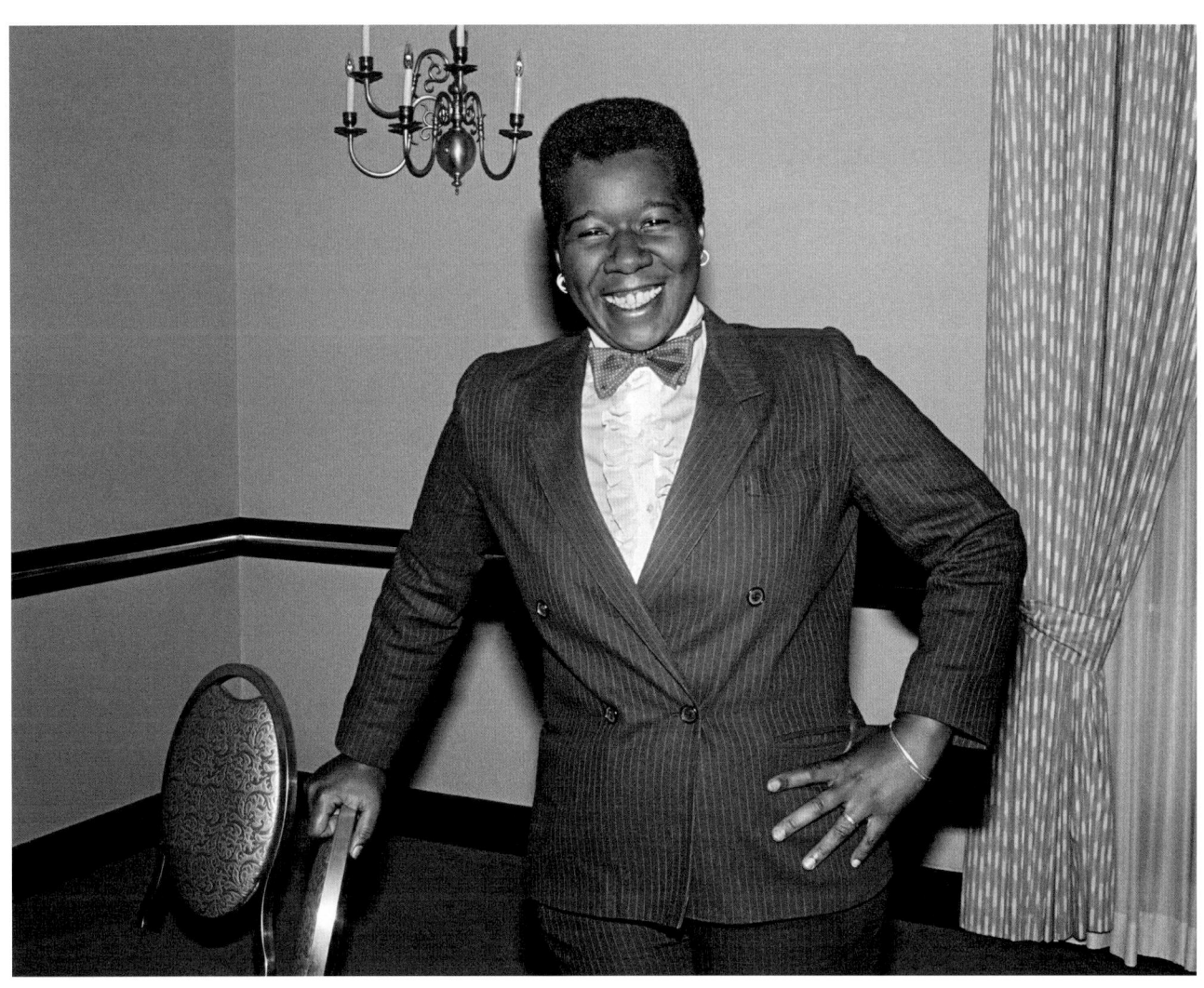

38

38. Colevia Carter, D.C. human
rights commissioner, poet, and
human resource developer for
the D.C. prison system, attends
the Human Rights Campaig.
Fund dinner in 1984. Colevia
also develops AIDS education
programs for the Black community
in Washington, D.C.

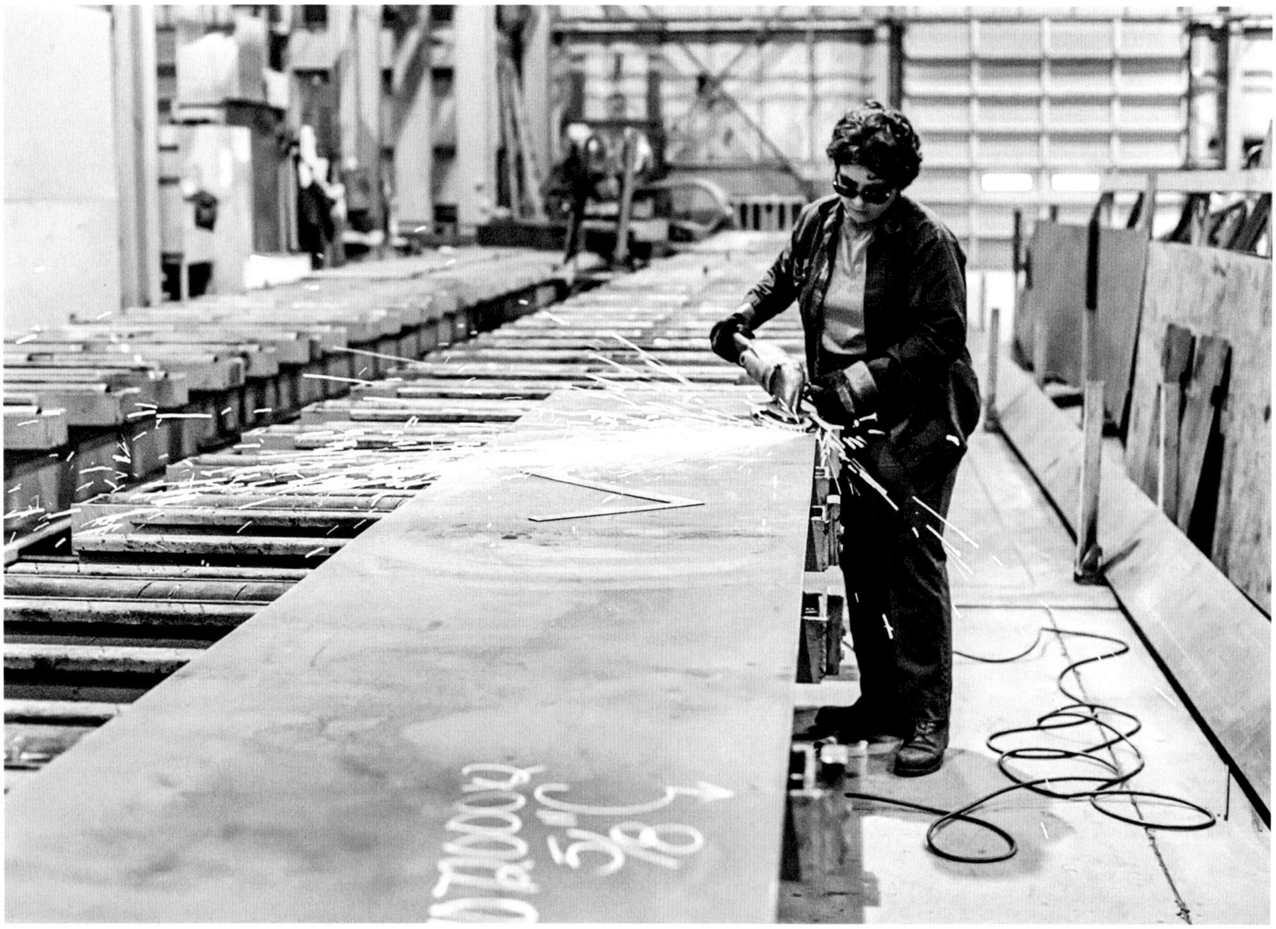

39

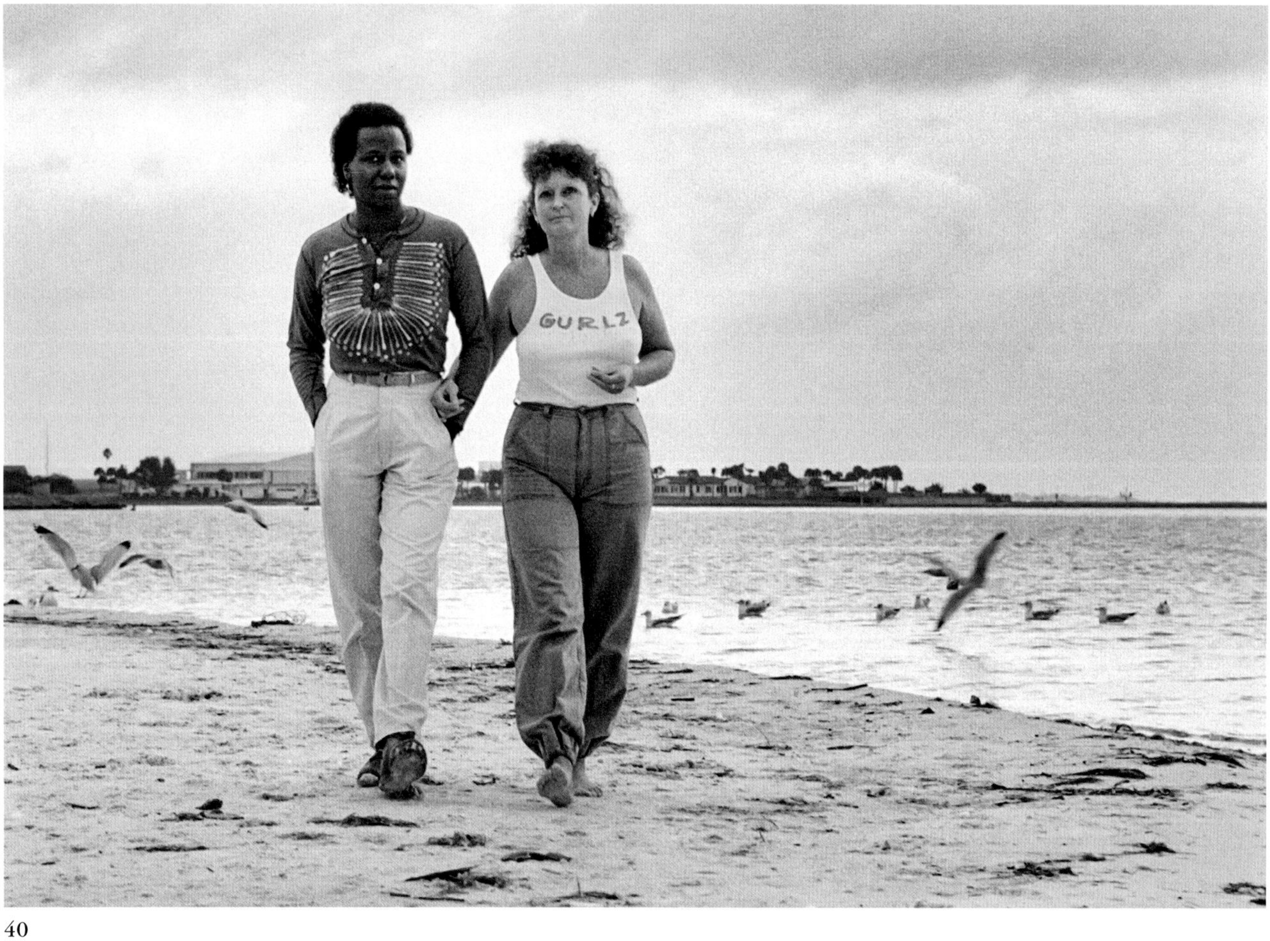

40

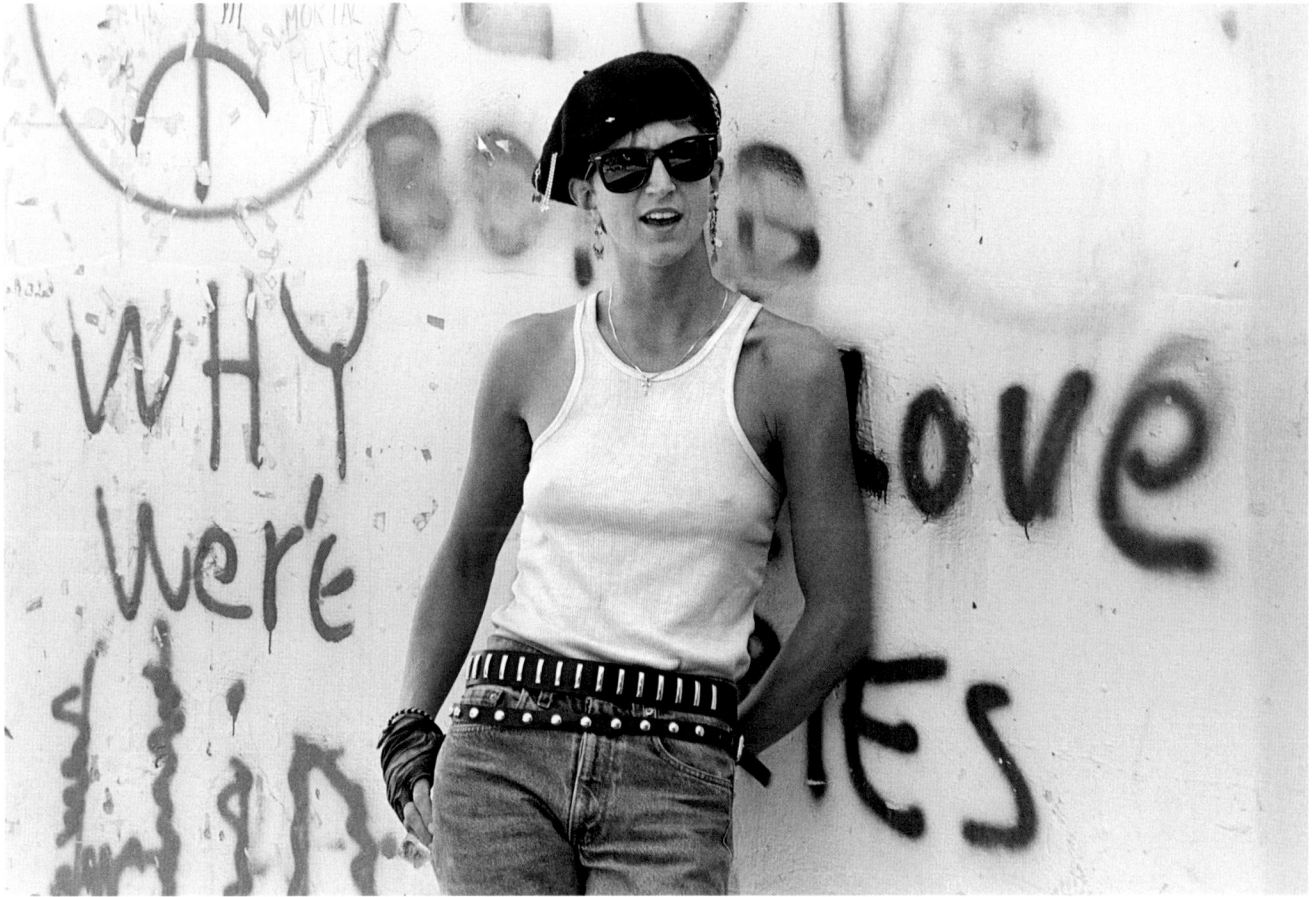

41

39. Anna Marie Rechichi works as a welder for a large crane manufacturer. She is an active member of Cleveland's Hard Hatted Women and Older Wiser Lesbians. Anna Marie also volunteers with Oven Productions, which produces women's cultural events in Cleveland, Ohio. 1986.

40. Pat Mason and Sunny Neal walk along Tampa Bay near their home in St. Petersburg, Florida. Pat counsels the families of abused and neglected children. Sunny works in physical therapy with trauma patients. They are both active volunteers with The Line, a gay and lesbian telephone hotline. 1987.

41. Mary Schultz, an abortion counselor in Missoula, Montana, loves punk music and plays the cello. 1987.

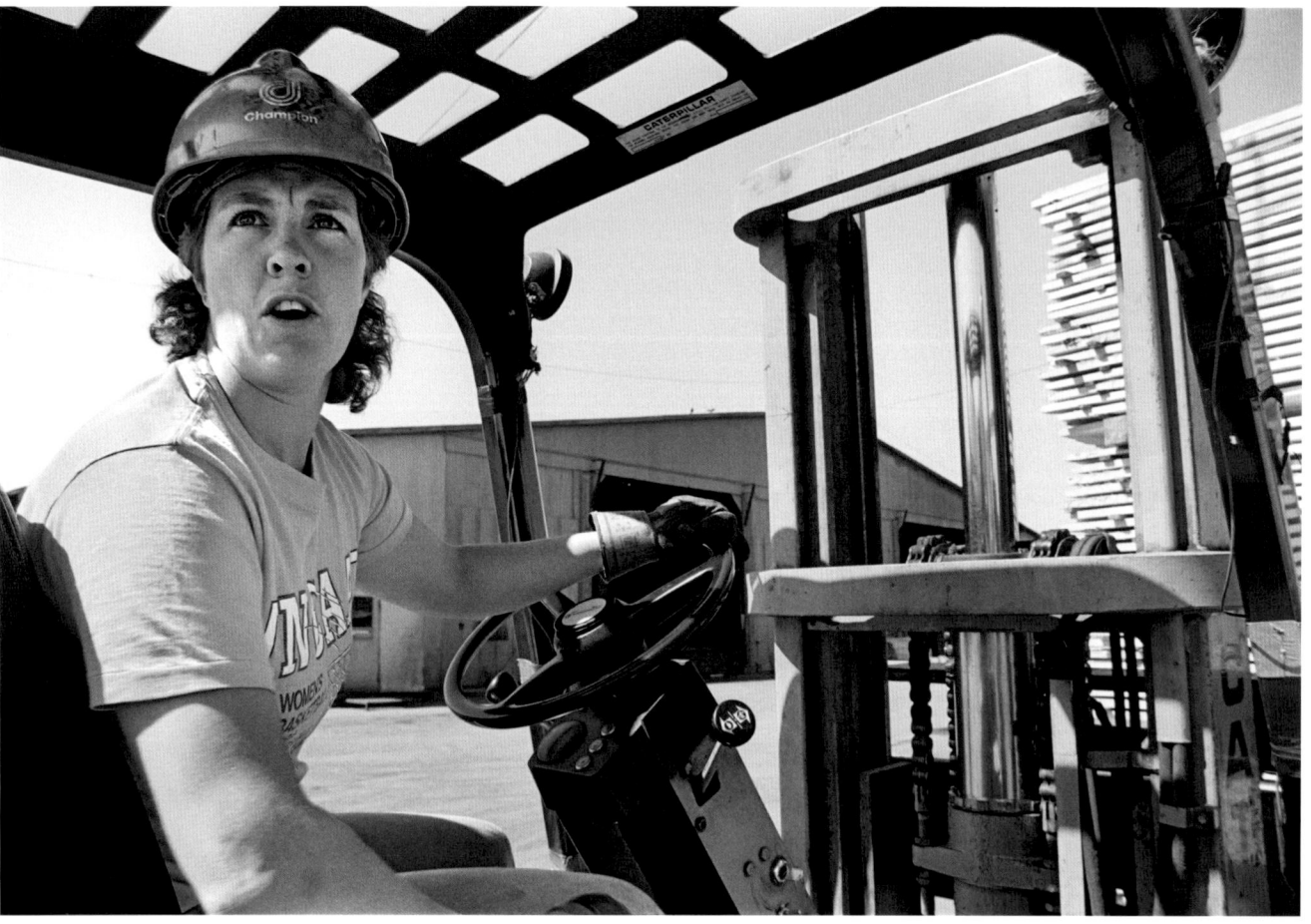

42

42. Shannon Morse loads boxcars at a lumber mill in Missoula, Montana. Shannon taught herself how to drive the forklift so she could get off the production line. 1987.

43. Abigail Johnson does the spring pruning at her 25-acre Christmas Tree Farm in northern Georgia. 1986.

44. Leslie Burgess plays the flute in Bass Creek Canyon, Montana, in celebration of her birthday. Leslie is a poet, a counselor, and a battered women's movement activist particularly concerned with survivors of incest and adult children of alcoholics. 1987.

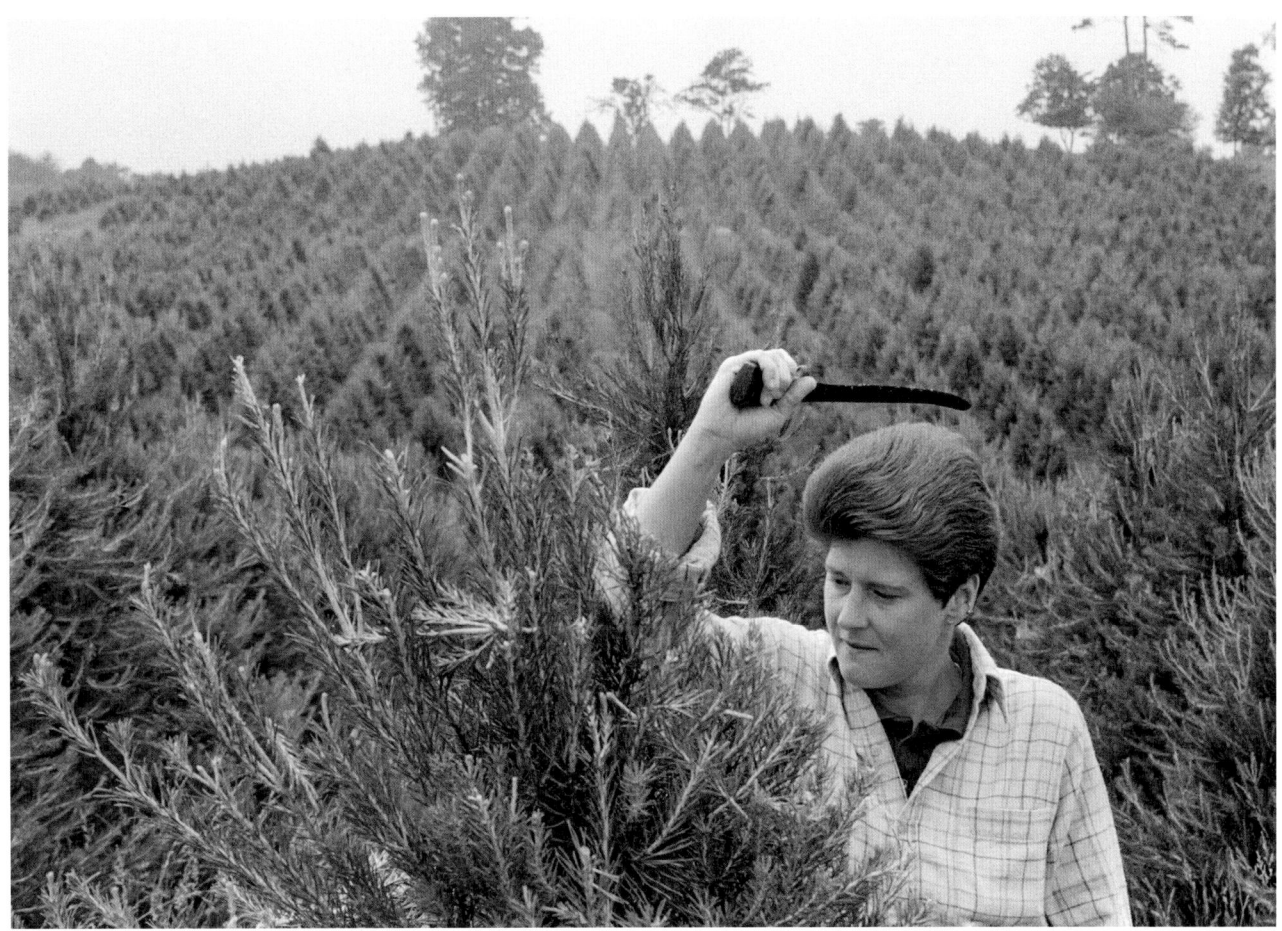

43

44

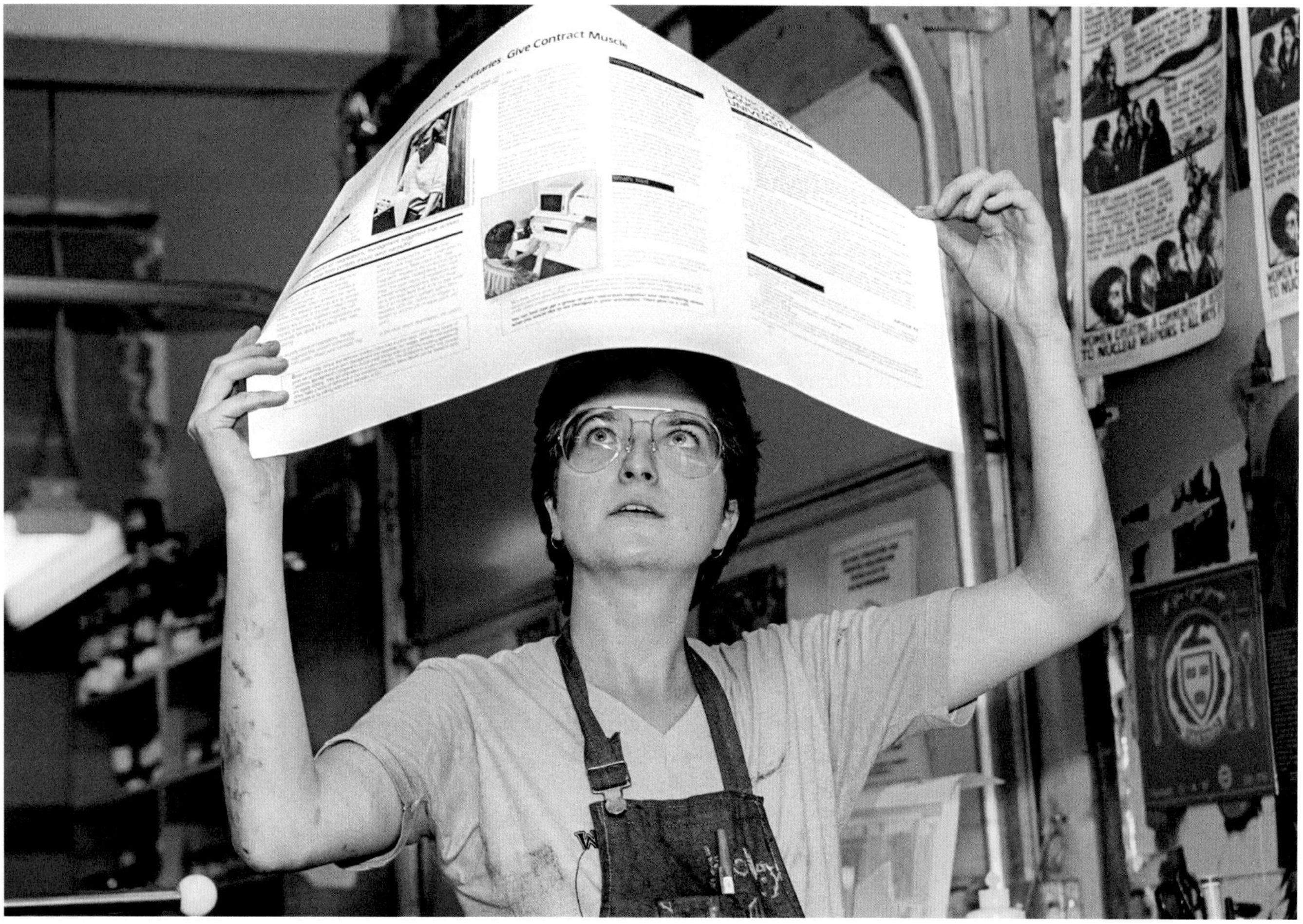

45

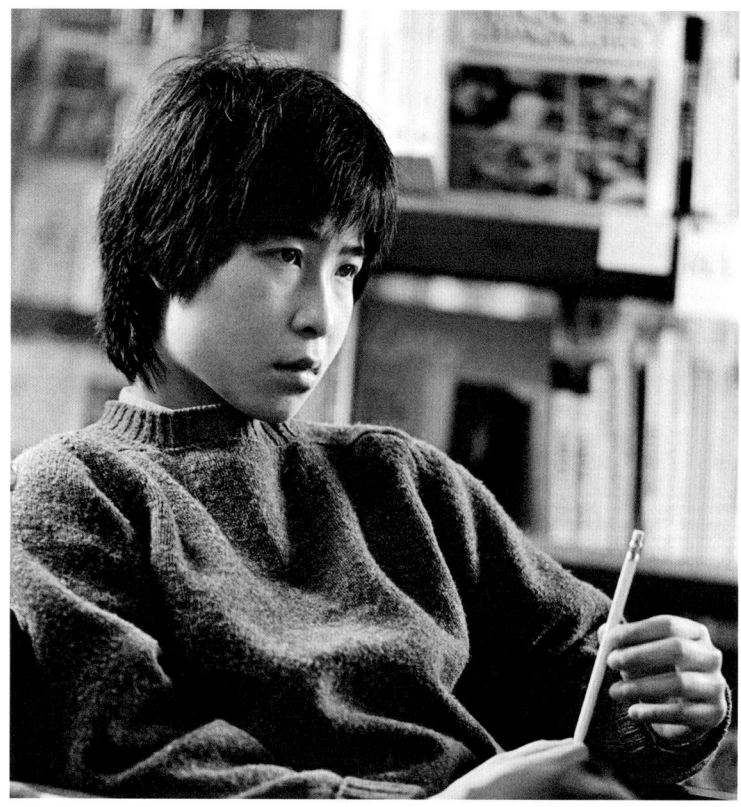
46

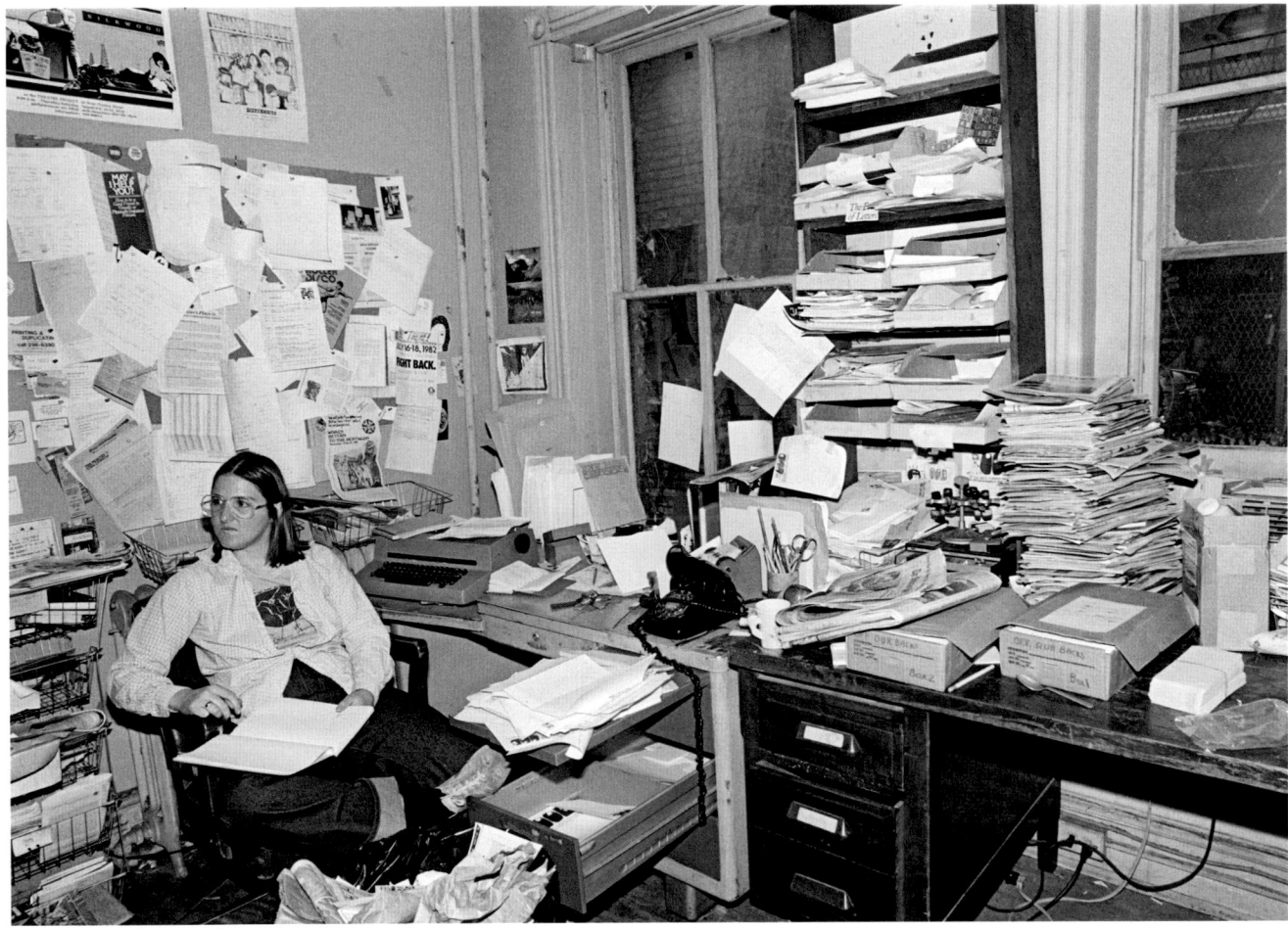

47

45. Kelley Ready inspects a sheet hot off the press at Red Sun Press, a worker-controlled collective and a union print shop committed to social change. Jamaica Plain, Massachusetts, 1986.

46. Kit Quan, at a collective meeting at Old Wives Tales bookstore, works at voicing the reality of immigrant working women like herself and her mother. Currently Kit is the office manager at Spinsters/Aunt Lute, a lesbian-feminist publishing company. San Francisco, California, 1982.

47. Office coordinator and collective member Tacie Dejanikus does the paper shuffle in the two-room Washington, D.C. office of *off our backs*. A national feminist newspaper begun in 1970, *oob* called this location home for nine years. 1981.

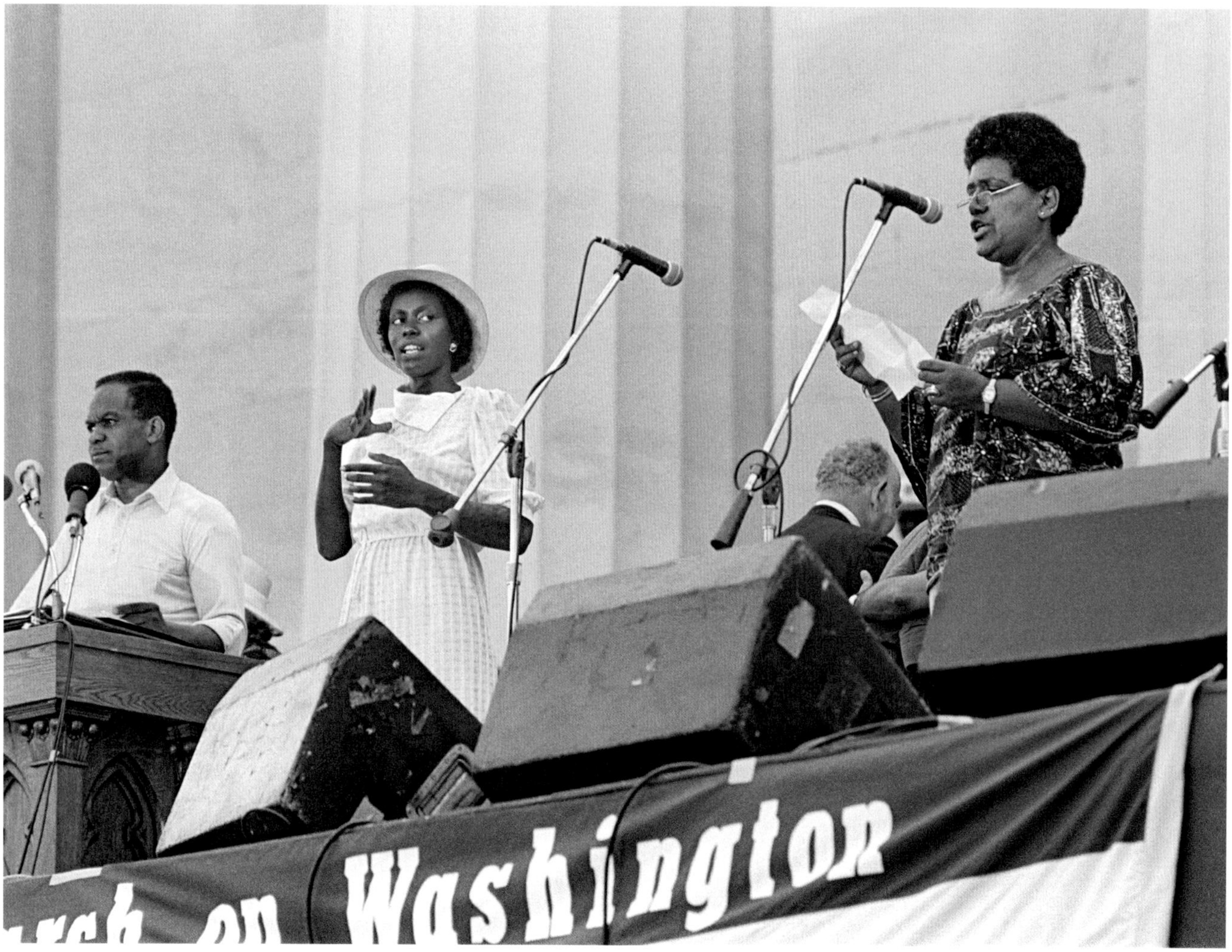

48

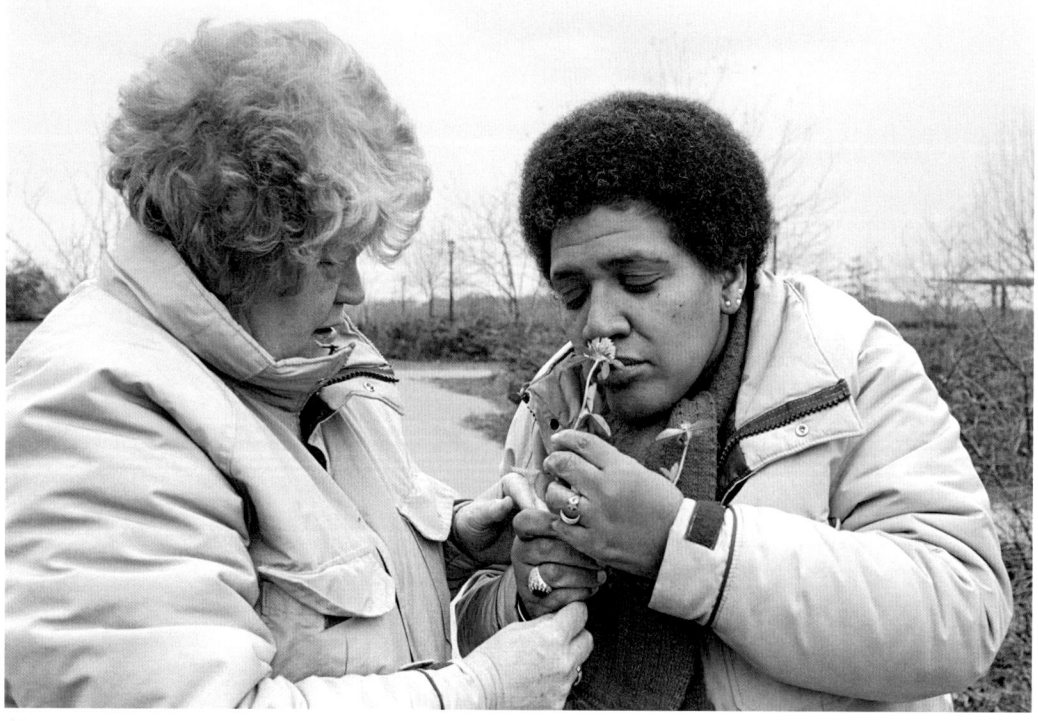

49

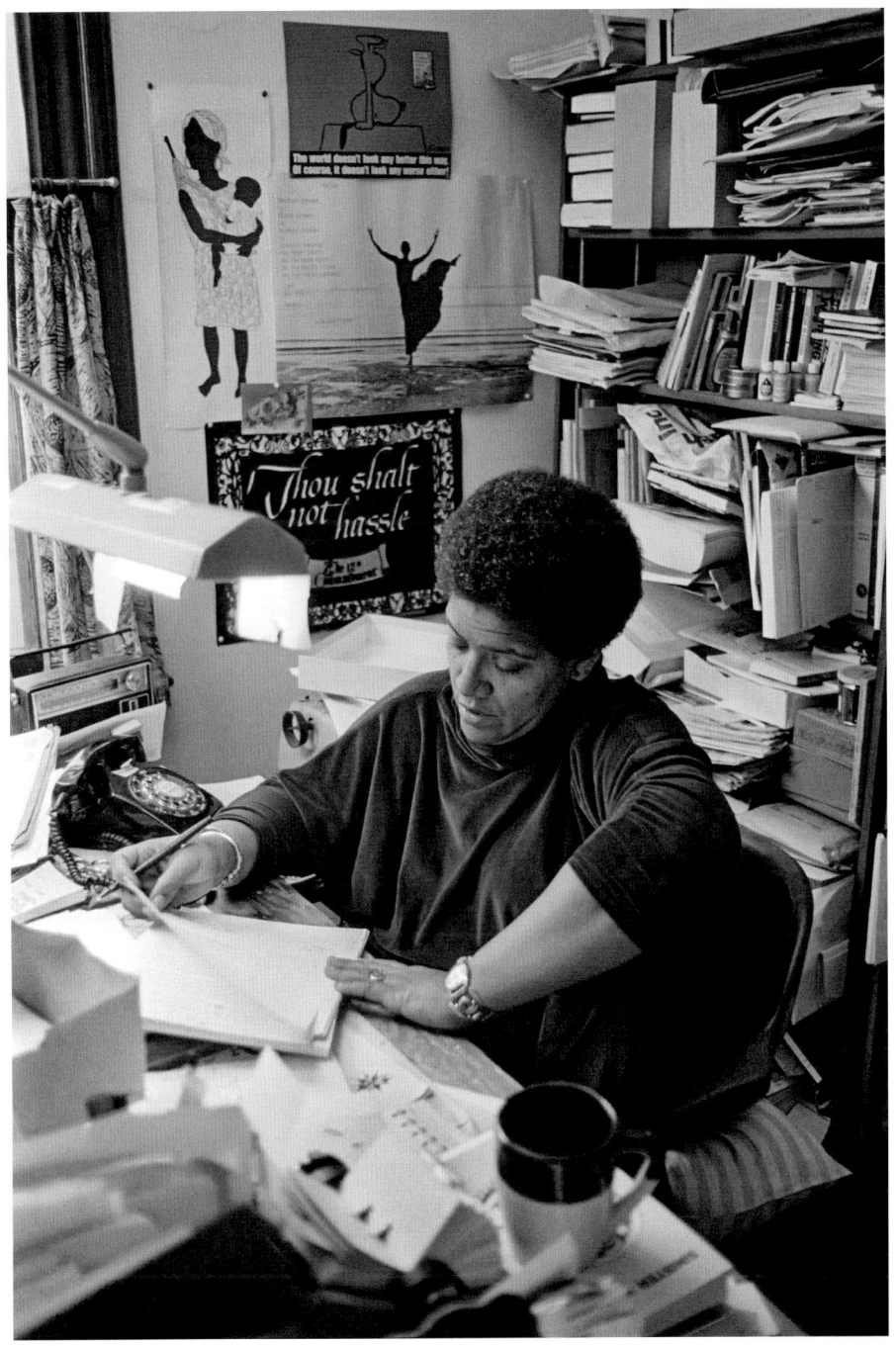

48. Audre Lorde (R), teacher, writer, poet, and activist, speaks from the steps of the Lincoln Memorial to 300,000 people who joined the 20th Anniversary March on Washington for Jobs, Peace, and Freedom, August 27, 1983. This was the first time that a representative of the lesbian and gay community addressed a major civil rights rally.

49. Audre and Frances Clayton (L) take a winter walk in the park. Staten Island, New York, 1981.

50. Audre reviews the final draft of *Zami: A New Spelling of My Name*, her biomythography. Staten Island, New York, 1981.

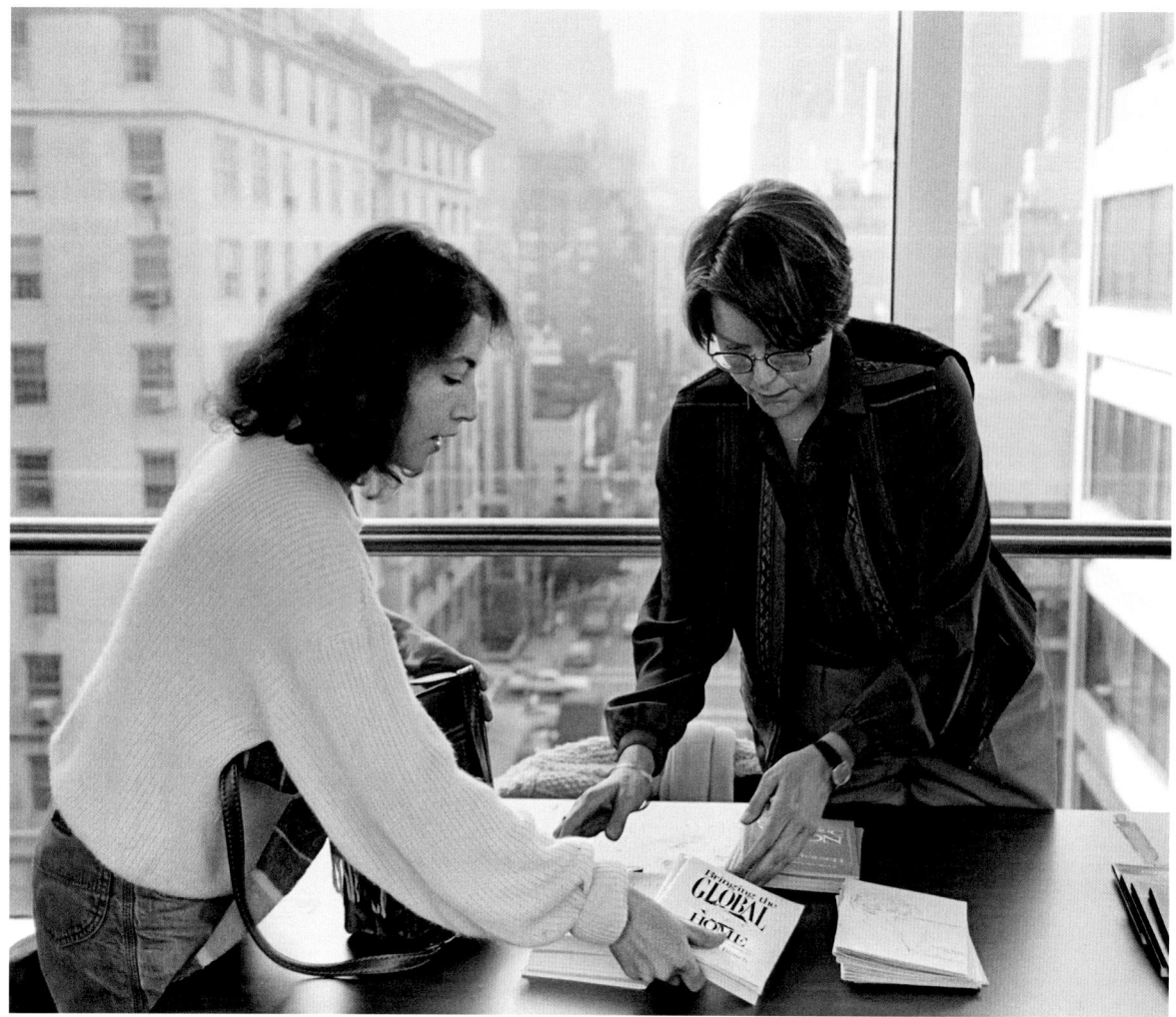

51

51. Claudia Hinojosa and Charlotte Bunch arrange a publications display at a conference on lesbian lives. Claudia is one of the first outspoken lesbian-feminist organizers in Mexico City. Charlotte has been an organizer, writer, and speaker in the U.S. women's movement for nearly 20 years. Together, they have presented lesbian and feminist issues in a global context at several events, including the 1980 Copenhagen and the 1985 Nairobi non-governmental forums held in conjunction with the United Nations Decade for Women. New York City, 1985.

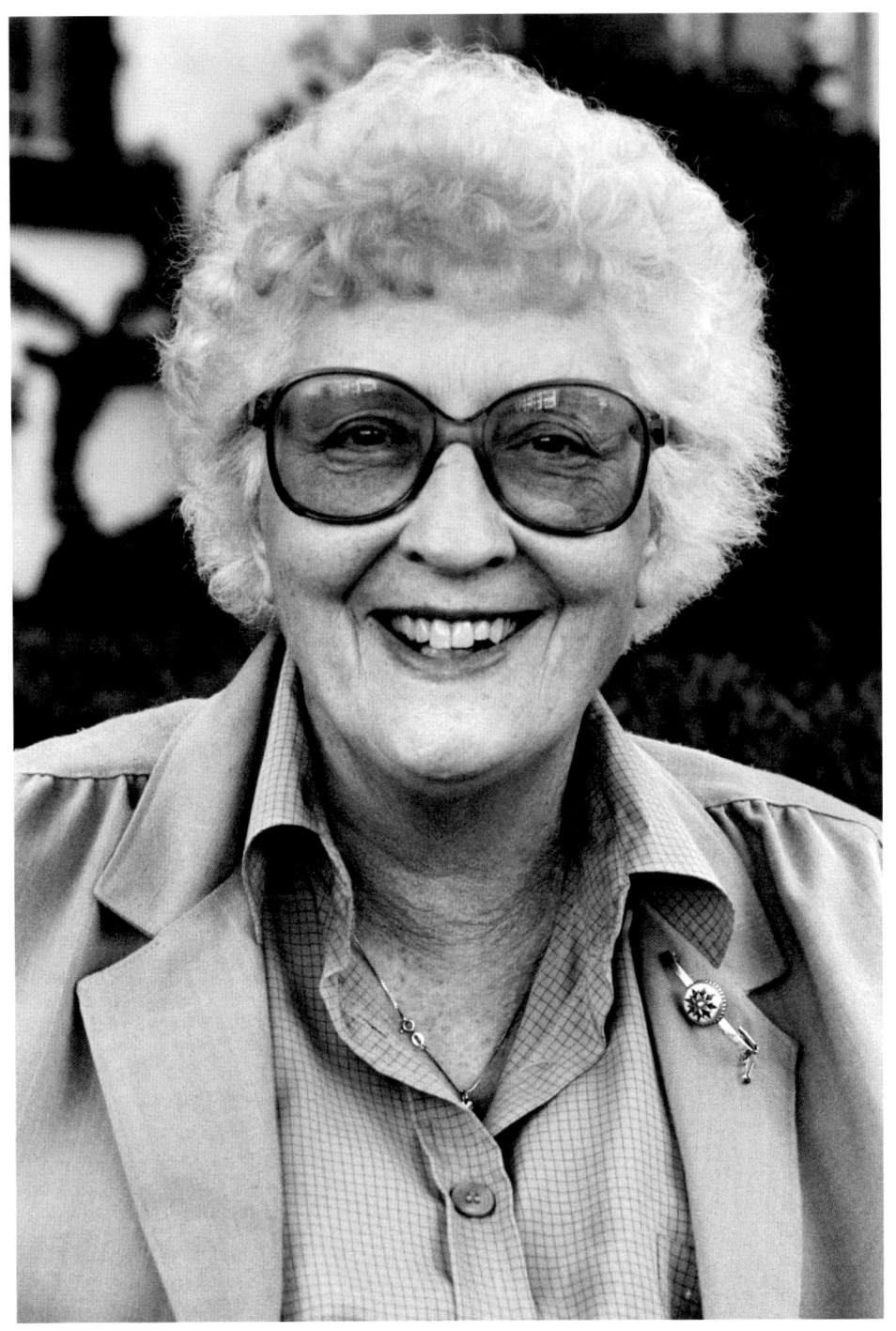

52

52. May Sarton, author of many
beloved volumes of poetry,
memoirs, journals, and novels,
most recently *The Magnificent
Spinster*, lives in Maine.
Washington, D.C., 1985.

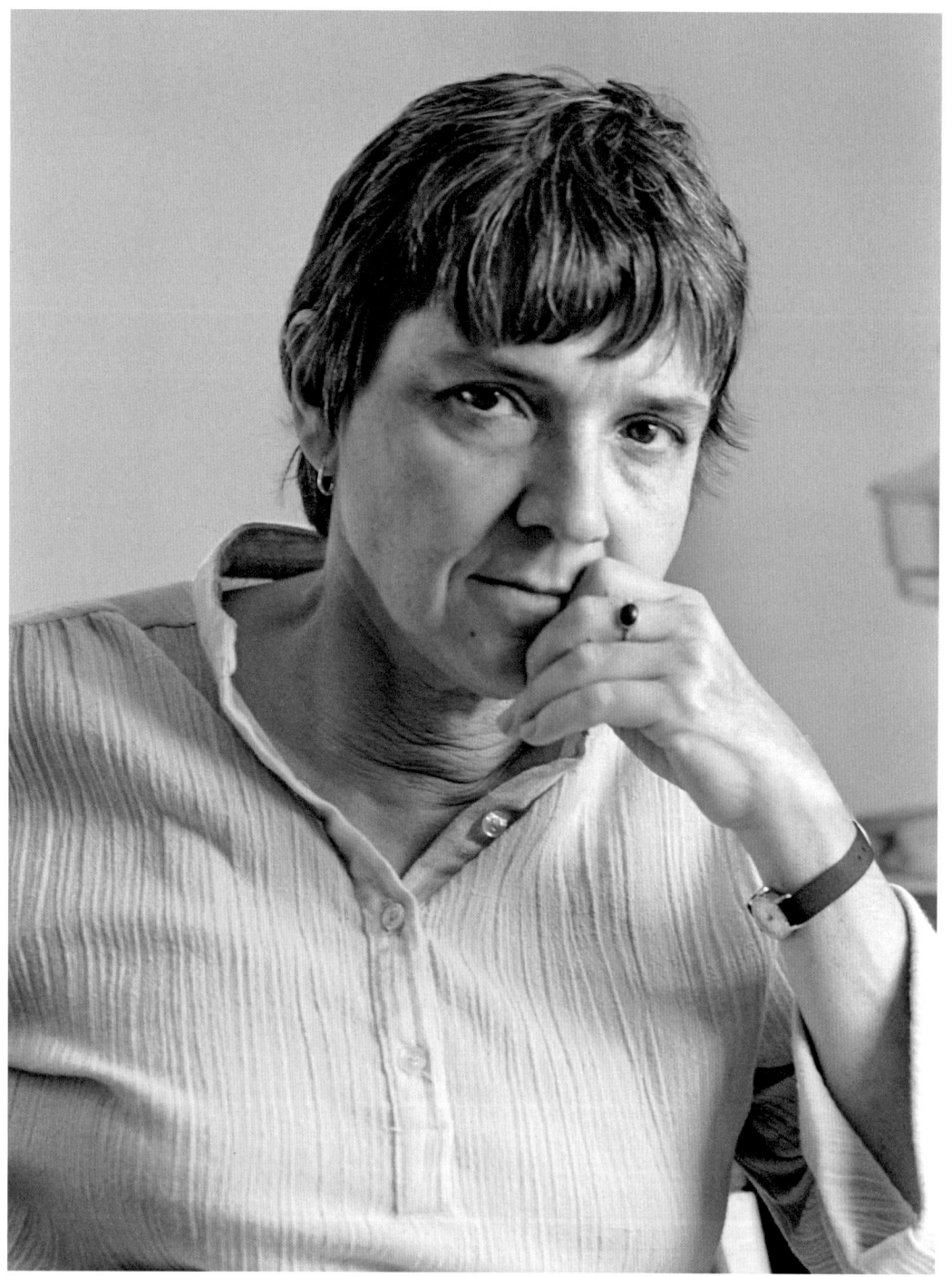

53

53. Adrienne Rich is a poet, activist, and writer. At this time, she and novelist Michelle Cliff were co-editors of *Sinister Wisdom*, a lesbian-feminist magazine. Montague, Massachusetts, 1981.

54. Adrienne reads her poetry at the University of Maryland at College Park on May Day, 1986.

55. Adrienne and poet Minnie Bruce Pratt leave Lammas women's bookstore with owner Mary Farmer after a book-signing party to celebrate Adrienne's *Your Native Land, Your Life*. Washington, D.C., 1986.

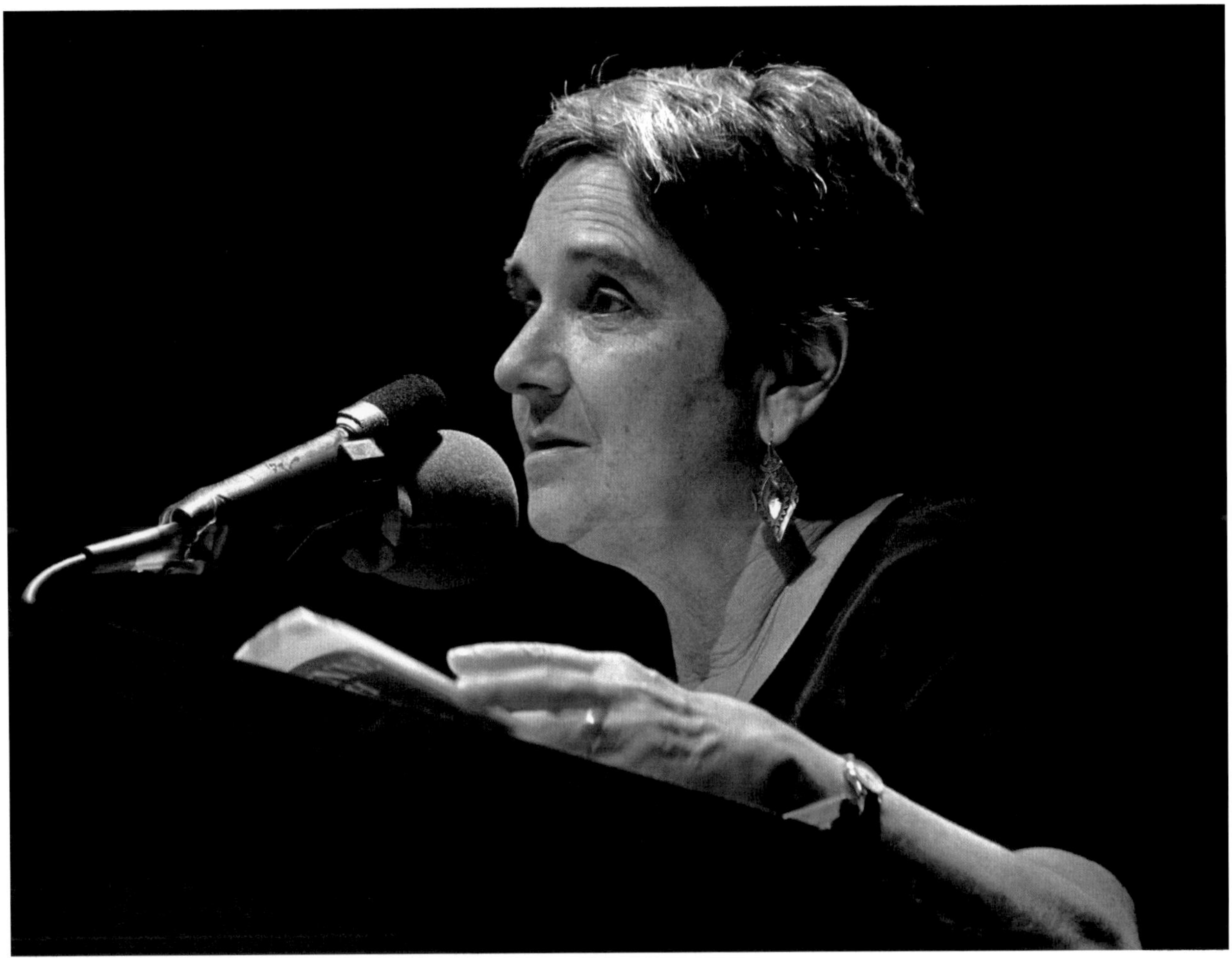

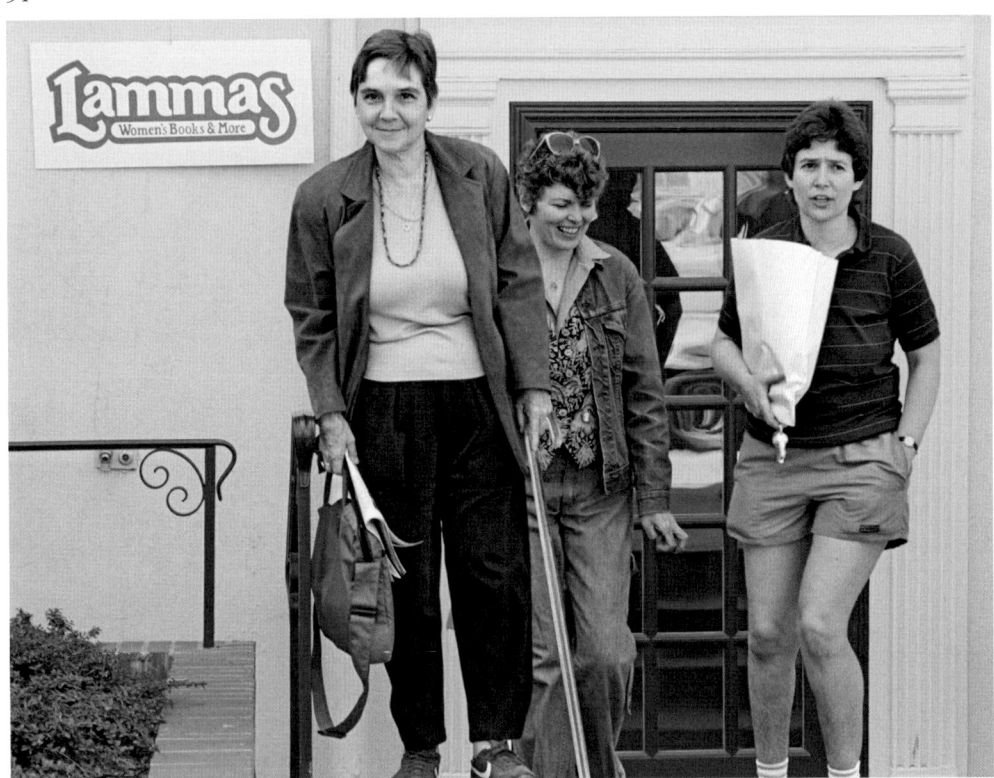

54

55

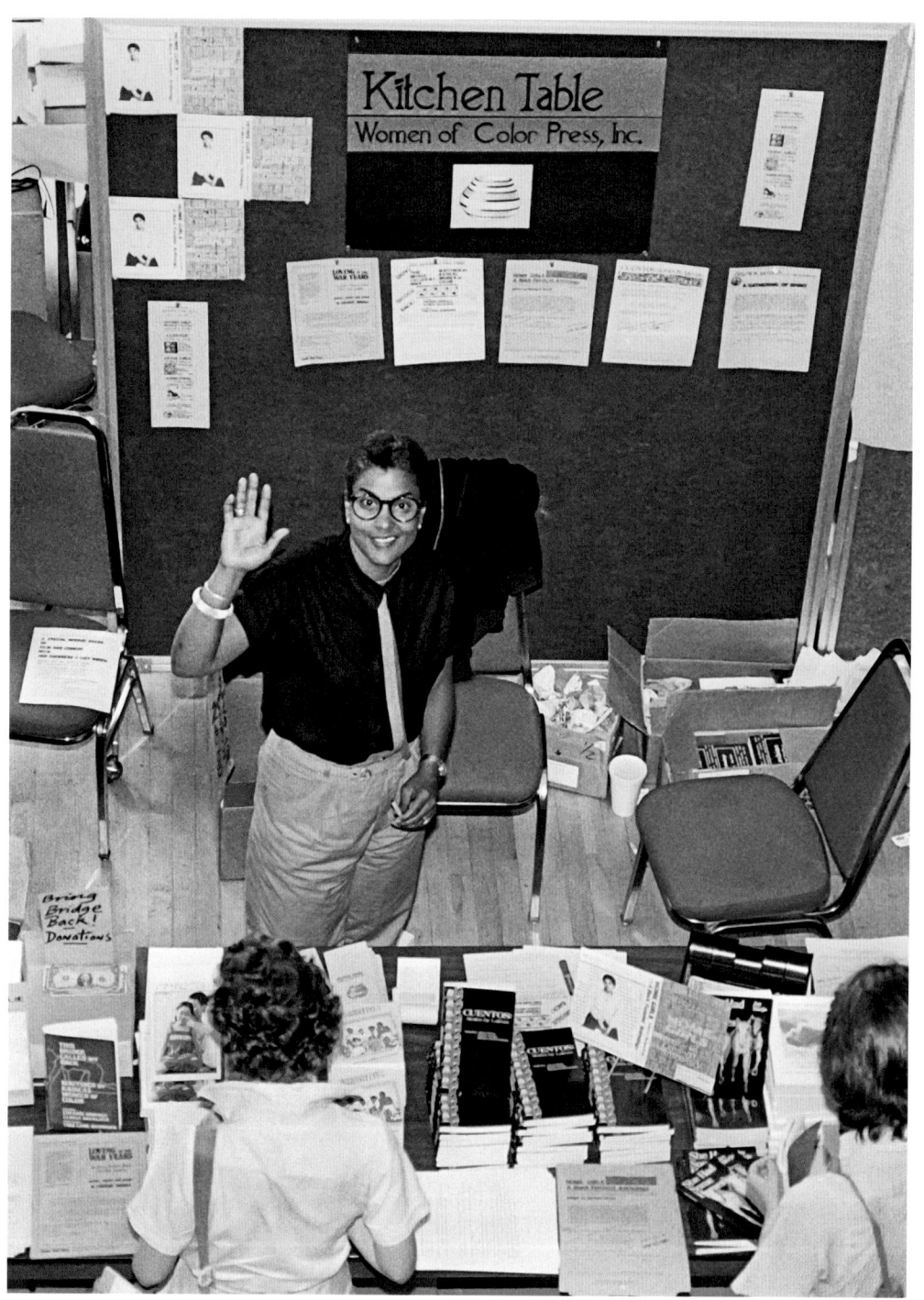

56. Poet Cheryl Clarke at the
Kitchen Table: Women of Color
Press book exhibit at the National
Women's Studies Association
Conference, Ohio State University,
Columbus, Ohio. 1983.

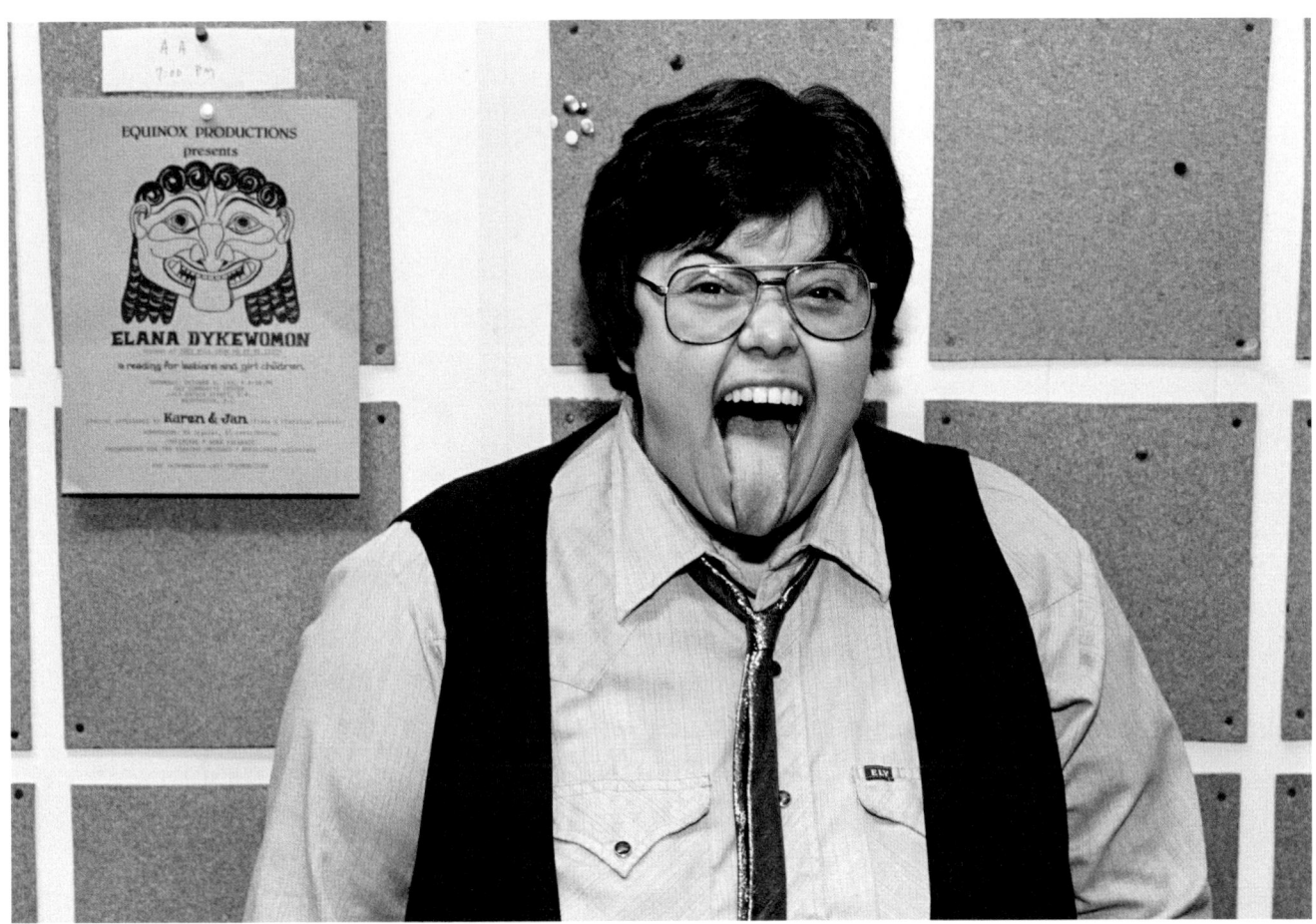

57

57. Elana Dykewomon as Gorgon
at the Washington, D.C. stop on her
1982 U.S./Canada reading tour for
lesbian-only audiences. In 1987,
Elana became the editor of *Sinister
Wisdom*.

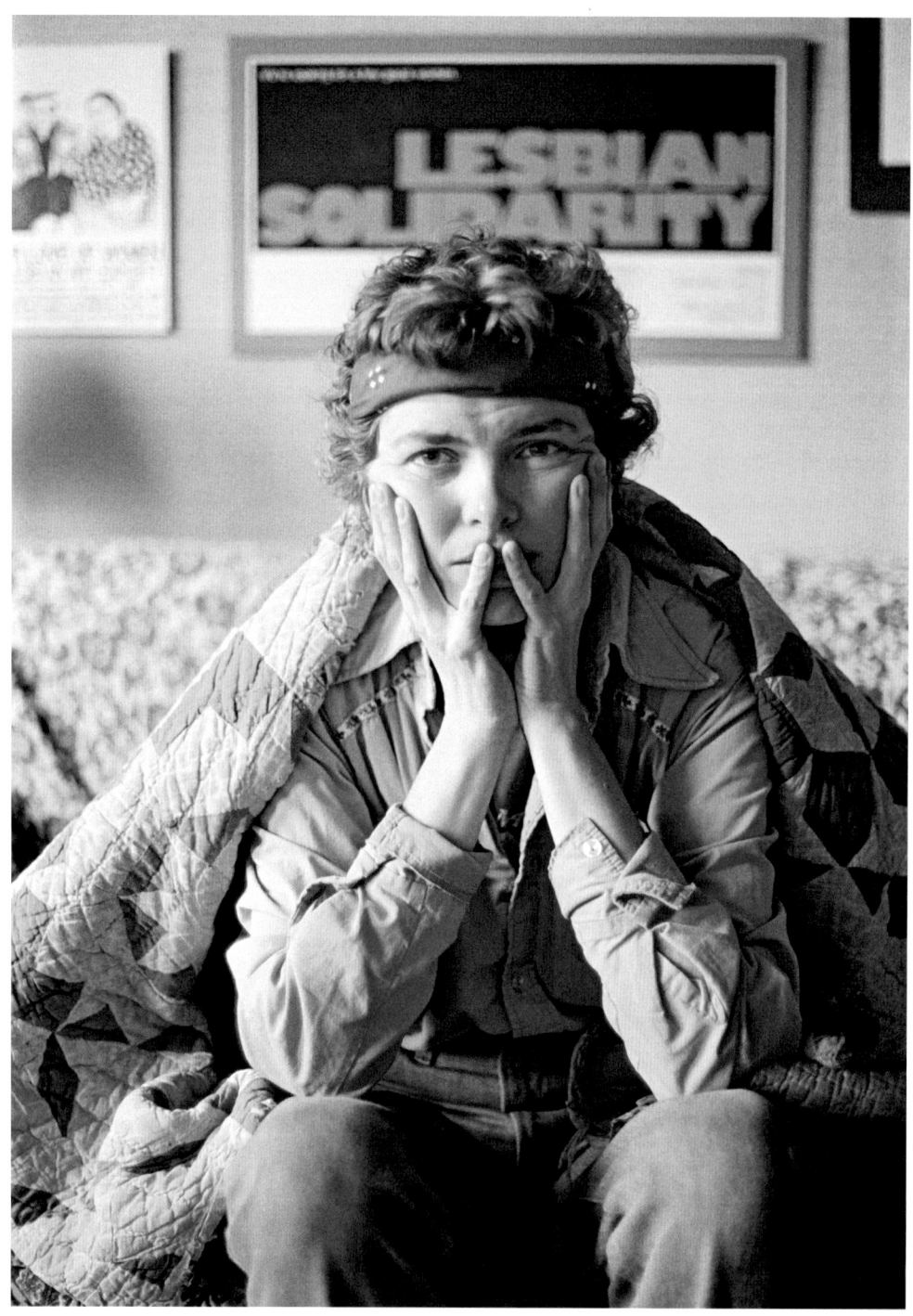

58. Minnie Bruce Pratt is a poet, essayist, teacher, and mother. During this time, she was working on poems for her book *We Say We Love Each Other*. Washington, D.C., 1983.

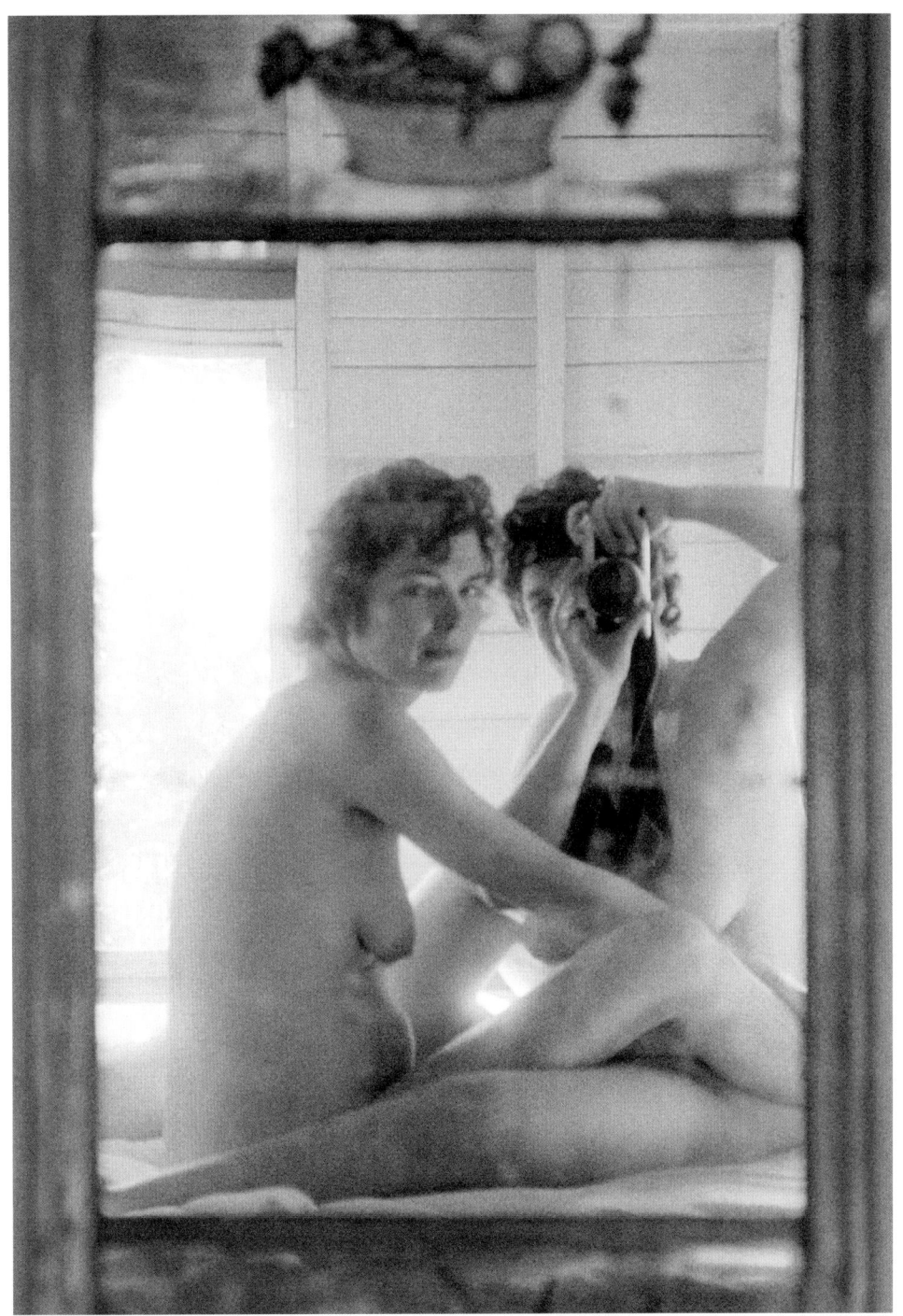

59

59. Minnie Bruce and Joan E. Biren
rest at the guest cottage of friends
in the Florida Keys. 1984.

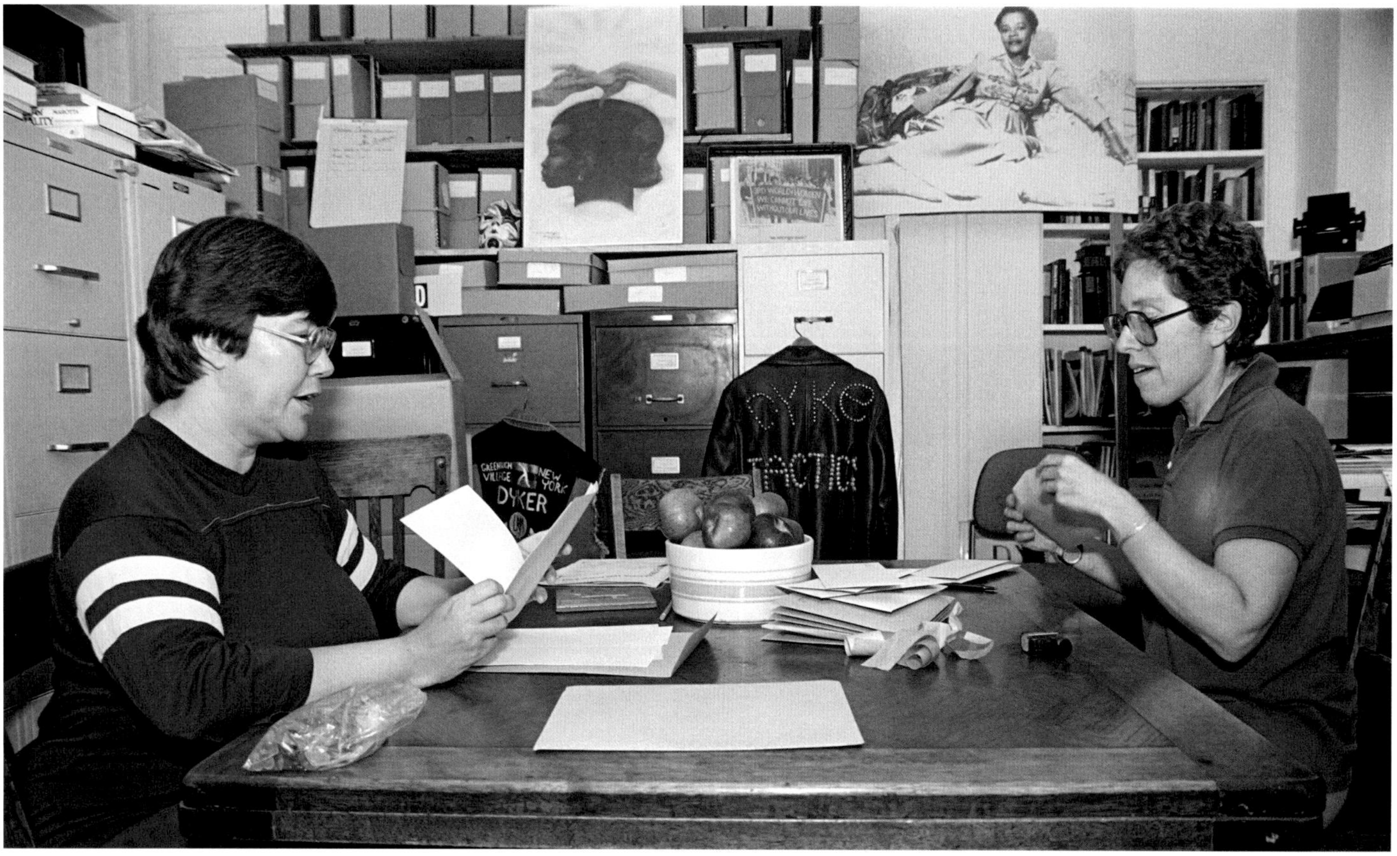

60

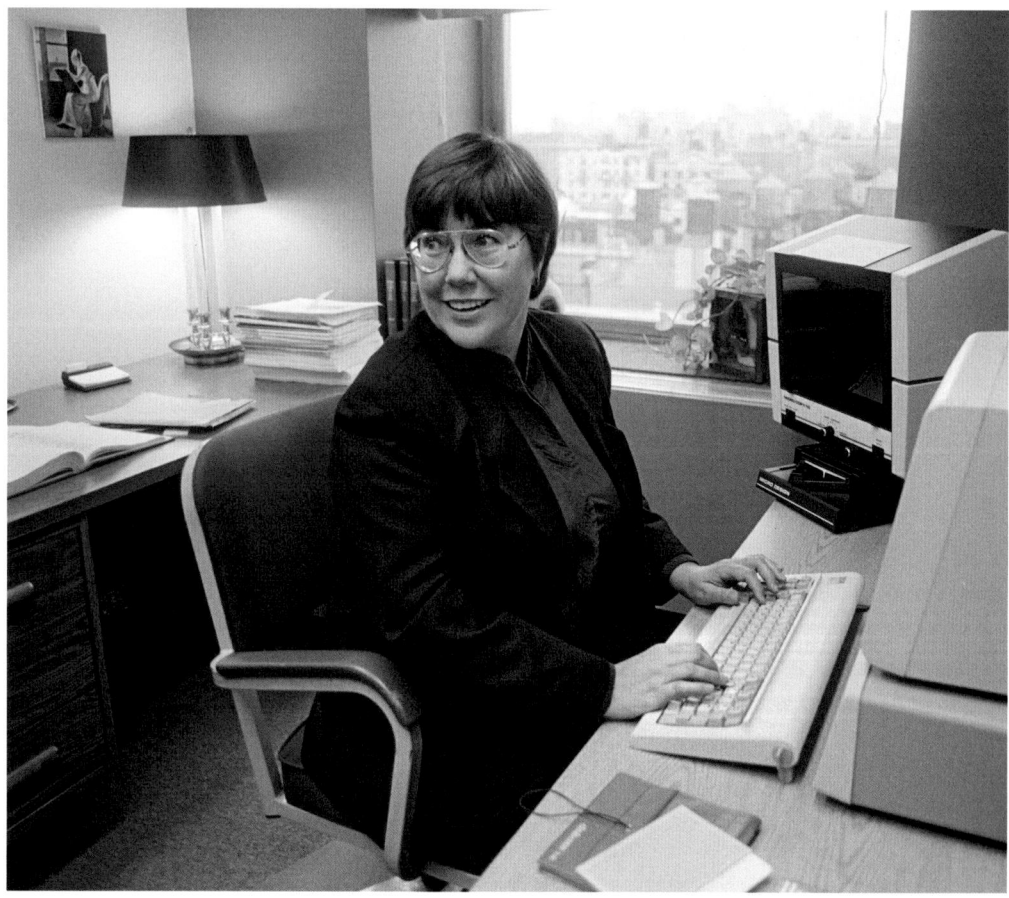

61

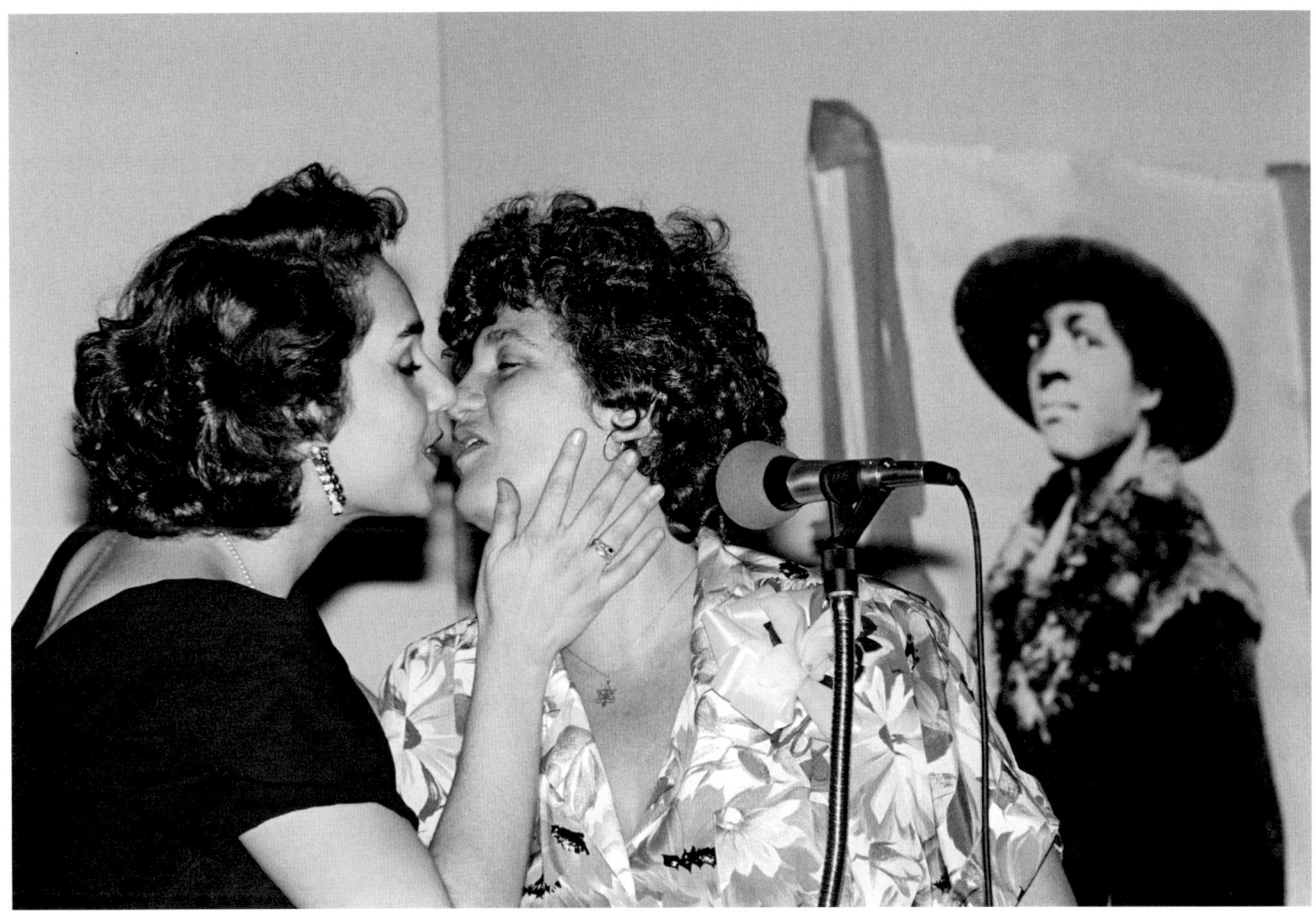

62

60. Judith Schwarz and Deborah Edel, two of the co-coordinators of the Lesbian Herstory Archives (LHA), answer requests for information on all aspects of lesbian life. They are surrounded by some of the Archives' diverse collection in its New York City home. 1986.

61. Judith is records manager for a New York City church organization. She learned how to use computers, micrographics, and optical scanning technology to help manage the vast collection of the LHA. 1986.

62. Claire Olivia Moed and Joan Nestle explore the varieties of lesbian ecstasy in front of 1500 women at the LHA's tenth anniversary benefit in New York City, 1986. Claire helps run W.O.W. (Women's One World) Cafe, a performance space. Joan is a co-founder of the LHA and the author of *A Restricted Country*.

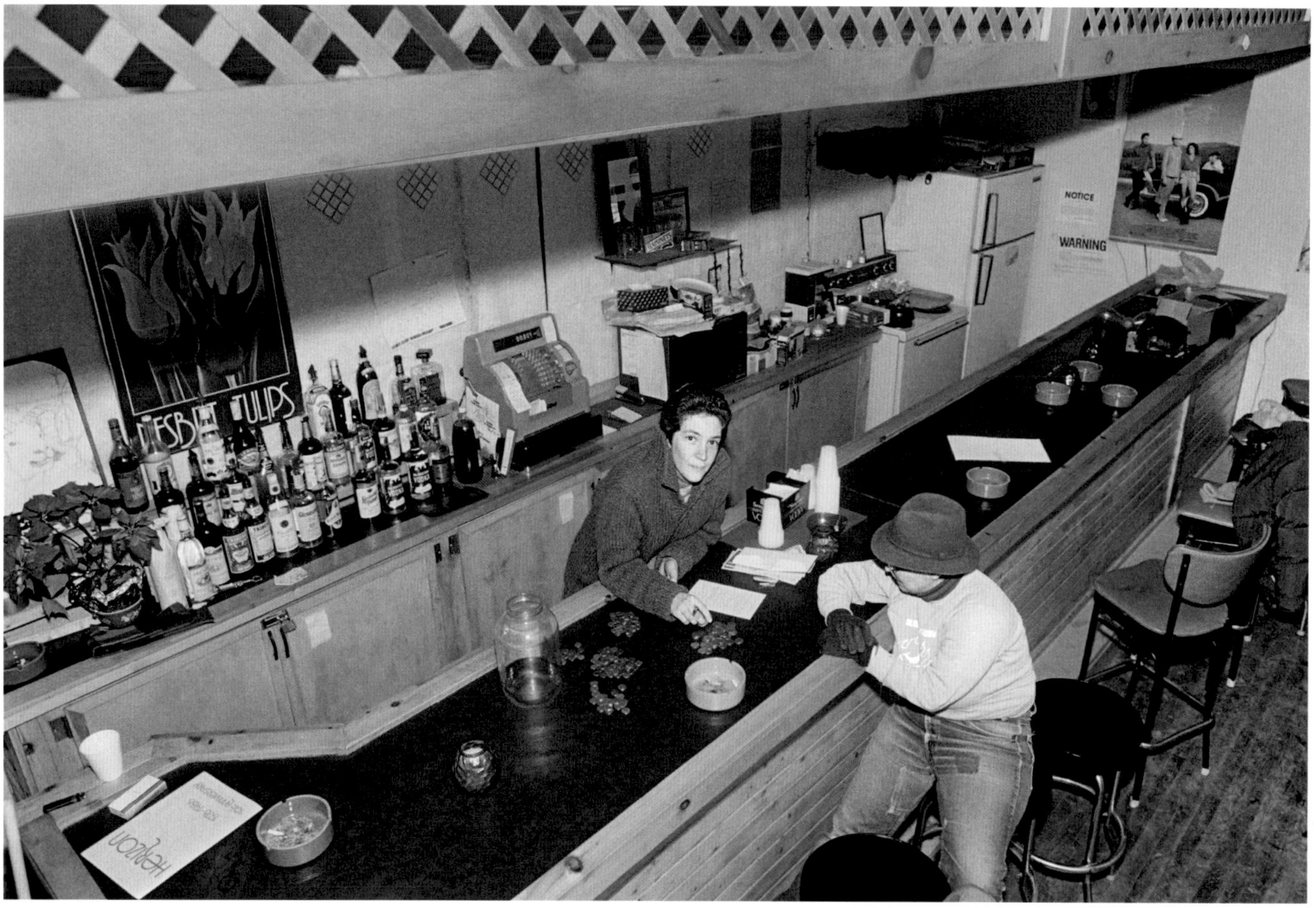

63

63. Herizon treasurer Marian Stern counts money from the donation jar while Faith Rogow waits to help construct a new wall for the women's social club in Binghamton, New York. Since 1976, Herizon has provided women-only space for events ranging from plays and concerts to slide shows and dances. 1987.

64. Longtime Atlanta Lesbian Feminist Alliance (ALFA) activist Jo Hartsoe (R) and visitor Minnie Bruce Pratt check on the progress of renovations at the new ALFA house, which was purchased in 1986. Founded in 1972, ALFA is one of the oldest lesbian-feminist organizations in continuous existence. Georgia, 1986.

65. Eleanor Smith, Dennie Doucher, and Bluebird celebrate ALFA's tenth anniversary. Eleanor had just cut the ribbon on the newly constructed wheelchair access ramp to the ALFA house. 1982.

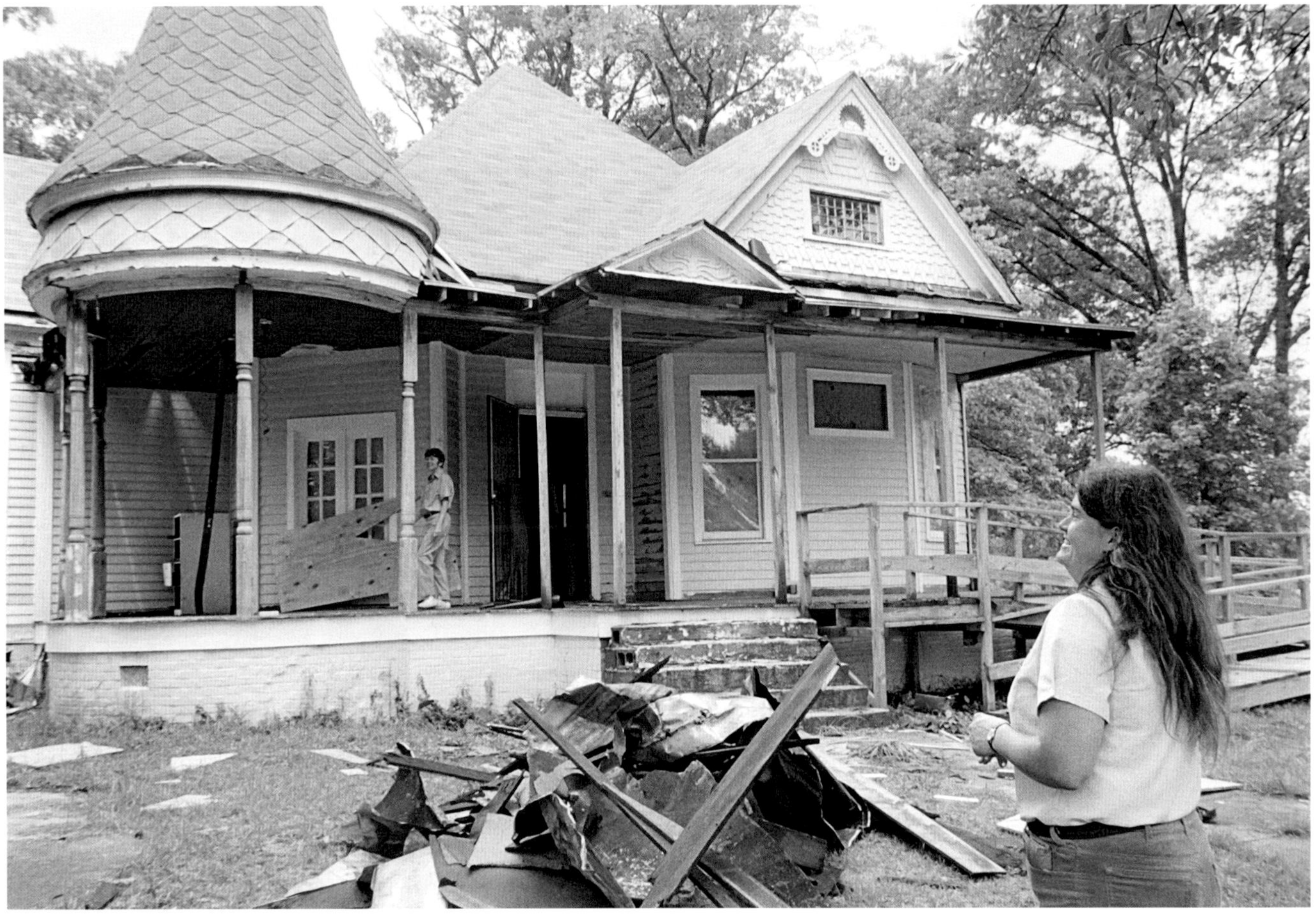

64

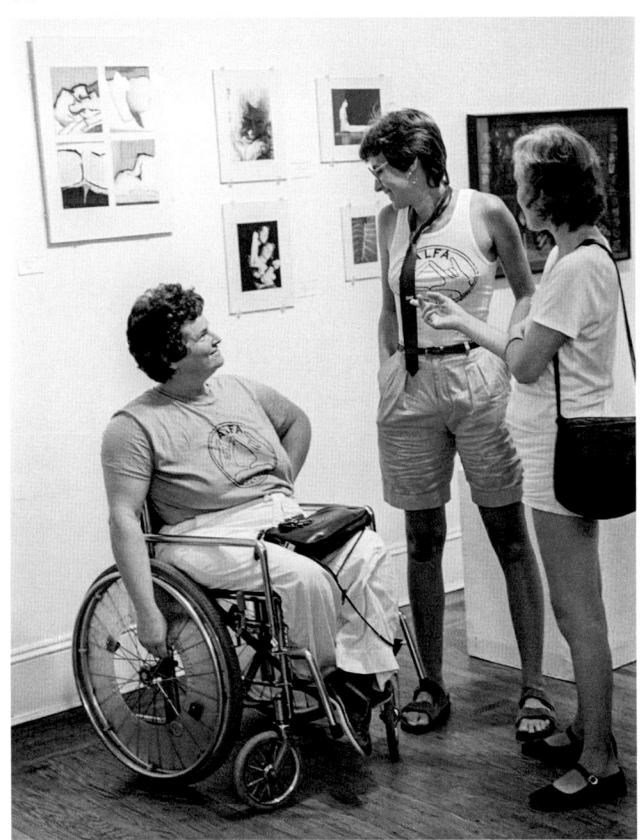

65

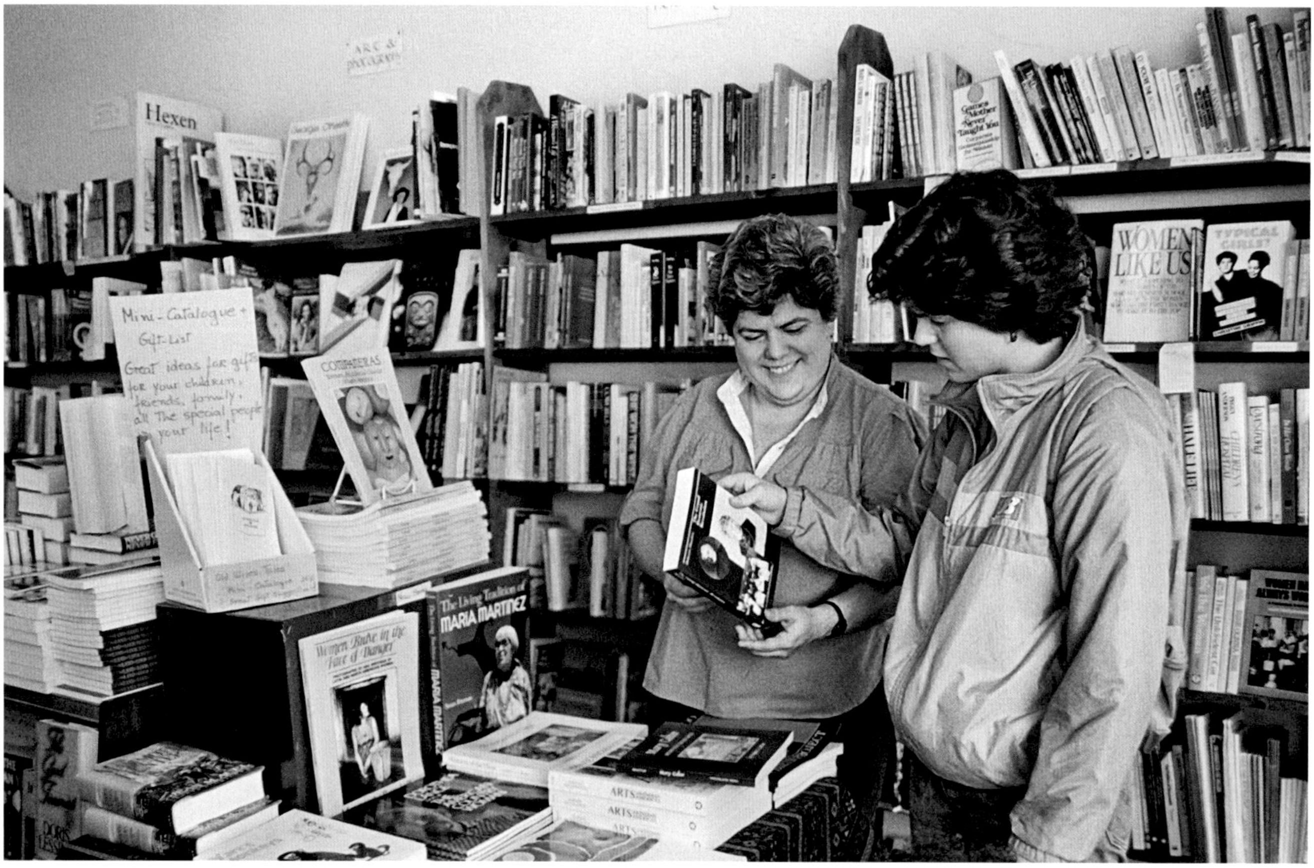

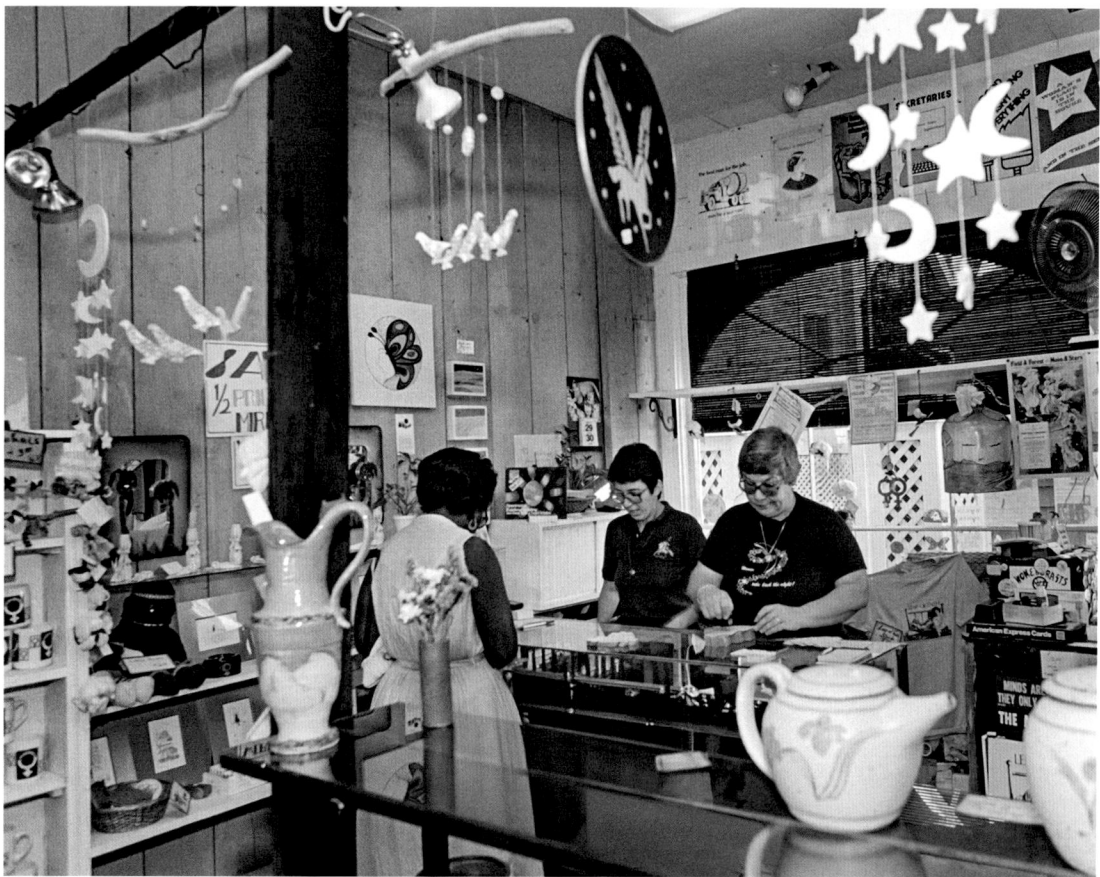

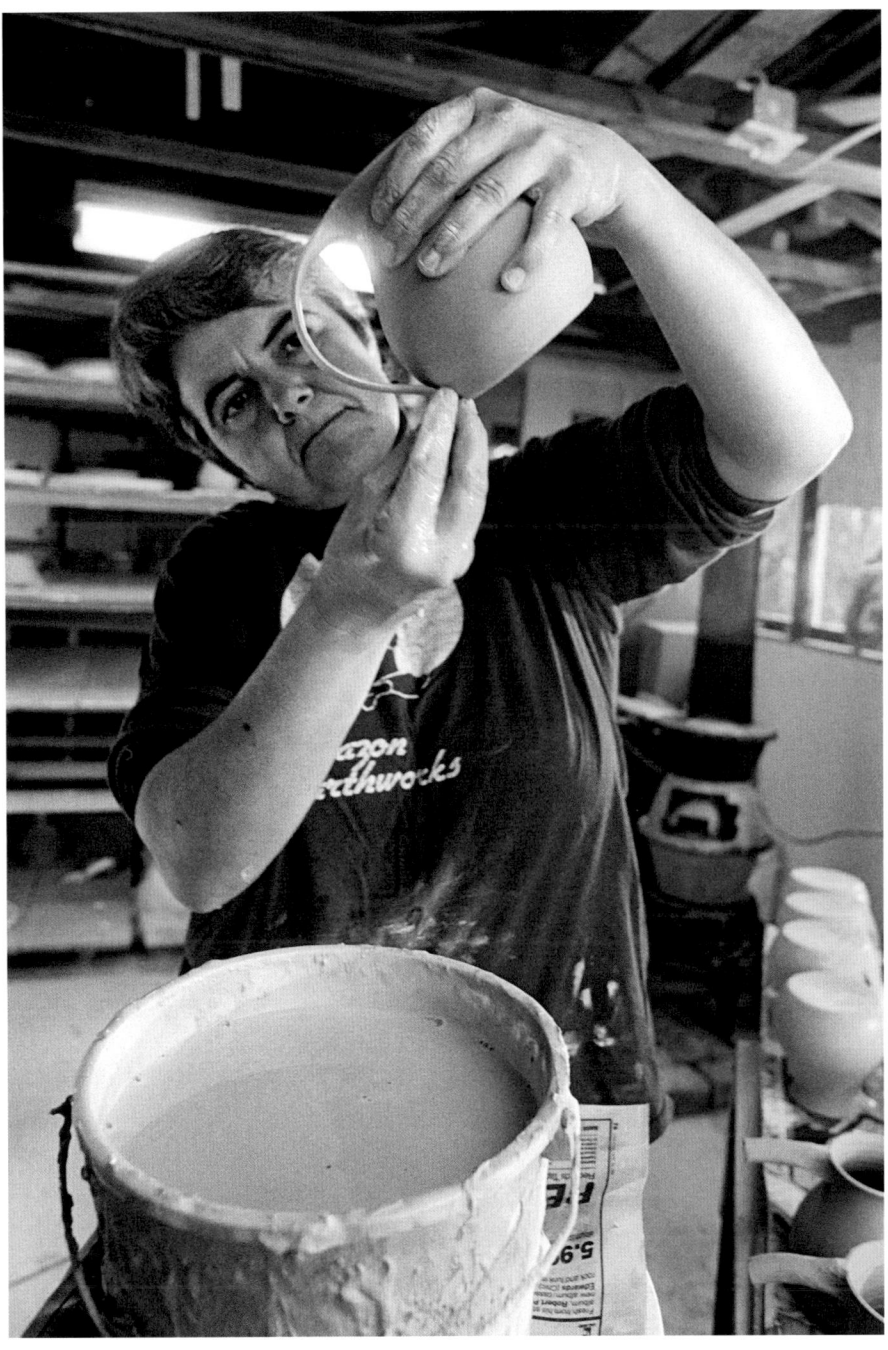

68

66. Tiana Arruda introduces a customer to a newly-arrived feminist book at Old Wives Tales, Women's Visions and Books. Tiana has been a member of the bookstore collective for six years. San Francisco, California, 1986.

67. Owners Carol Karlmann and Joie Deall help a visitor at their lesbian-feminist shop, Womancrafts, in Provincetown, Massachusetts. Women come to the shop for information, gifts, and the 5% discount given to those who identify themselves as dykes. 1981.

68. Marguerite Kotwitz puts the finishing touch on a cup in her Amazon Earthworks studio in Benicia, California. Next she will add her unique drawings of women, and then glaze and fire. 1986.

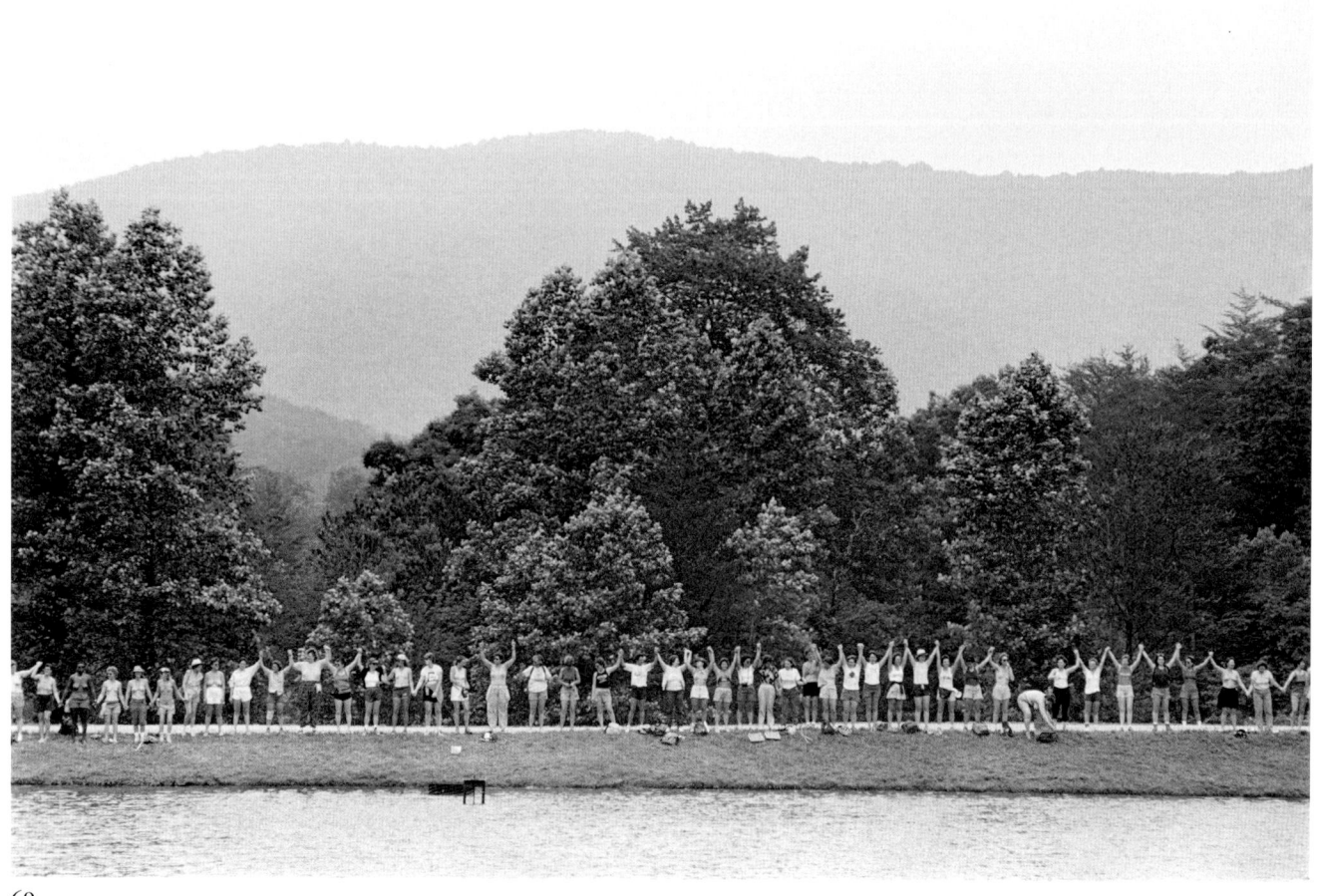

69

69. Women attending the third annual Southern Women's Music and Comedy Festival join hands in a two-mile circle around a lake in northeastern Georgia on May 25, 1986, to coincide with Hands Across America. Organizers asked for "a dollar a dyke" and raised $1600, which was donated to the Georgia Network Against Domestic Violence.

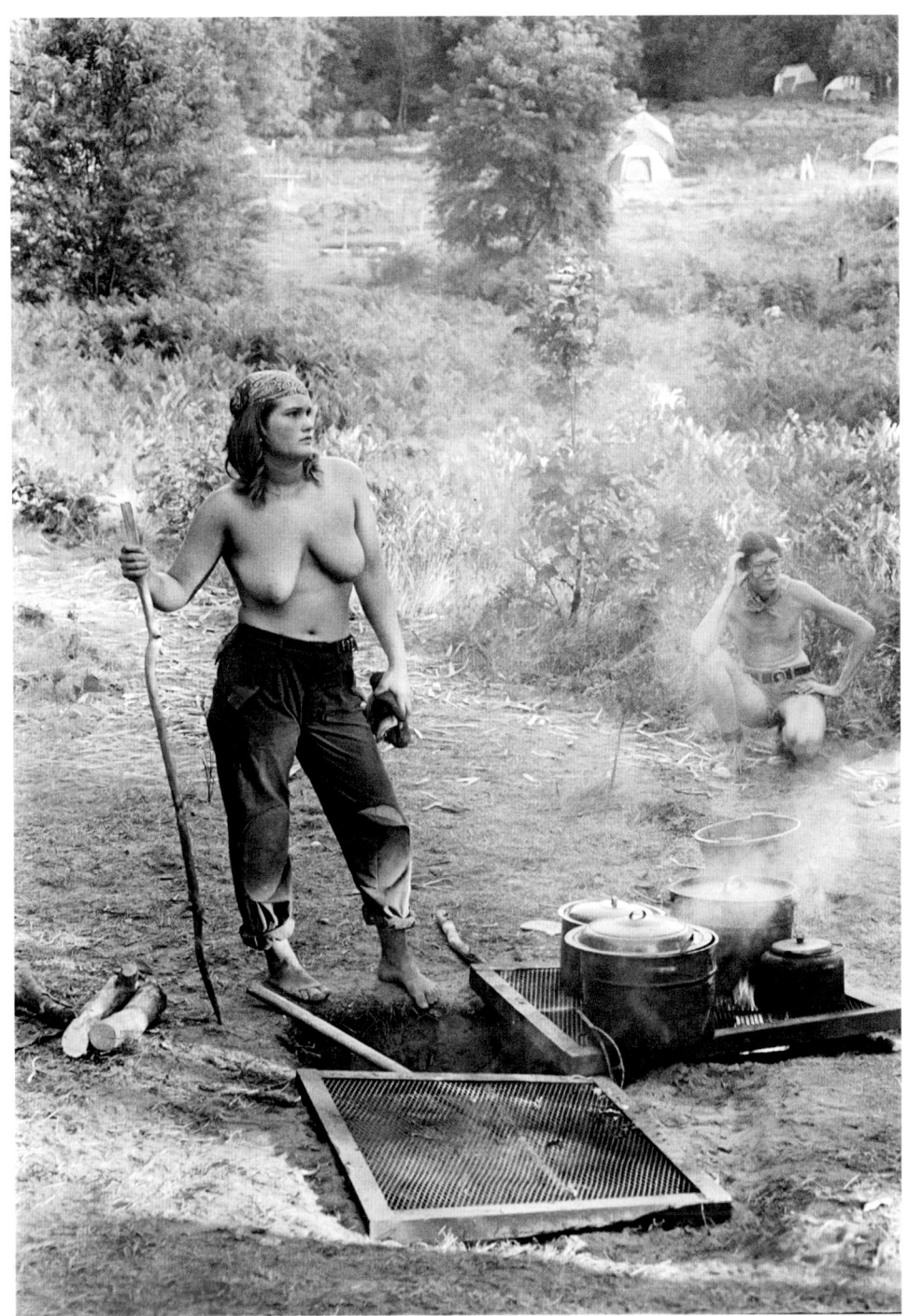

70

70. Amie Laird and J. Finch tend the
fire in the workers' kitchen at the
Michigan Womyn's Music Festival
in 1983.

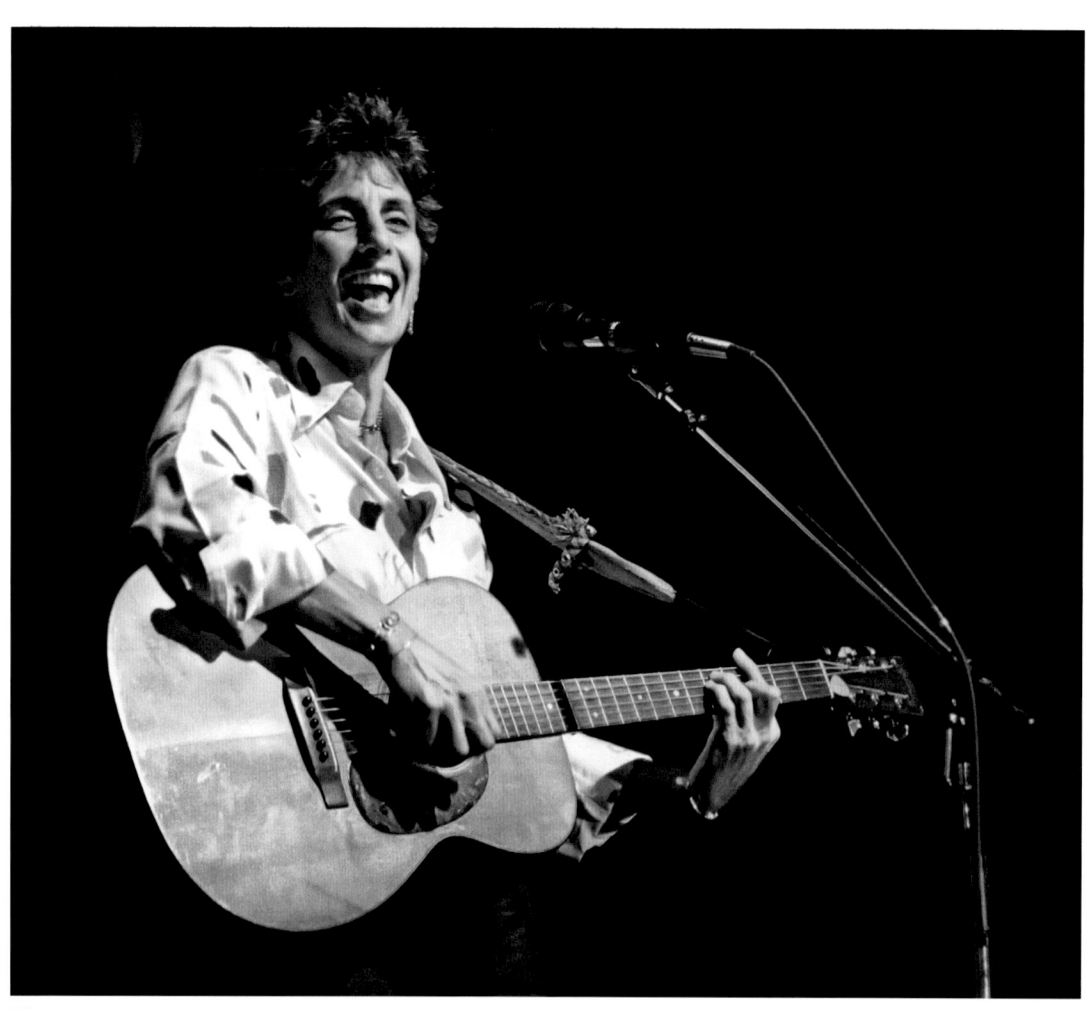

71

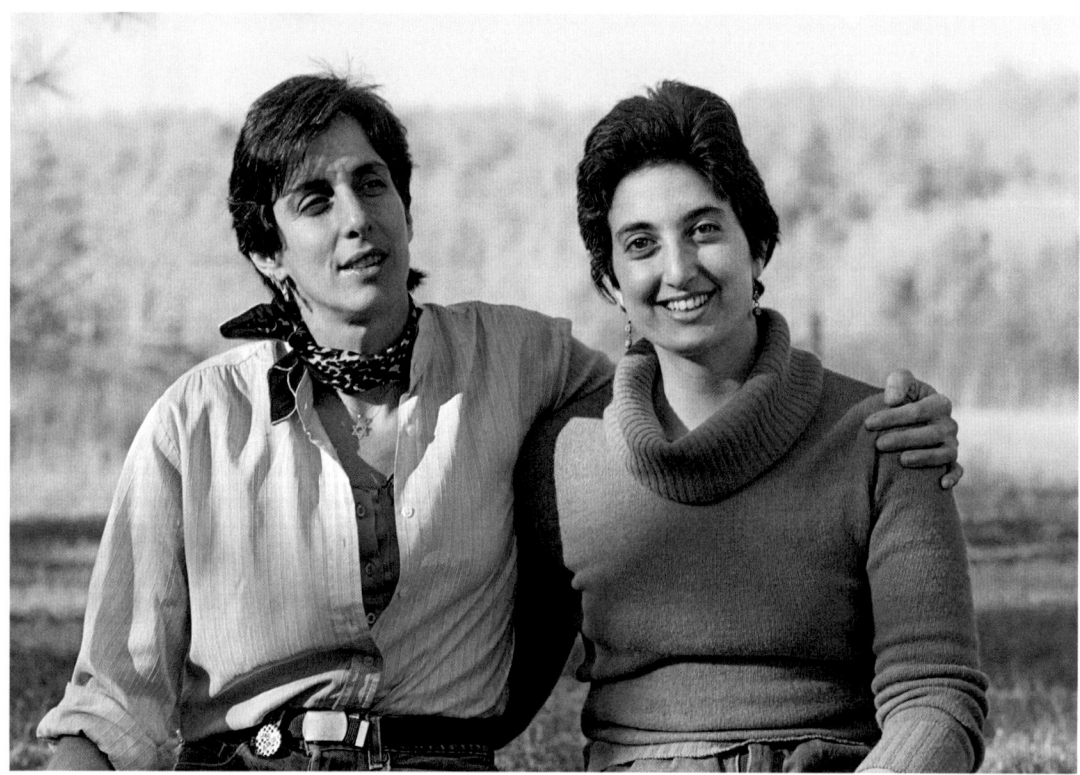

72

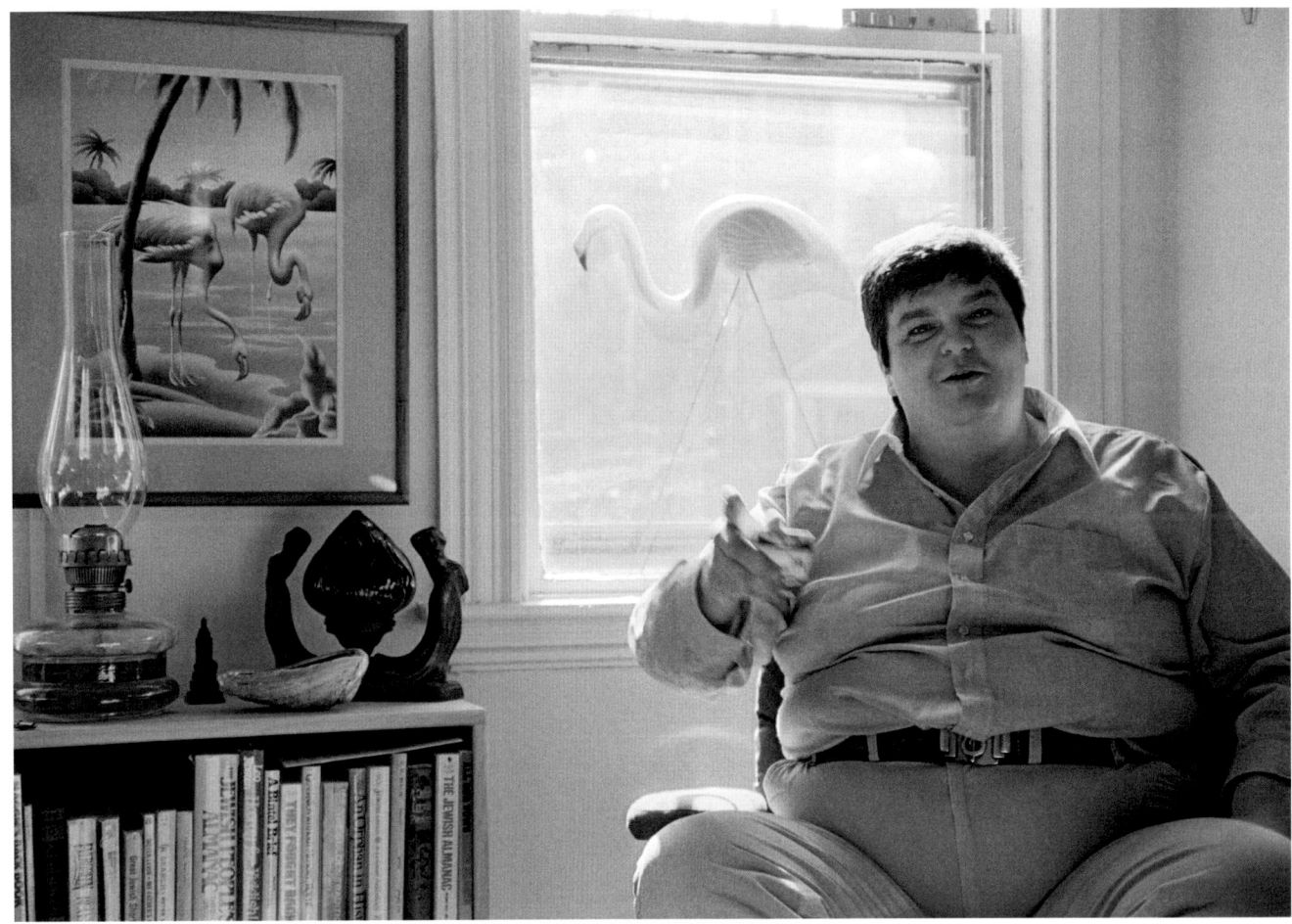

73

71. Alix Dobkin, who has been writing and singing music for women since 1970, tells us that it has *Never Been Better* at the third annual Southern Women's Music and Comedy Festival in northeastern Georgia. 1986.

72. Alix and her sister Julie Dobkin visit at a friend's farm in upstate New York. Julie is a masseuse and manages Osento, a woman-only bathhouse in San Francisco. Julie says "a sister is a sister is a sister." Alix says "a lesbian sister is a blessing." 1983.

73. Maxine Feldman makes her point, with humor, in her Boston home in 1985. What is now called women's music began in 1969 with the release of Maxine's proud lesbian recording "Angry Atthis."

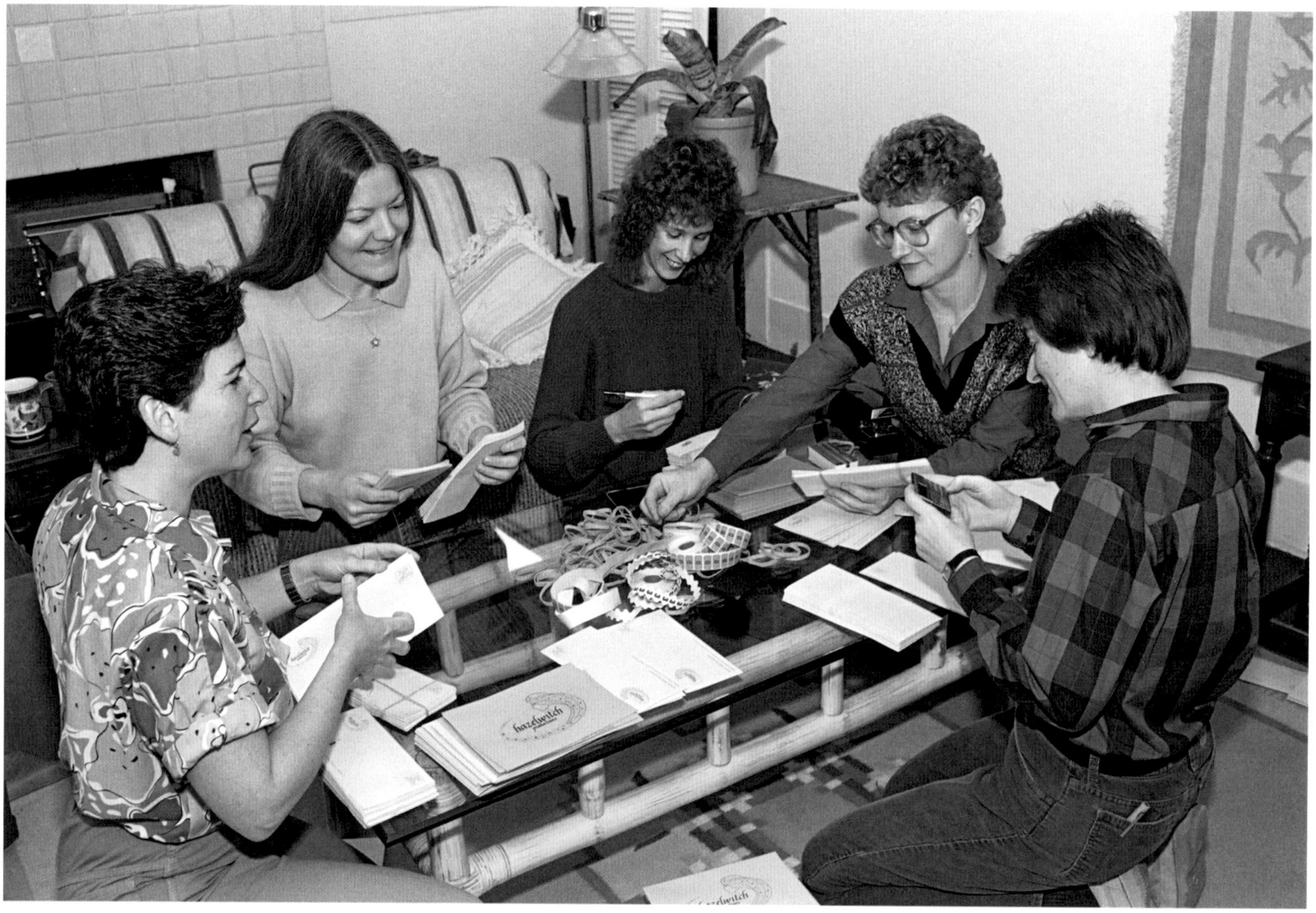

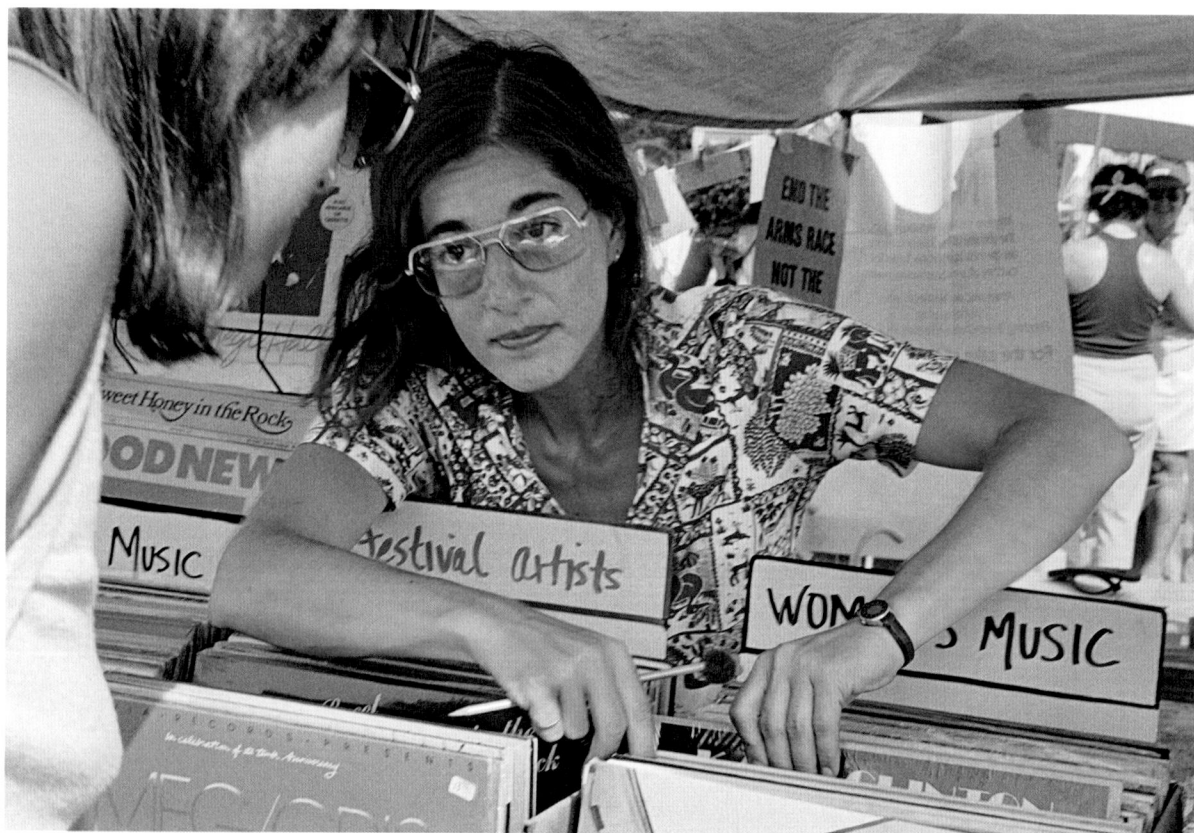

74

75

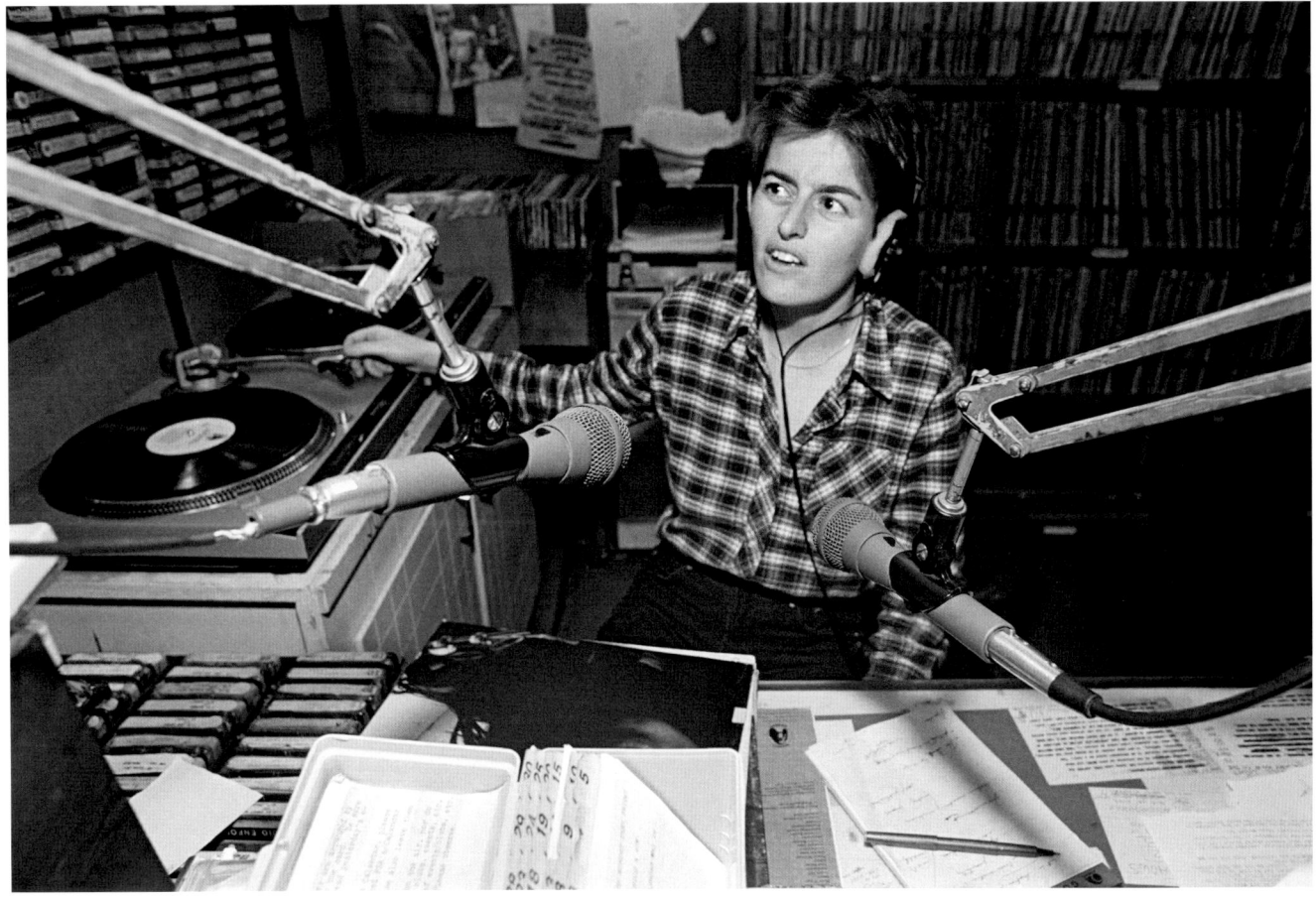

74. In the tradition of the quilting bee, Gail Eldridge, Sherry Collier, Janice Reed, Cherry Wolf, and Pokey Anderson of Hazelwitch Productions mail out information on the next women's cultural event in Houston, Texas. Hazelwitch member Tori Williams is not pictured. 1987.

75. Laurie Fuchs of Ladyslipper assists a customer at the 1983 Sisterfire festival, a multi-cultural celebration of women artists held just outside Washington, D.C. In 1976, Laurie founded Ladyslipper, the largest national distributor of recordings by women.

76. One of the most popular shows at community radio station KPFT in Houston, Texas is the lesbian-feminist show, *Breakthrough*, co-produced each week since 1981 by Pokey Anderson and Cherry Wolf. Here Pokey serves up her special blend of women's music. 1982.

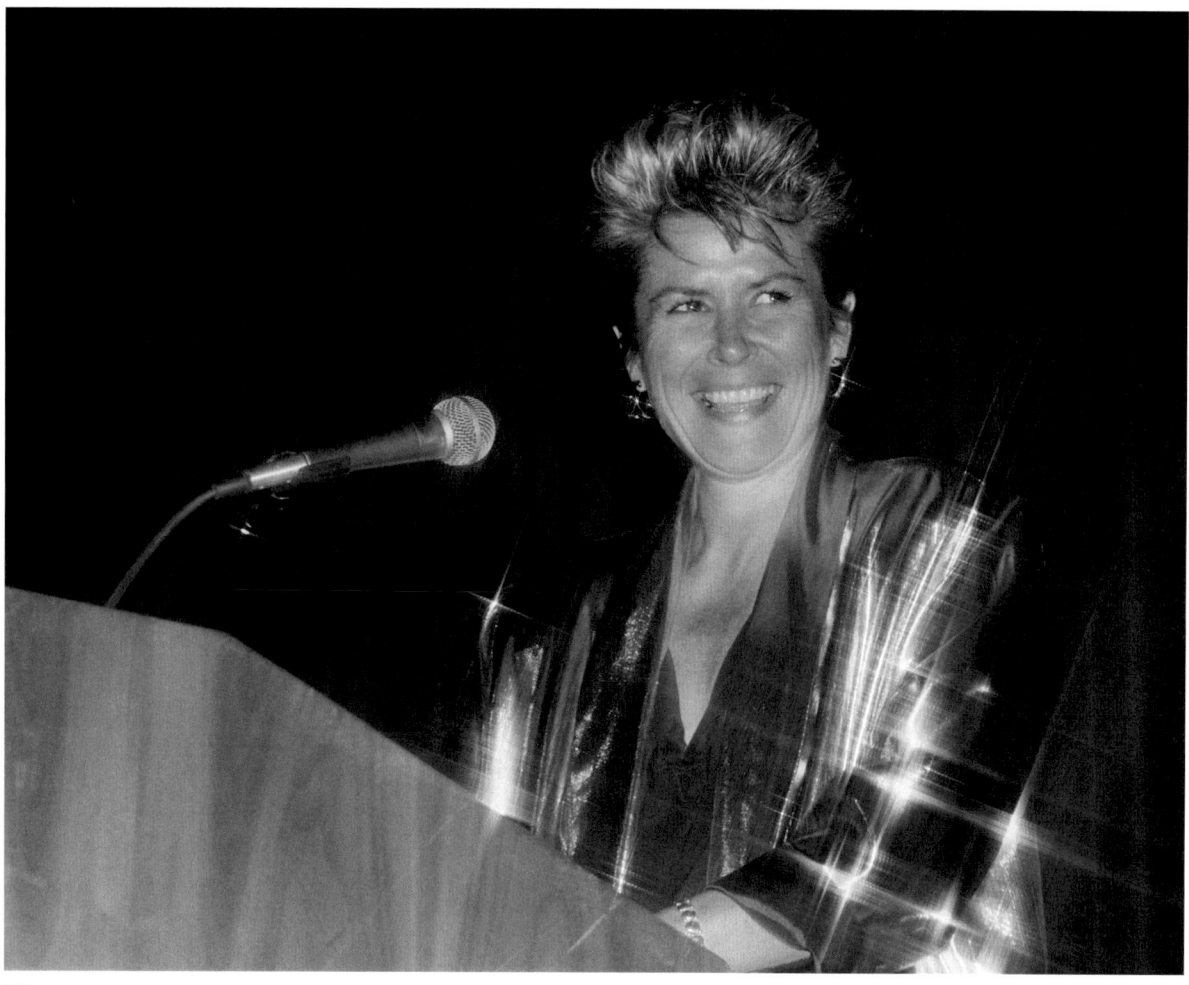

77

77. Fumerist (feminist humorist) Kate Clinton co-emcees the third annual Human Rights Campaign Fund Gala at the Sheraton Ballroom in Washington, D.C., in October, 1986. Kate's sharp political and sexual satire filled the room with laughter.

78. Boden Sandstrom, president and chief engineer of City Sound Productions, does her job at Washington, D.C.'s 1987 Gay and Lesbian Pride Day festival. Boden has been providing sound engineering to the community for more than 12 years.

79. Boden gets rowdy between sound checks at the 1984 Michigan Womyn's Music Festival while digging ditches for the large outdoor kitchen.

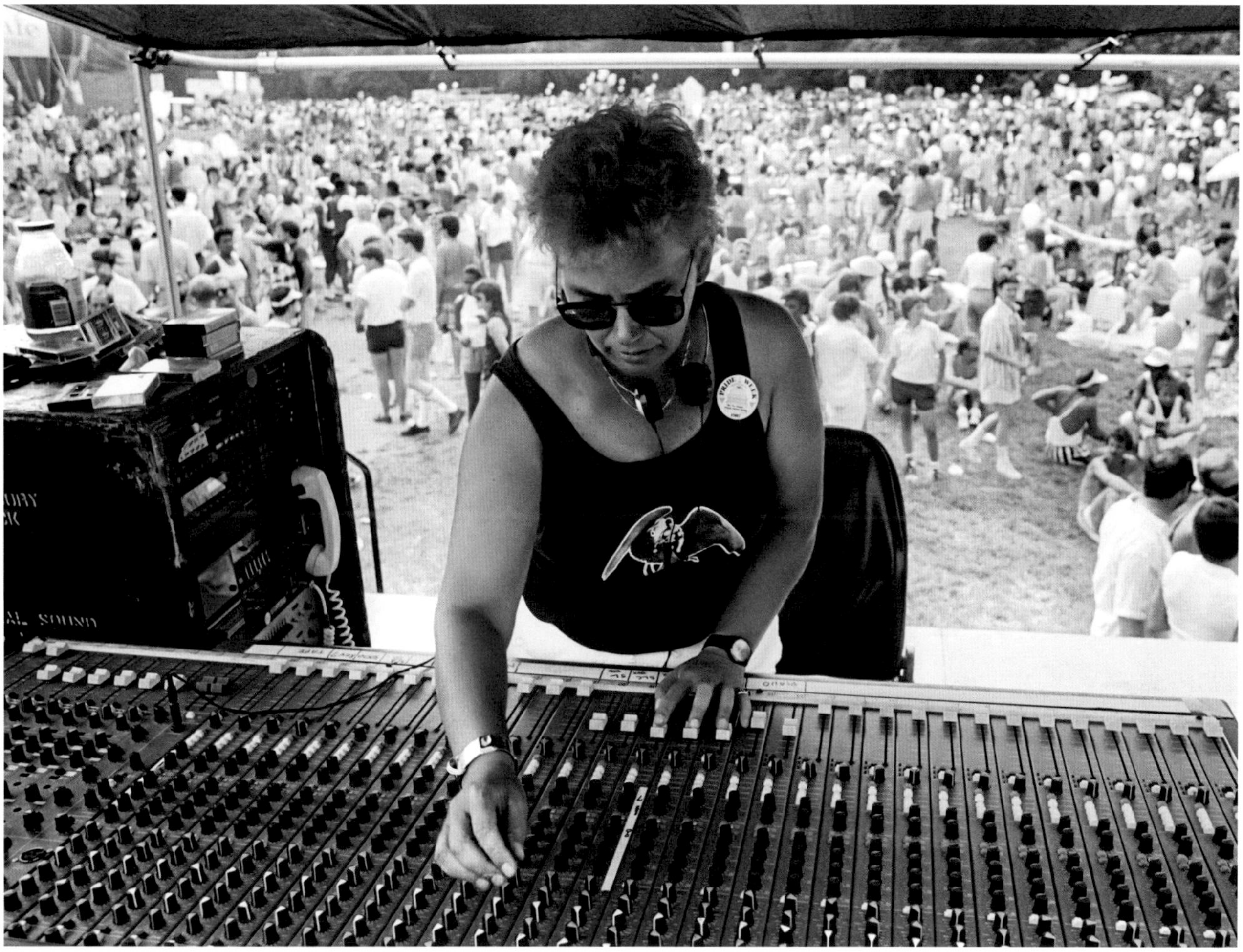

78

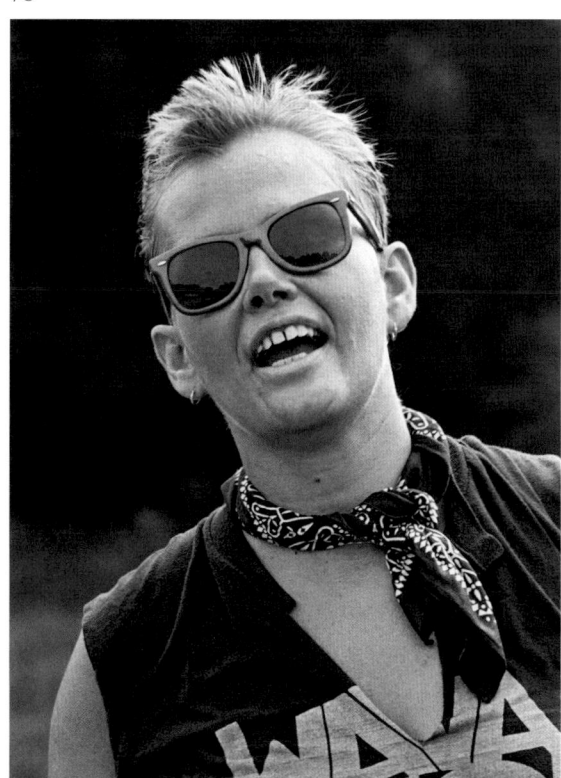

79

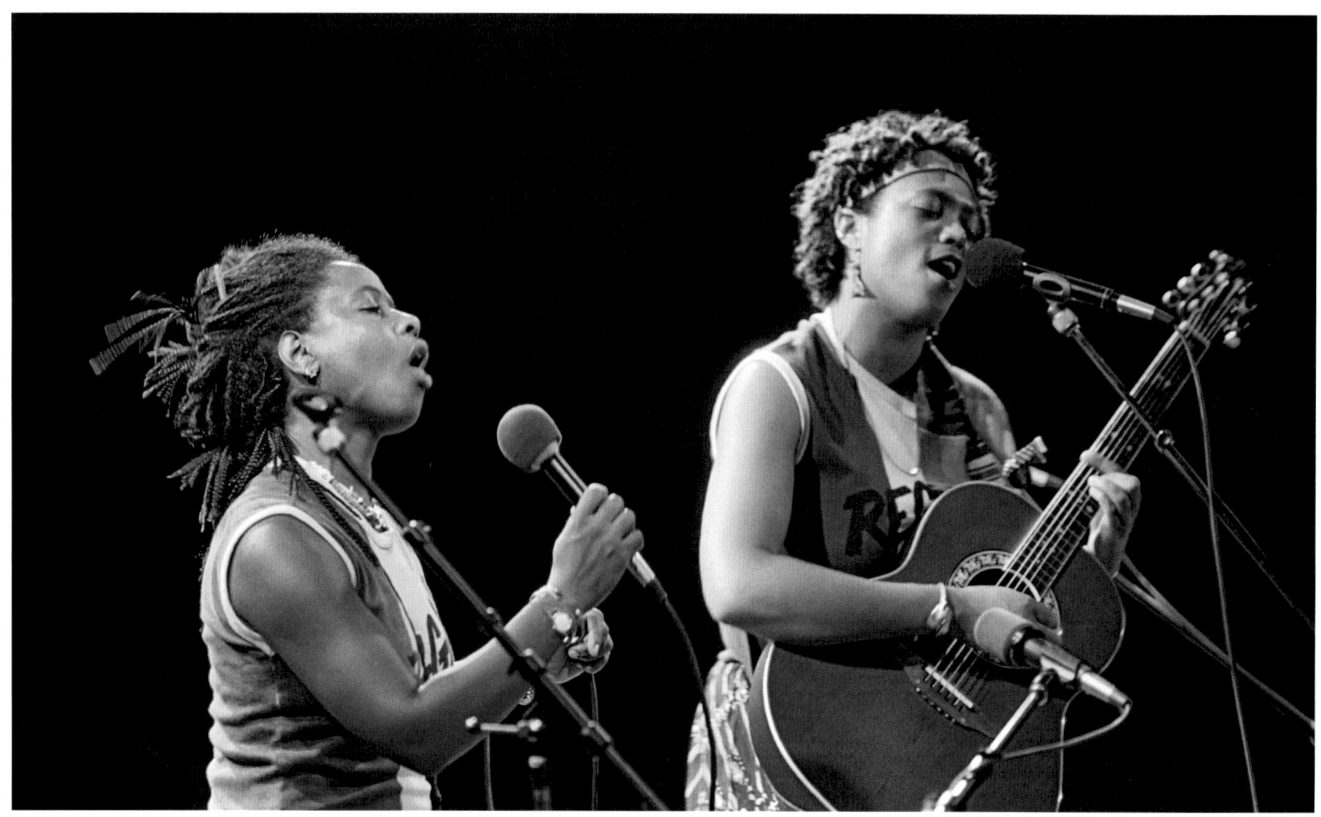

80

80. J. Casselberry (R) and Jaqué
DuPreé create an original musical
synthesis that "proudly reflects
our connection with the long
bloodline of serious Black women
musicmakers." Michigan Womyn's
Music Festival, 1984.

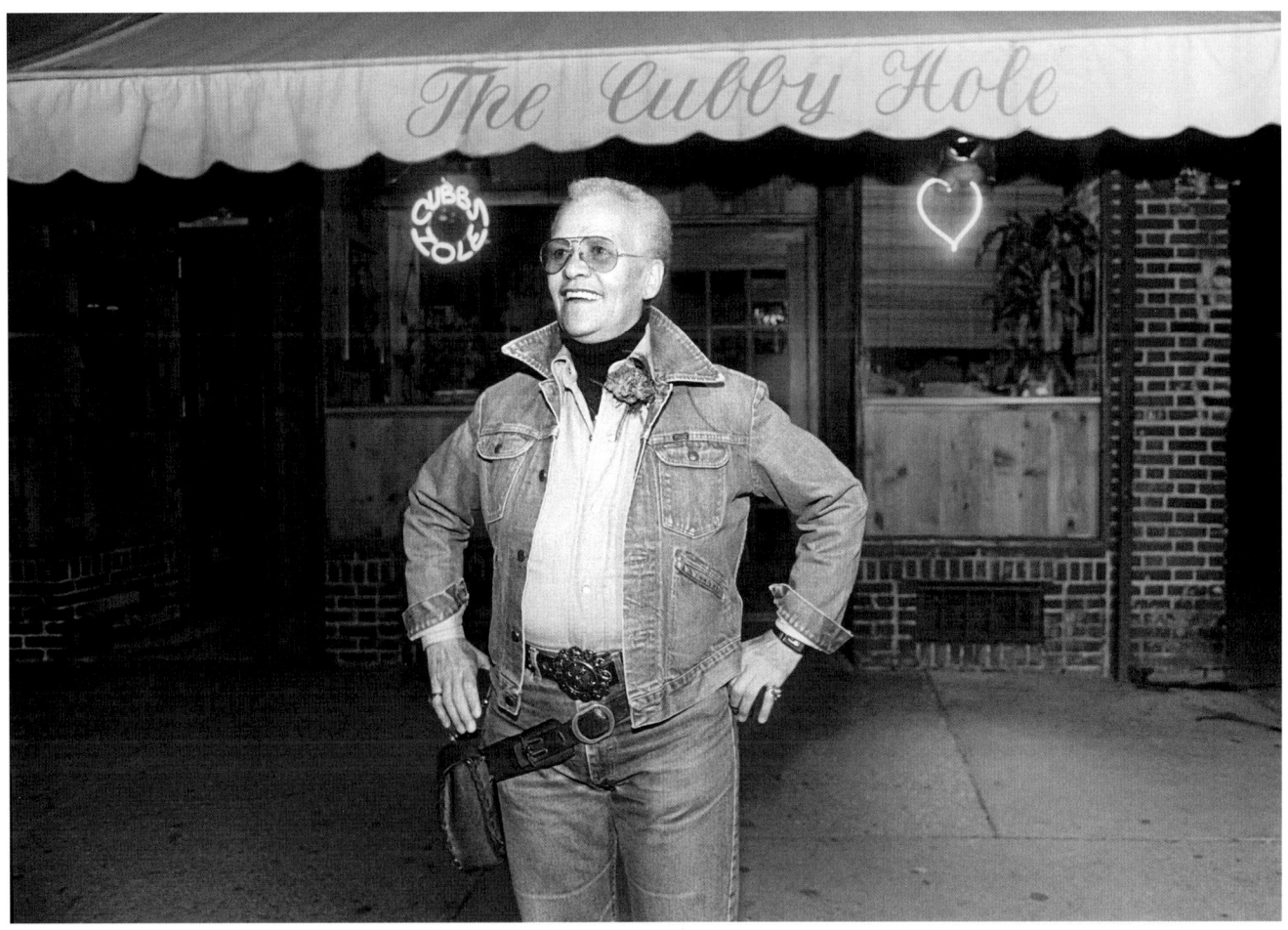

81

81. Stormé DeLarverié greets
women coming to The Cubby
Hole, a lesbian bar in New York's
Greenwich Village, where she
is the bouncer. For many years,
Stormé perfected the art of illusion
when she performed as a male
impersonator with The Jewel Box
Revue. 1986.

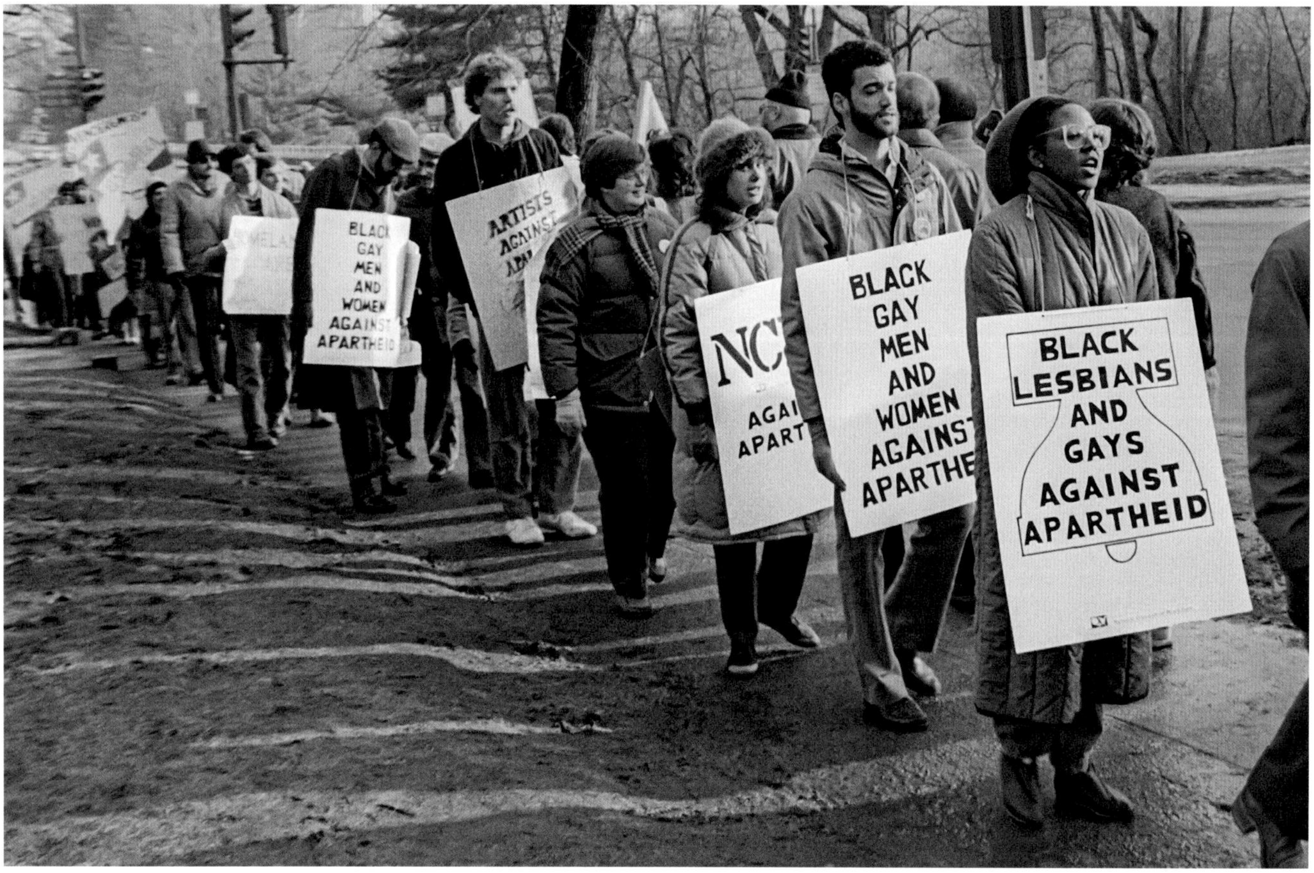

82

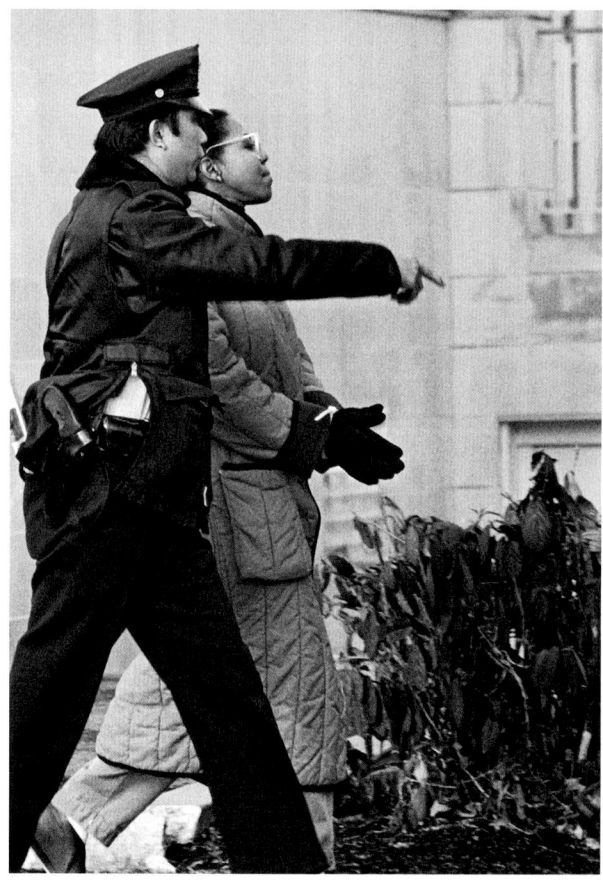

83

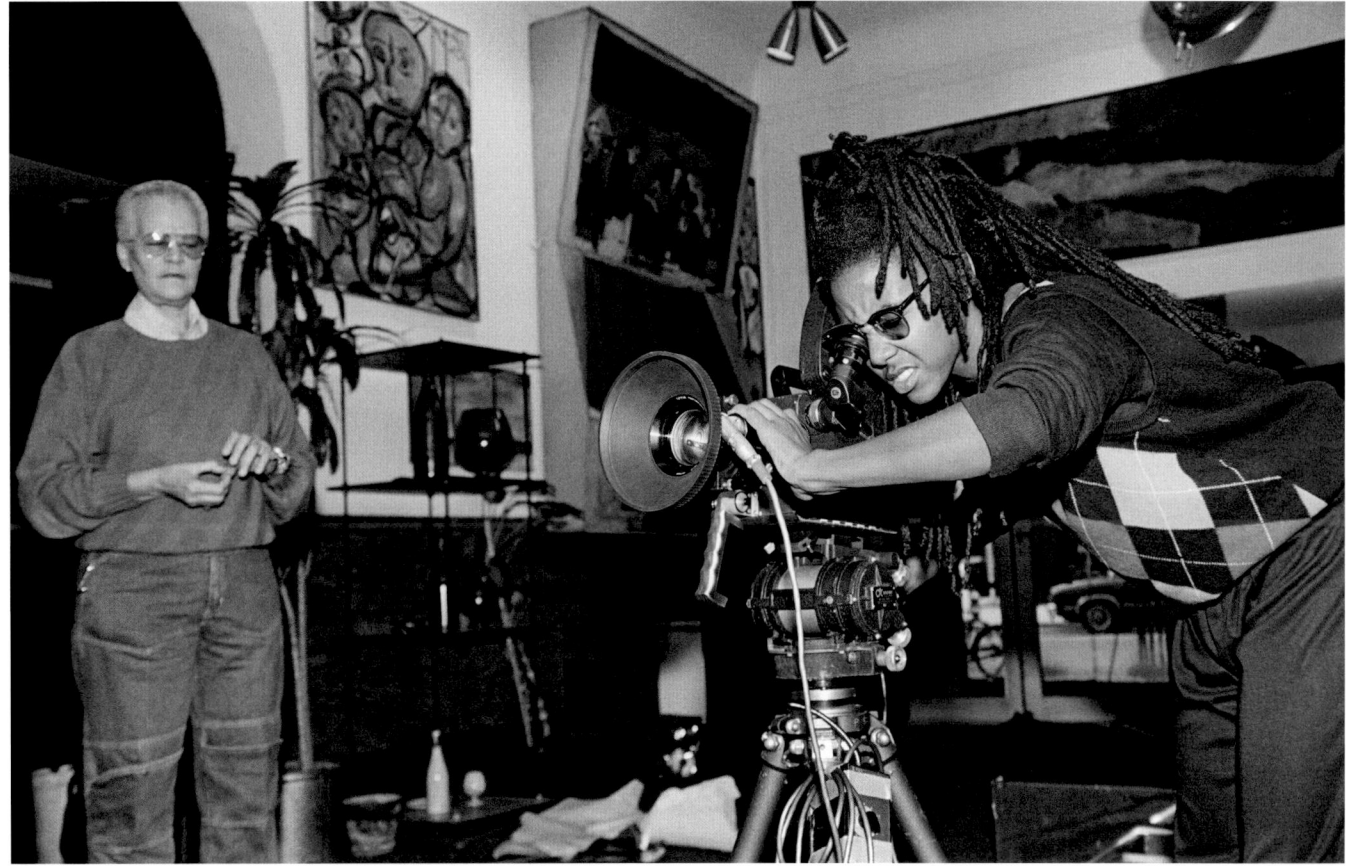

84

82. Michelle Parkerson (R), co-chair of the National Coalition of Black Lesbians and Gays, joins demonstrators near the South African Embassy in Washington, D.C., 1985.

83. After the picketing, Michelle is arrested in front of the embassy for protesting apartheid in South Africa. 1985.

84. Michelle (R) on location at the Chelsea Hotel, New York City, during the filming of *Stormé: the Lady of the Jewel Box*. Michelle directed and produced the film, which features Stormé DeLarverié (L). 1986.

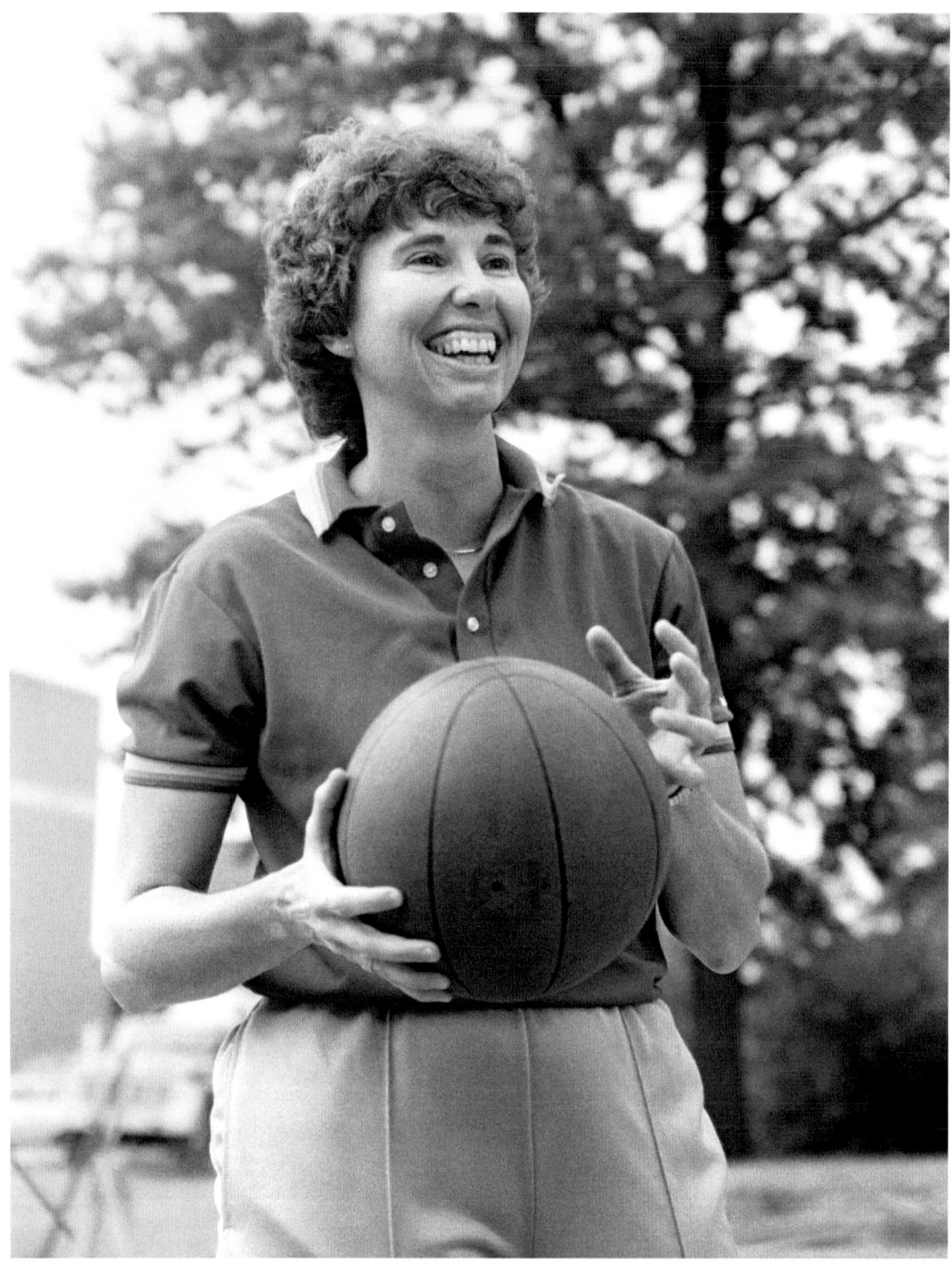

85

85. Karen Thompson is an assistant professor of physical education and recreation at St. Cloud State University in Minnesota. Karen lived with Sharon Kowalski for four years in a committed, loving relationship before Sharon was severely disabled in a car accident; Sharon's father won guardianship in a highly contested legal struggle, and has prevented Karen from seeing her. To bring attention to the violation of Sharon's civil rights, Karen has been speaking to groups around the country. College Park, Maryland, 1986.

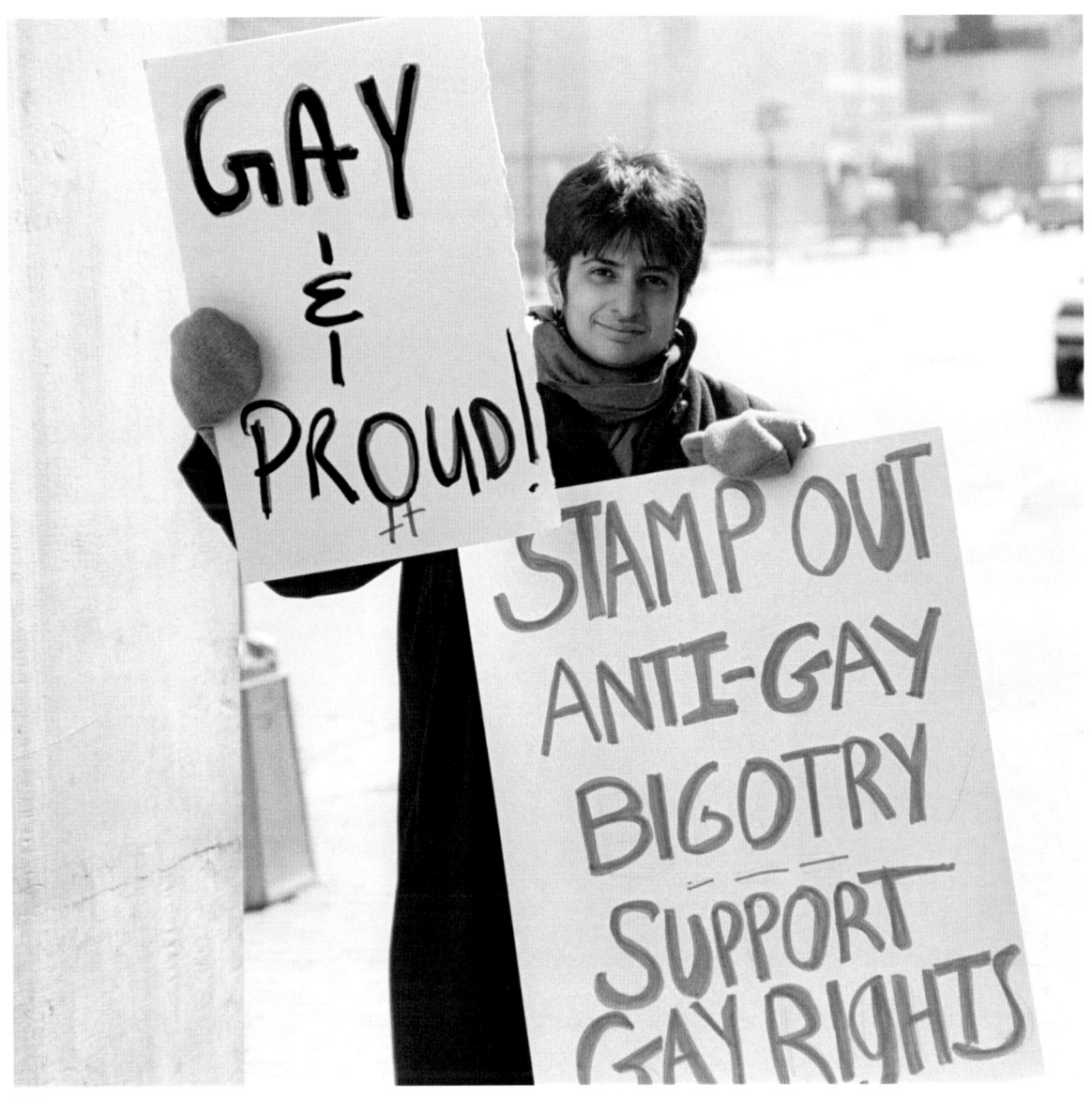

86. Urvashi Vaid pickets a right-wing, anti-gay conference in Arlington, Virginia. Urvashi is one of the founders of LIPS, a lesbian-feminist action group that uses tactics including guerilla theater, leafleting, and picketing to educate the public about sexism, racism, and homophobia. 1987.

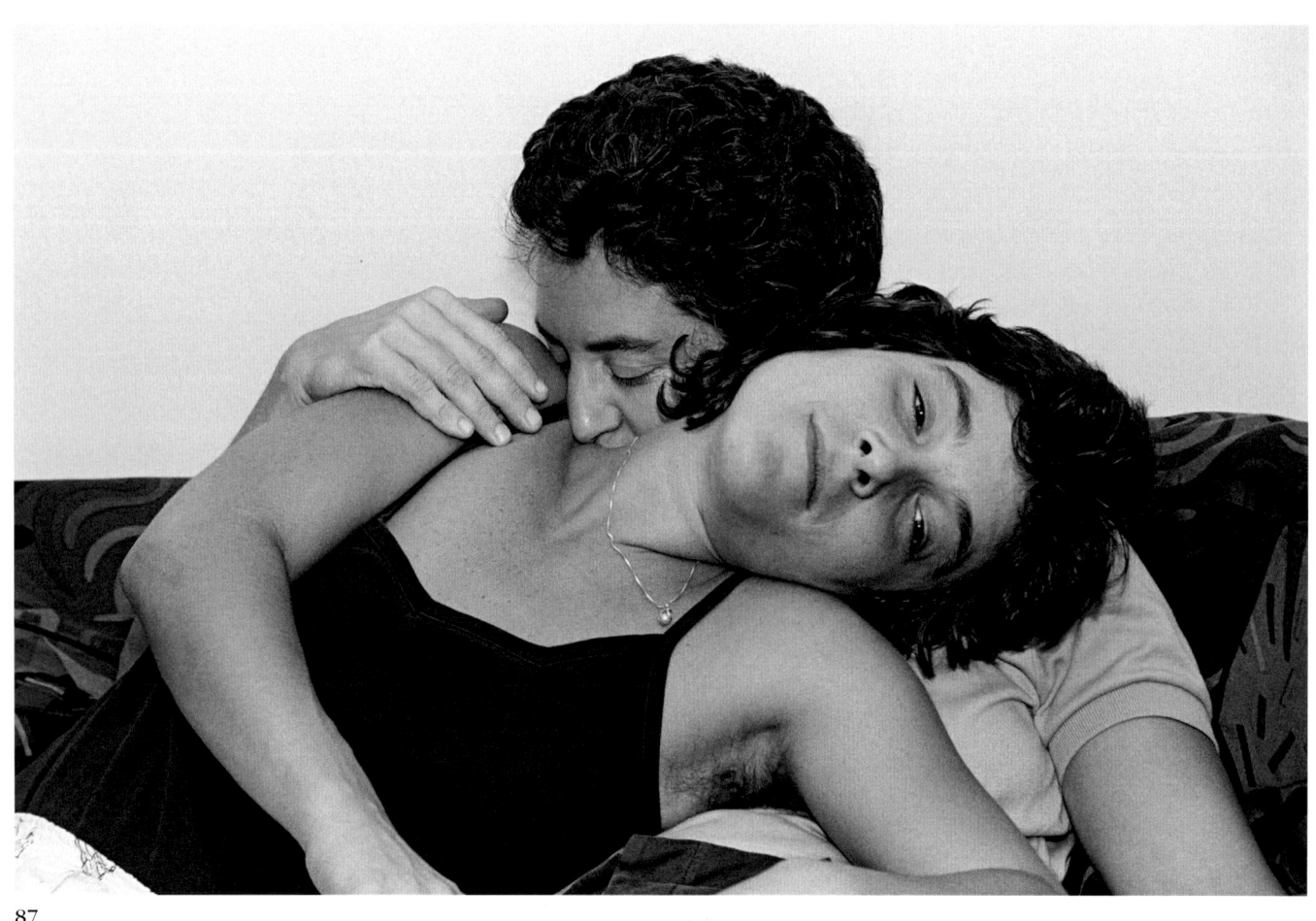

87

87. Jenifer Firestone (front) and
Sue Hyde at home in Cambridge,
Massachusetts, in 1986. Jenifer
tours with *The Ten Percent Revue*,
a musical celebration of lesbian
and gay life. Sue, who works for
the National Gay and Lesbian Task
Force, is organizing full-time to
overturn the sodomy laws that still
exist in 25 states.

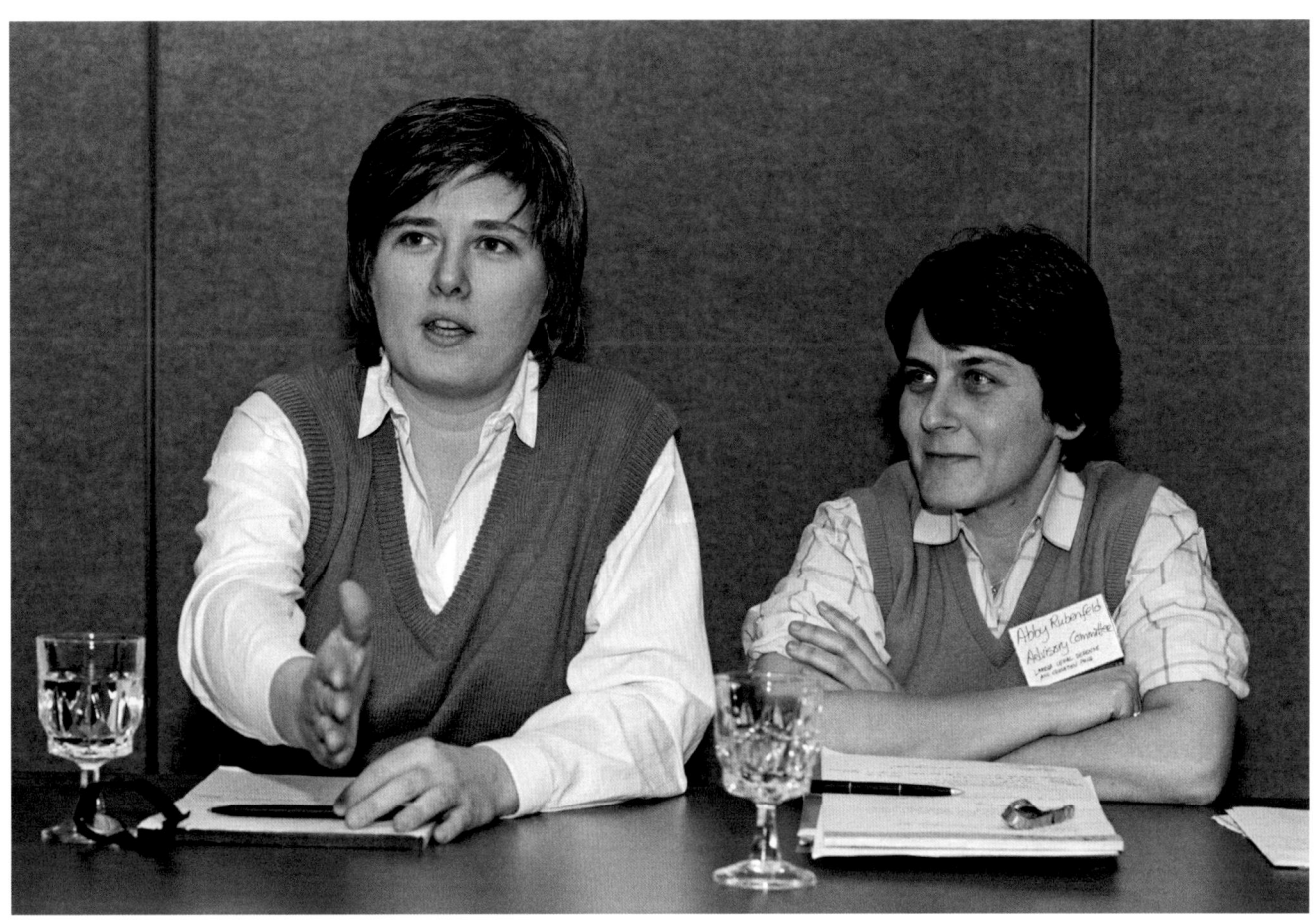

88

88. Nan D. Hunter, director of
the Lesbian/Gay Rights Project
of the American Civil Liberties
Union, and Abby R. Rubenfeld,
legal director of Lambda Legal
Defense and Education Fund, lead
a workshop on the importance of
lesbian rights in the age of AIDS
at the 1987 National Conference
on Women and the Law in
Washington, D.C. Nan and Abby
say, "Butch lawyers wear sweater
vests."

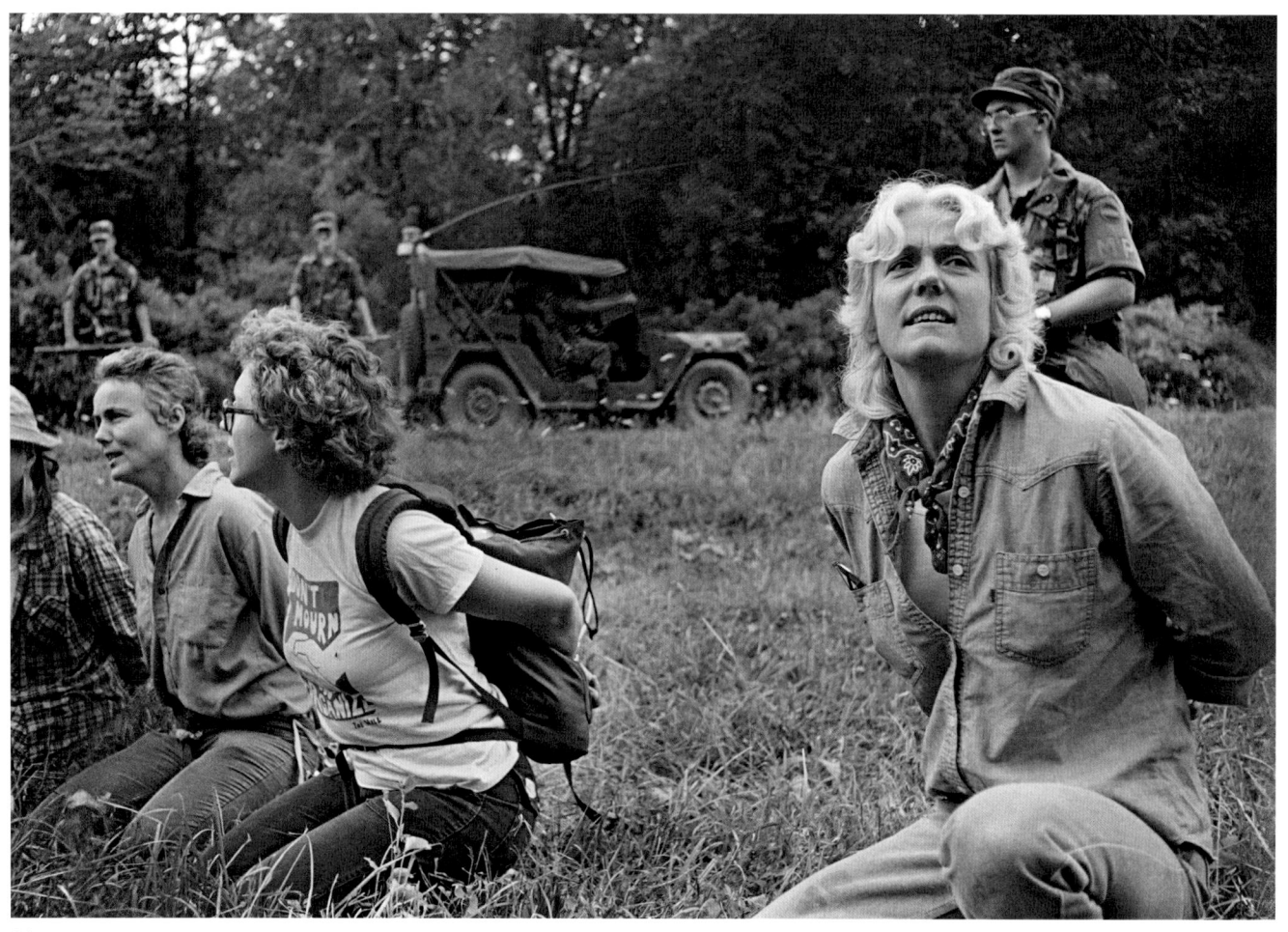

89. Deborah Jones (R) protests the deployment of nuclear weapons to Europe inside the Seneca Army Depot. Deborah climbed over the barbed wire fence with women from the Ithaca Women's Affinity Group on August 1, 1983, when more than 500 women committed acts of civil disobedience at the Depot in Romulus, New York.

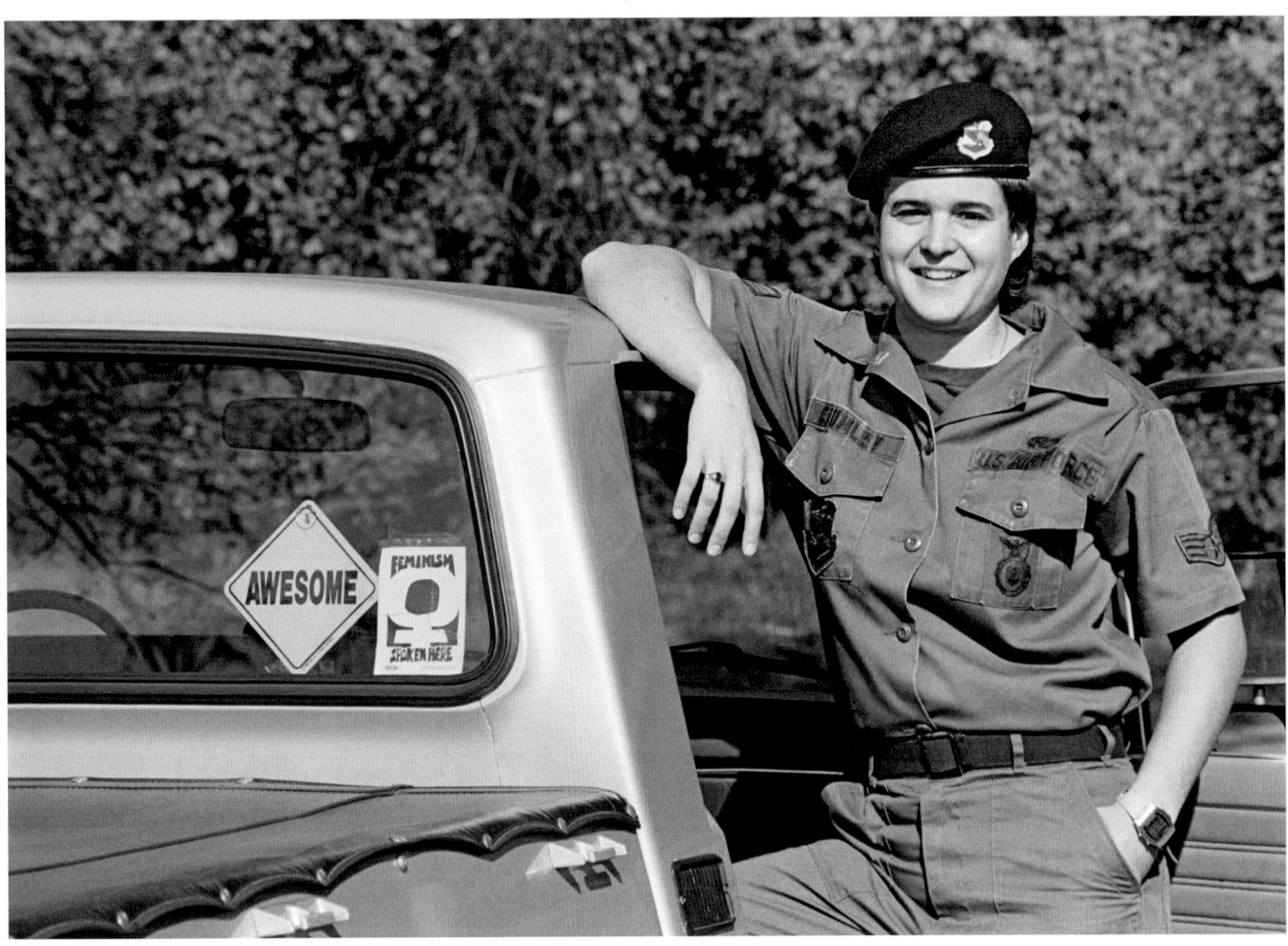

90

90. Brenda Crumley is a staff
sergeant with the Ohio Air National
Guard and a sociology graduate
student. Columbus, Ohio, 1986.

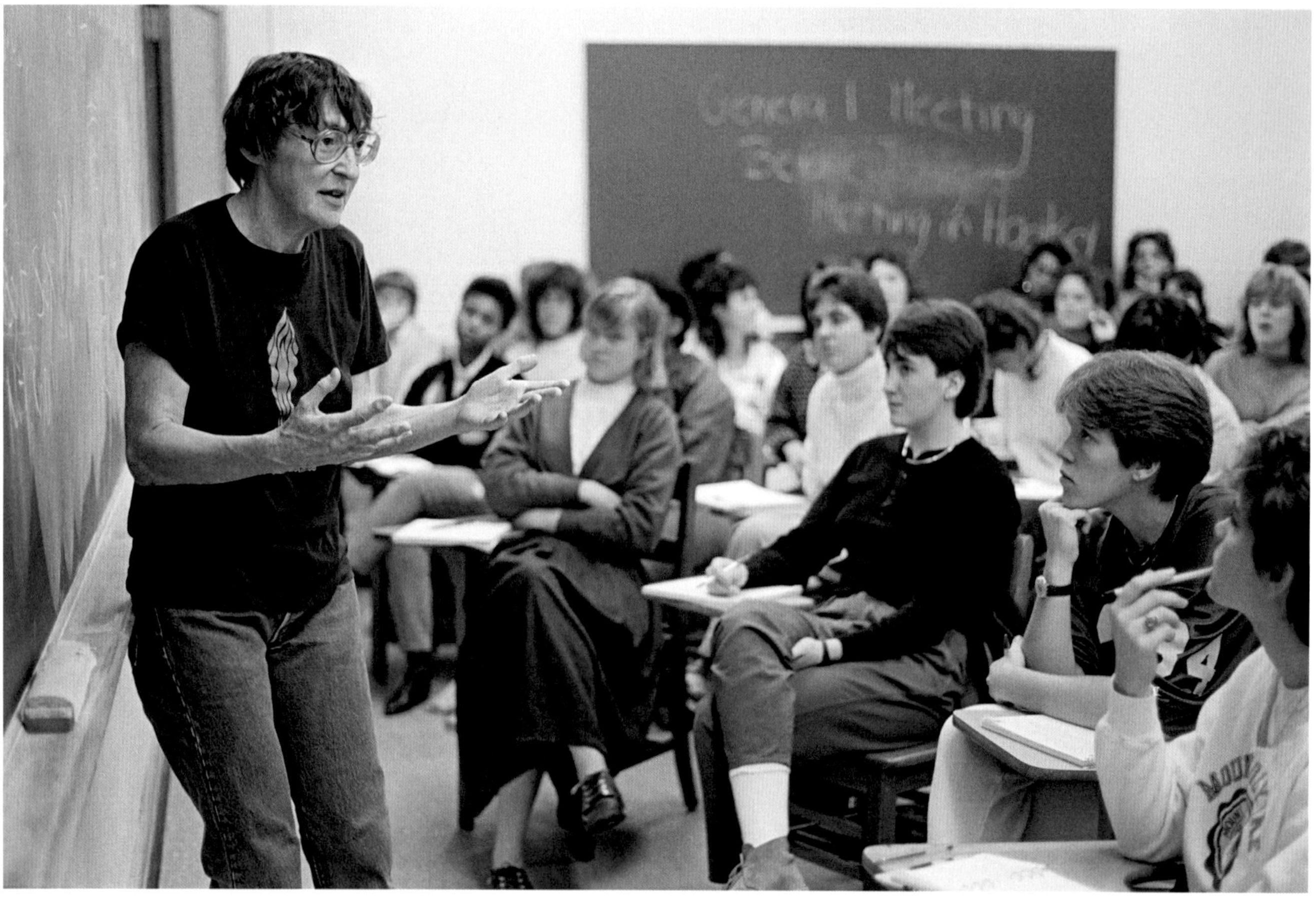

91

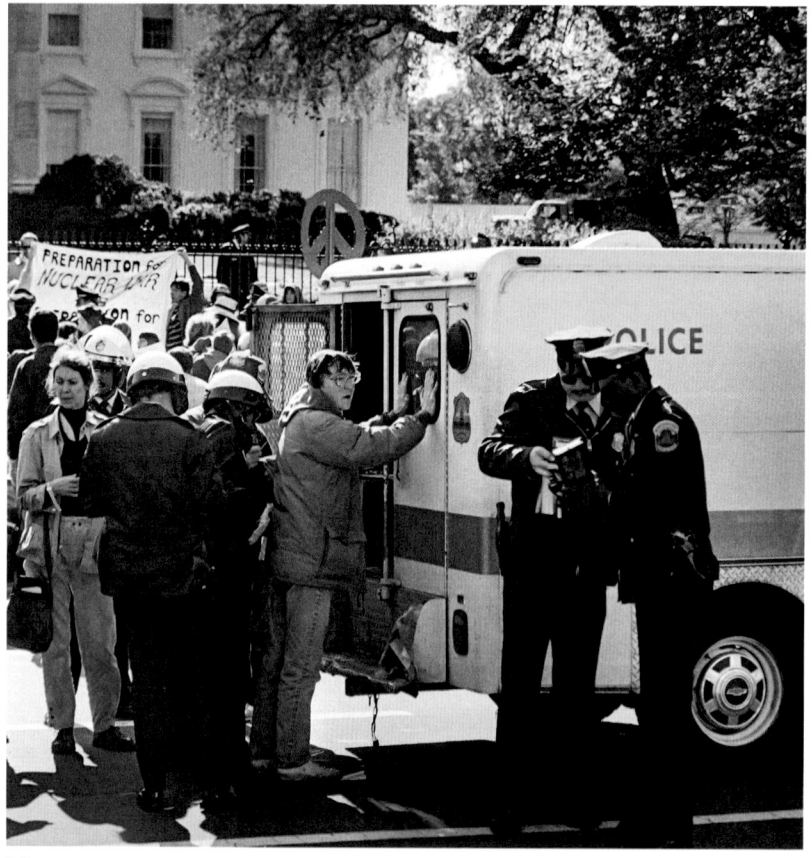

92

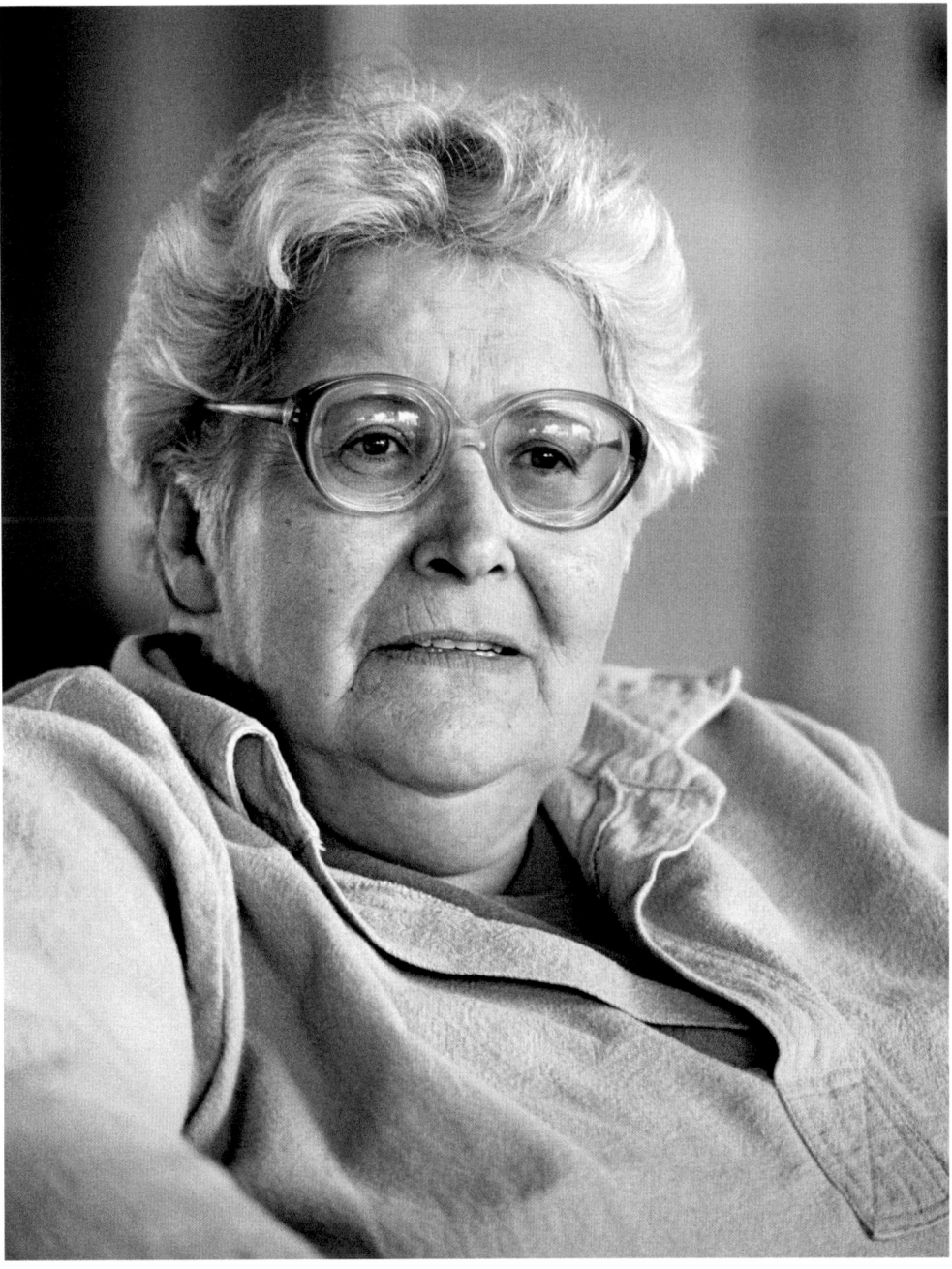

93

91. Jean Grossholtz, professor of political science at Mount Holyoke College, teaches the "Politics of Patriarchy." The course, an introduction to women's studies, is known for its lively discussion of controversial issues. South Hadley, Massachusetts, 1986.

92. Jean places her hands on the paddy wagon after being arrested in front of the White House for protesting the increase in homelessness brought about by military spending. 1984.

93. Renee C. Hanover, at the age of 61, is still involved in political work, which began for her at age 16 when she helped organize a local union. In the late 1960s, Renee became the first "all-out" lesbian attorney in the U.S. Chicago, Illinois, 1987.

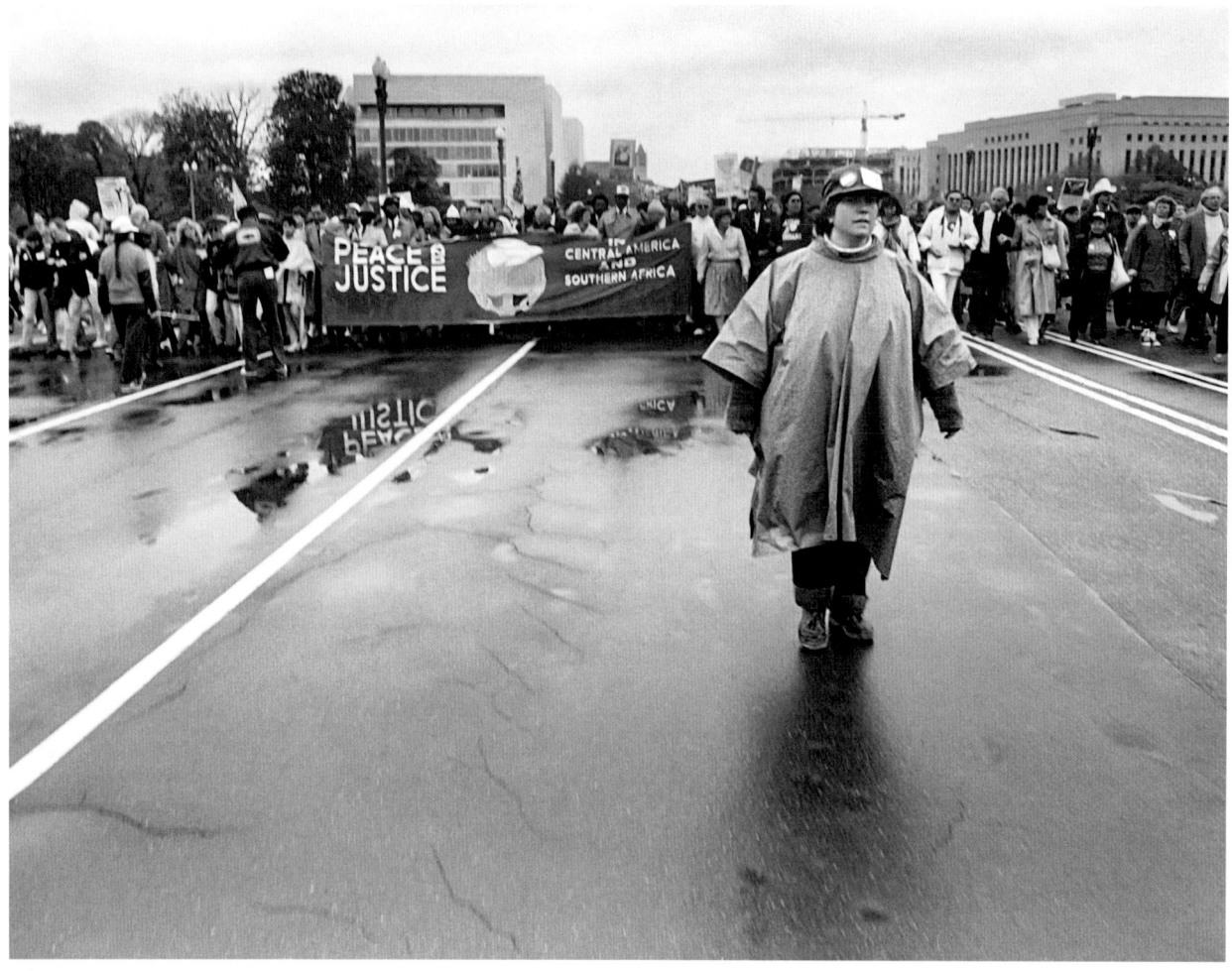

94

94. Leslie Cagan, national
coordinator of the April 25–27
Mobilization, leads 150,000 people
on a march to the Capitol to protest
U.S. policy in Central America and
Southern Africa. Participants in
the coalition included Reverend
Jesse Jackson, Eleanor Smeal, Ed
Asner, Randy Forsberg, Reverend
Rosemary Radford Ruether, Bishop
Thomas Gumbleton, Vernon
Bellecourt, and Kenneth Blaylock.
Washington, D.C., 1987.

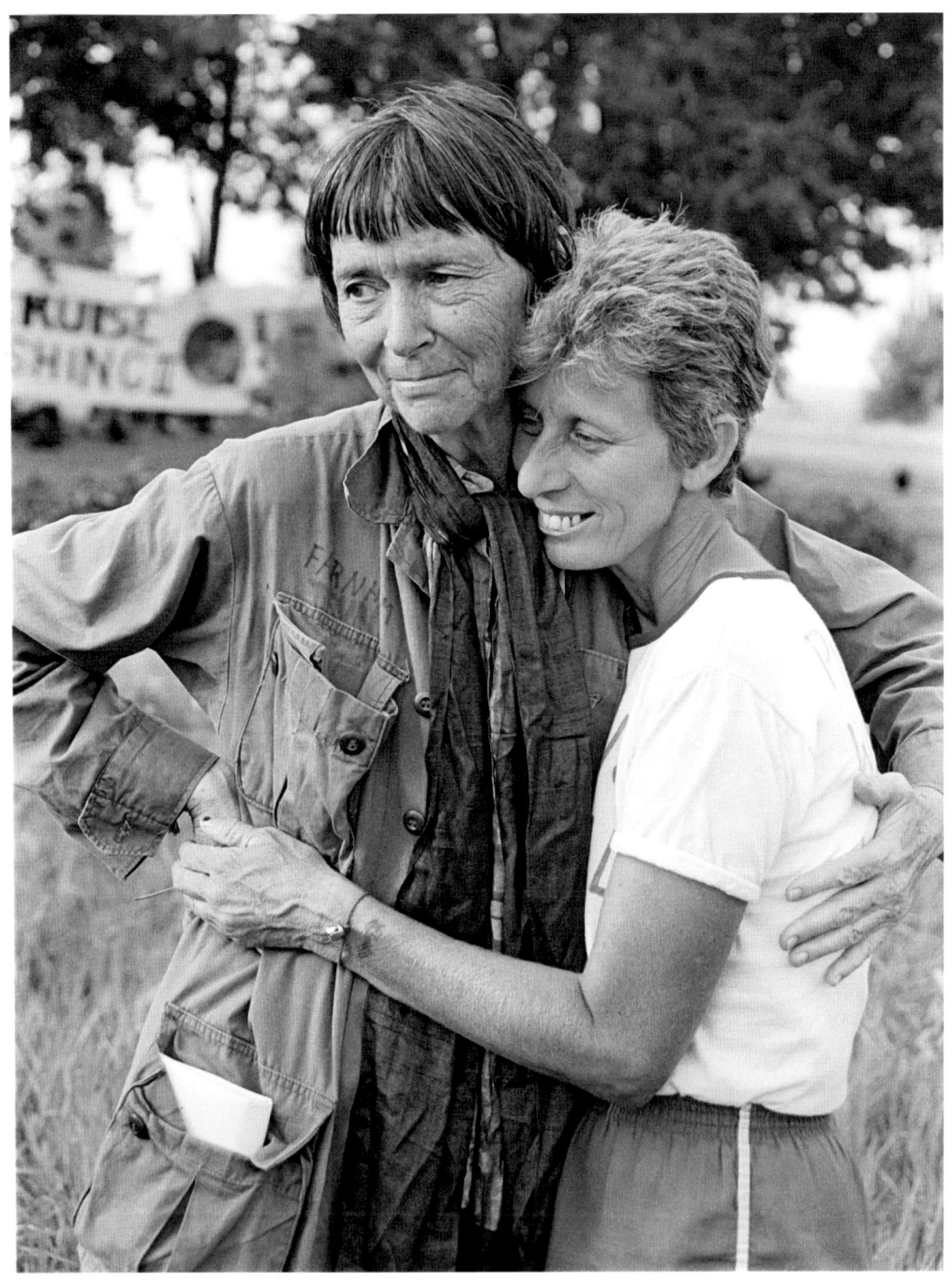

95

95. Friends Barbara Deming and
Blue Lunden at the Seneca Women's
Peace Camp, Romulus, New York,
shortly after being released from
five days in jail. They were among
54 women on a walk honoring
women's history, from Seneca
Falls to the Peace Camp, who
were arrested when townspeople
blocked the route. 1983.

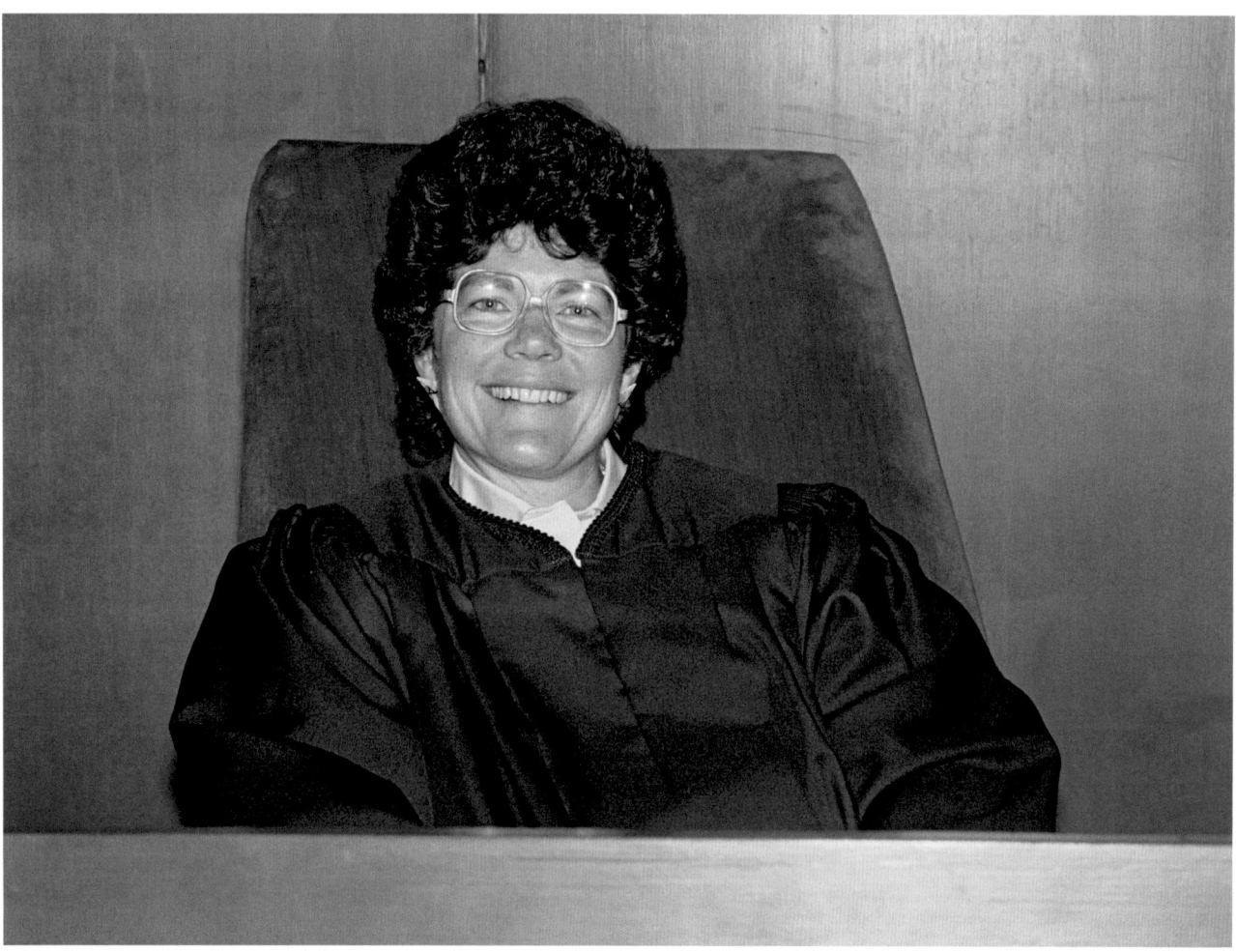

96. Mary Morgan was appointed to the bench in 1981. In 1987, her colleagues elected her presiding judge of the Municipal Court of San Francisco. Here Mary is in Chicago for a conference on sexual orientation and the law. 1987.

97. Dale McCormick, president of the Maine Lesbian/Gay Political Alliance, tallies the votes of the other Maine delegates on the floor of the 1984 National Democratic Convention in San Francisco, California.

98. Gwenn Craig, co-chair of the National Association of Gay and Lesbian Democratic Clubs and co-chair of the Gay and Lesbian Caucus of the 1984 Democratic National Convention, brings the meeting to order.

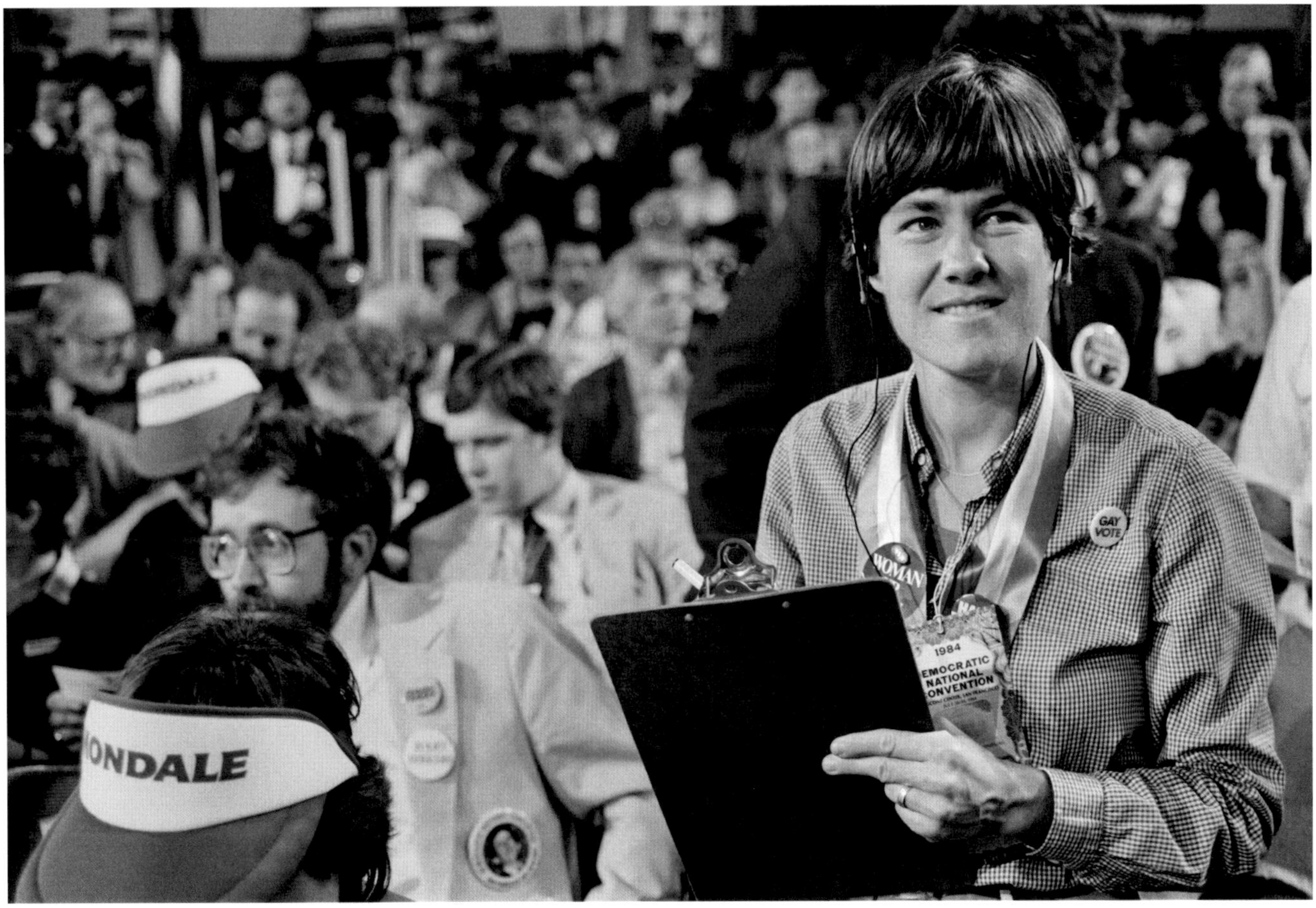

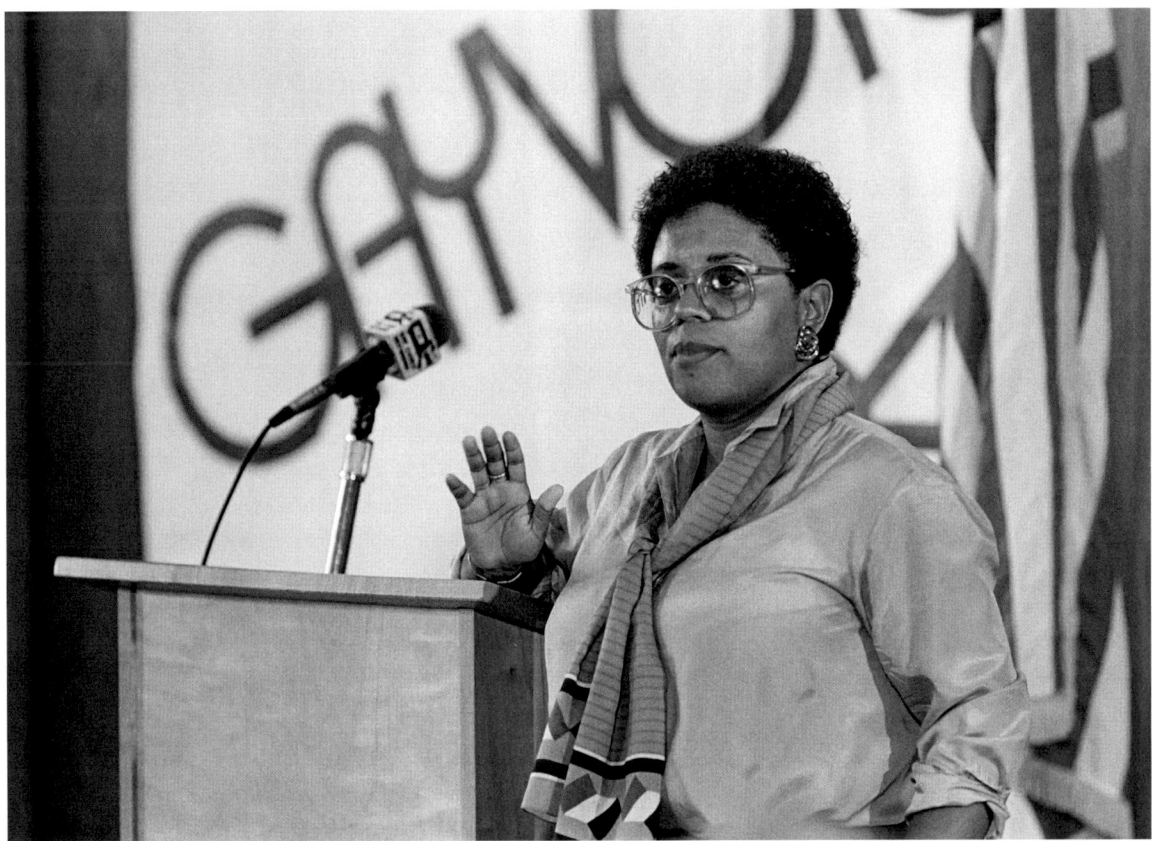

97

98

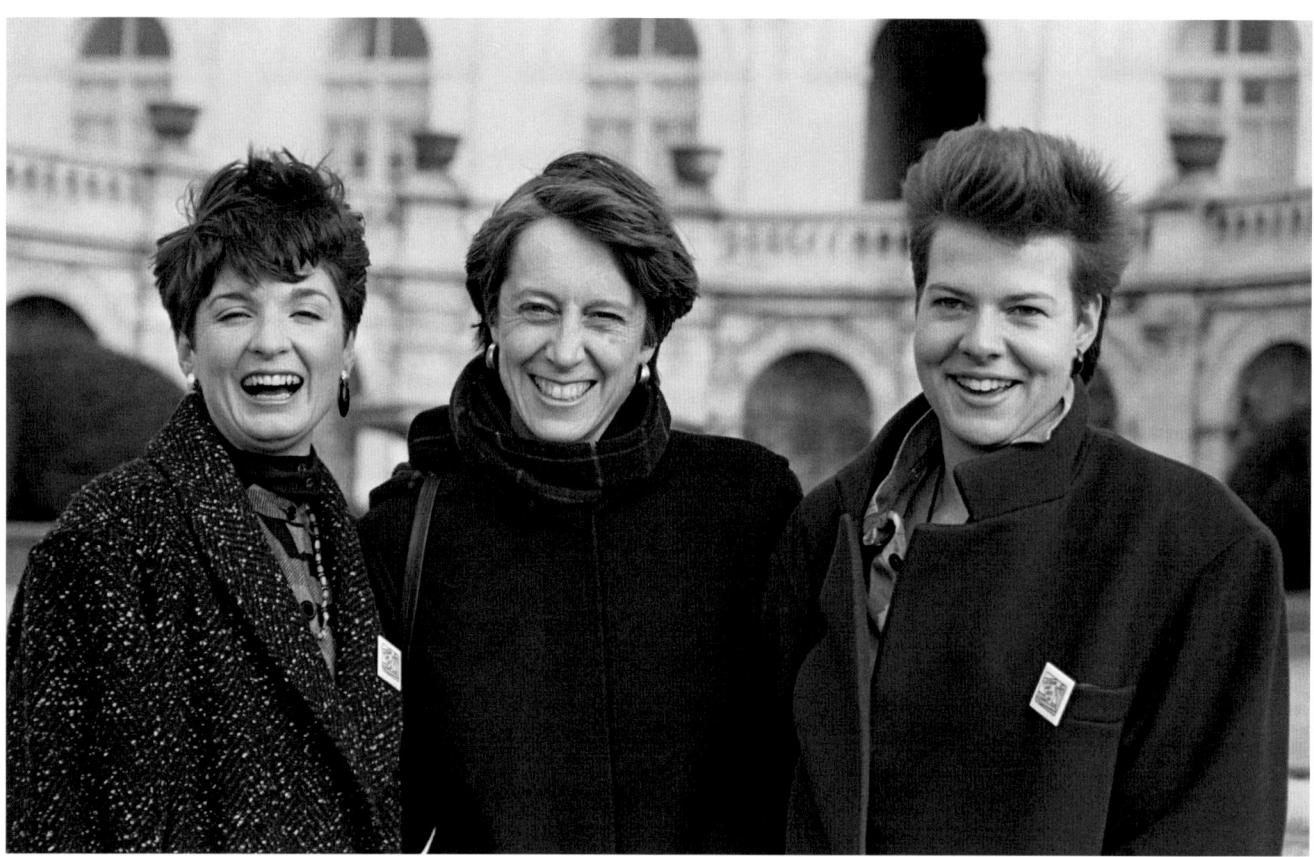

99

99. Dane County, Wisconsin, board supervisors Kathleen Nichols (L) and Tammy S. G. Baldwin (R), and Minnesota state representative Karen Clark (center) meet on the U.S. Capitol steps during the second conference of openly gay and lesbian elected officials. 1986.

100. Virginia "Ginny" Apuzzo addresses a rally at the site of the Democratic National Convention. Ginny was then the executive director of the National Gay Task Force and one of a group of activists who successfully worked to get the words "lesbian and gay" mentioned in the Democratic Party platform for the first time. San Francisco, California, 1984.

101. Ginny is arrested for protesting President Reagan's failure to respond in any positive way to the AIDS crisis. The civil disobedience action took place in front of the White House in May, 1987.

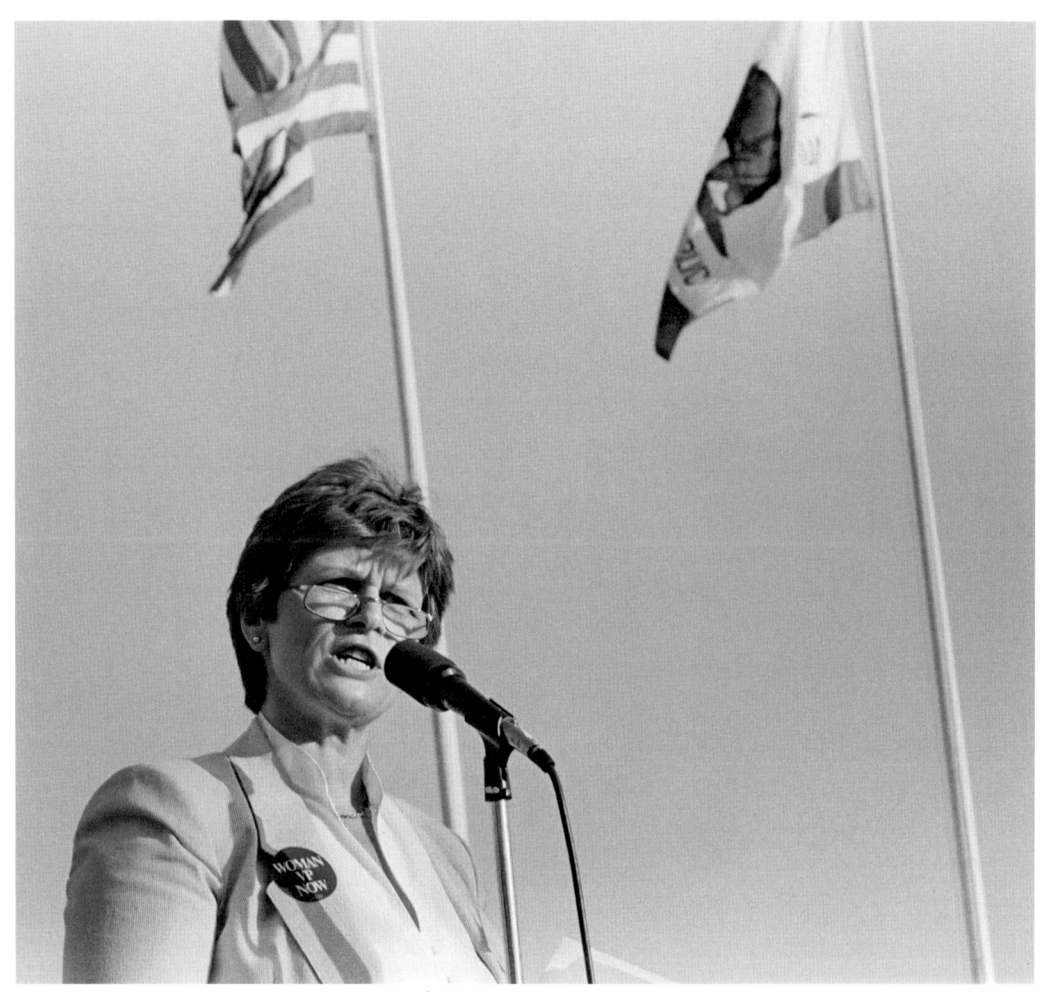

100

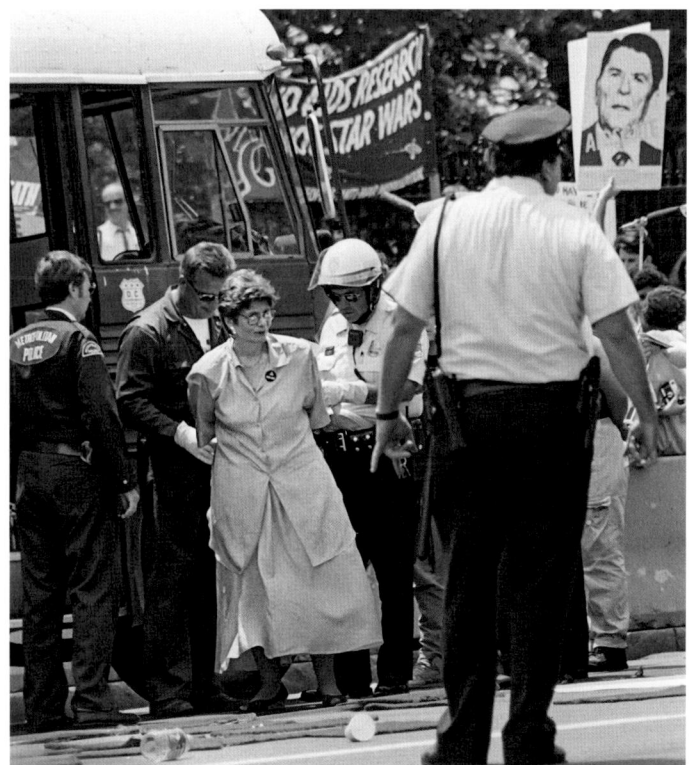

101

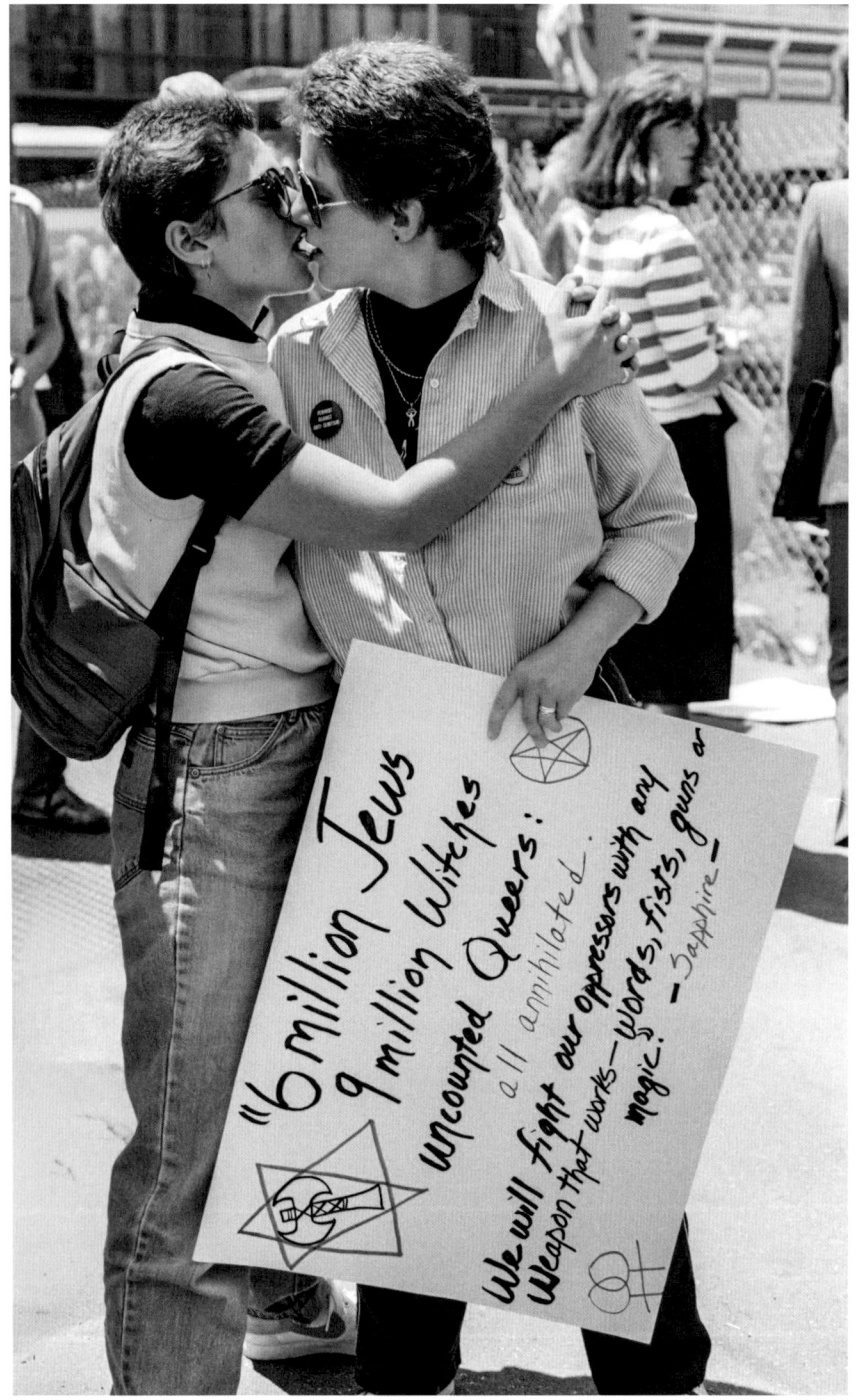

102

102. Joyce Newstat and Katherine Alfieri take a break during a demonstration to stop the Ku Klux Klan from marching. San Francisco, California, 1984.

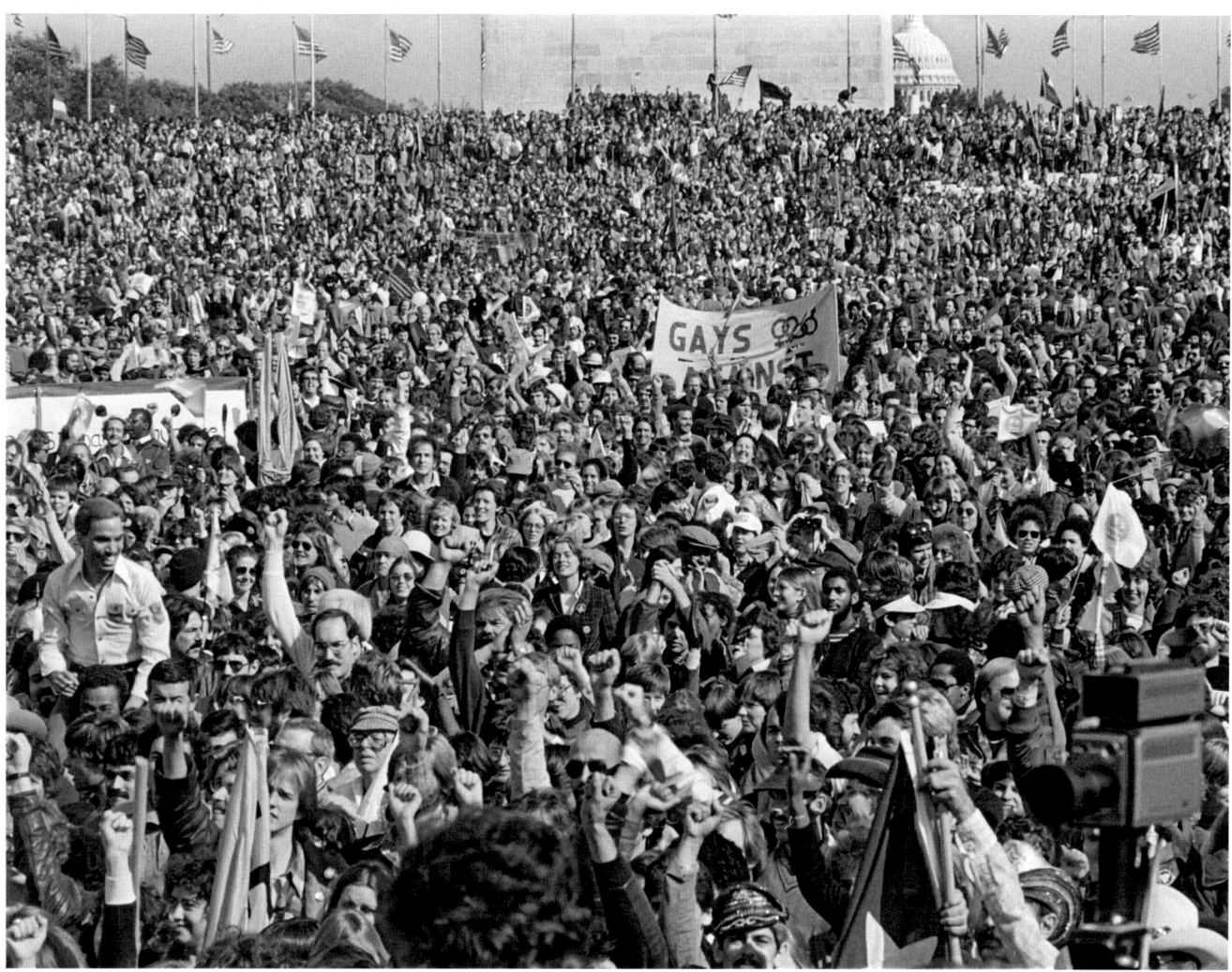

103

103. In October, 1979, we came
out for the First National March on
Washington for Lesbian and Gay
Rights (above). In October, 1987,
we said: *For Love and For Life,
We're Not Going Back!*

SPEAK OUT

FOREWORD. SARAH THORSEN

*M*y daughter, Song, is the joy of my life. Because of her I researched child-rearing and became a Montessori teacher. My job with pre-school children (2 1/2 to 6 years old) is the most important thing I do, although there's little prestige to be had in the wimmin's community from such a low-paying, traditional job.

Song was four years old in the spring of 1977 when I died to men, and sprung to wimmin. Now it's 1987, she's 14, and the impact of a decade of feminist wimmin in her life shows in her character. She has a healthy sense of her power when relating with her boyfriends. She speaks her mind about her political beliefs, has a strong sense of what's right and wrong, and cares about exposing our government for its hypocrisy. Song is talented in acting, ballet, singing, and has an incredible imagination in her writings.

1 & 2. LYNDA SUZANNE

*A*fter being involved in a wicked bad car accident I knew I needed to leave the cold climate of upstate New York and heavy work with the chain saw to relocate in Florida warmth. Insurance money enabled me to buy a 27-foot sailboat and study full-time learning to sail. After several years living on board and cruising in Florida, I got my captain's license and started Whelk Women Sailing Charters to support myself in my new lifestyle. Moving from nearly full-time involvement with the northern lesbian feminist community to life on southern waters, where it is so obviously a white man's world, was an isolating experience at first. Now, with the quickening growth of both the Florida west coast lesbian community and my woman-focused charter business, I'm feeling much more comfortable and rooted here. I long for the day, though, when I won't be so unique as to have boats change their course to inquire "Are there only women on board?"—"You bet, sure are!"

3. KIMBERLY SAMSEL

*W*hen I was five years old my parents took me to see *The Sound of Music*. I carried a torch for "Maria" (Julie Andrews) for months. That was the beginning of a steady progression of infatuations for women throughout my childhood and adolescence. Even after my mother told me that my feelings were "unnatural" and not normal for a young woman my age (at 17), I never felt ashamed or doubted my feelings, nor did I ever wish to change. At the age of 18, trapped in suburbia with no contact with a lesbian community (where do they hide?), my role models came from the library of books I kept under my bed and treasured. The more I learned about my heritage as a woman and as a lesbian, the prouder I became. Even though I had not yet met any of these women I so fervently read about, I knew I was in good company. When I came out not long after that, it was with my head held high and my fist in the air. I think it is important that we keep our history alive and that we celebrate our lesbian identity—for those of us who know, for those who want to know, and for those who need to know.

3. ROBIN CHING

*A*lthough I'm from California, I've been living in the D.C. area for the past five years now. There are so many beautiful and interesting womyn here on the east coast. It is difficult for me to go back to sunny California. I have been profoundly deaf since birth. I lipread well and of course I communicate with sign language. I am a hair designer and graphic artist. My sign is Gemini. When I first became aware of my Lesbianism, my favorite high school teacher asked me to write a report about homosexuality. (Special thanks to my high school teacher.) When I learned more about the world of womyn, I understood why I had always felt something was missing in my life. In my very first week at California State University,

Northridge, I had my first sexual experience with a woman. It felt so wonderful and equal. I am very happy and proud that I am a Lesbian.

4. ARCHENE TURNER

*W*hen I hear the song "There's a Place for Us," I think of a dream I have. A world where Black lesbian couples are recognized and valued. We are all sculptors of our world. As an artist starts with a block of stone and diligently chips away until the mistresspiece is completed, so must we come out to form the world and make it our own.

4. LYNN WALKER

I have been an out-of-the-closet lesbian for seven years and love every minute of it. It's a wonderful feeling to not have to be something that you are not. I have learned that many heterosexuals live their lives worrying and wondering what everyone thinks of them. I no longer have that problem because I know what I am; I am a black lesbian and loving it.

5. FAITH STAYER

*W*hat we experience in life is the direct result of our conscious and unconscious choices and visualizations. When I was 20, I dreamt of making love with another woman. The dream was so powerful and beautiful that I became obsessed with finding out all I could about lesbianism. My inner voice suggested an alternate path. I listened. I chose a life in which women play the leading roles. Through this process, I have learned to love myself and value my differences. One of the most important things in my life is the immediate and extended family of women I have created for myself through living in various places, traveling, going to festivals, and networking. I've learned that I do not have to live in the same geographic location to be interconnected with others with whom I am spiritually or culturally bonded. This insight has been a major source of comfort and strength to me during the time I've spent by myself, separated from my "immediate family," in a new location.

By trade, I am an educator—a special educator. I have worked with children experiencing emotional conflicts and significant behavioral problems. I am currently teaching others how to work with/help/teach children and adolescents who have difficulty coping with parental and societal demands. I believe that learning positive ways of coping with stress and frustration associated with lifestyle or job-related demands is essential to maintaining physical, emotional, mental, and spiritual health. The best coping resource I have found to deal with these pressures is the Radiance Technique. I apply this technique to myself daily to balance my energy, to prevent stress from accumulating, and to adapt to change in my life.

6. KRIS KLEINDIENST

*N*ine years ago I started running. I had never done anything athletic before. My first race was an all-women event, a five-mile course with Grete Waitz in the lead! Two years later I ran a marathon, finishing second in my age division. But my secret fantasy was to run track—to sprint, to run all out until I couldn't. I got my chance in San Francisco at Gay Games I, where I ran 400 and 800 meter races. I had never competed, barely knew the rules and I finished fourth both times. I returned in 1986 to run in Gay Games II and placed second in the 200 and 400 meter sprints. The Gay Games without a doubt are the best, most affirming experiences of my life.

I have always lived in St. Louis. In 1972 I was 19 and had been out for two years. I helped start the Women's Coffeehouse and *Moonstorm*, a lesbian periodical. Later, I wrote a feminist column for a (straight) local paper. In 1974, I co-founded Red Tomatoe and produced women's concerts for six years. For the last twelve years

I have been a co-owner, along with a small group of men and women, gay and straight, of Left Bank Books. Left Bank is what we call a progressive, general bookstore with a strong feminist and gay emphasis. When I am not there, or running, or playing softball, or working in my yard, I am writing and sometimes publishing. I live with my lover of five years, Debi Law, who is a health-care activist, horticulturist and long-distance cyclist. We share the house we are buying with two cats and a Great Dane.

7 & 8. JAMIE HECKER

I am a 38-year-old lesbian-feminist and a member of the Hag House Collective. Since 1973, the work I've done in Cleveland has been to create and make visible/accessible a community for women, and to participate in groups and organizations that work to empower women. For relaxation, I like to travel, work out physically and read.

8. HAG HOUSE COLLECTIVE

*T*he Hag House Collective is Debra Hirshberg, Jamie Hecker, Sally Tatnall, and Phyllis Balcerzak. Of the original five members, three are hanging tough. We first came together in 1978, to build a structure that would encourage us as radical women, through the creation of a revolutionary unit. Our commitment was sparked by the shared idea that "together we could change the world, but alone we could only change our hairstyles." The result of this idea is our individual and collective participation with other women in the creation, organization, maintenance, and support of: Ohio Chicago Art Project, which brought Judy Chicago's "The Dinner Party" to Cleveland; OVEN Productions, feminist production company; National Radical Thought Conference for Women, 1987; Women's Building Project, subsidized space and services for women's groups; Feminist Forum, early discussions of theory; The Land Project, women's land group;

Public, woman-only disco parties for 100–900 women; Three of Cups, women's restaurant and bar; Women's Community Fund, local women's foundation; Cleveland's Annual Women's Variety Show; Mary Daly discussion group; Local Lesbian Feminist Conference, 1975; Local Radical Feminist Conference, 1981; Preterm, abortion clinic; Cleveland Women's Counseling and Referral Service; Gold Flower Defense Committee, to subsidize legal fees for women who killed their husbands; Womanspace, coalition of women's groups; DYKE: Dykes You Know Everywhere; The Women's Fitness Center, women-only gym; *What She Wants*, local women's community newsletter; and The Wellness Center (in process).

As a collective, we open our house to the entire community. We plan women's celebrations, parties, and share our home with traveling feminists. We are pet-free and proud. One of the current concerns we have as radical women is how to move each other through burnout, back to changing the world. We have experienced the collective as the best process going.

9 & 10. LANA WALL

I've founded a shelter for battered women, played eight years of professional women's football, gotten a master's degree, bought 1 and ⅓ houses, and am now a therapist/healer working with women who have been victimized. I guess I've done a lot in my 35 years. I am proudest of my life with Judy and Chris. I've heard it said—mostly in movies—that "it all means nothing without my love," and I always thought that was a little corny. Well, I wouldn't sell myself as short as to say that I'd be nothing without my *loves*, but I sure wouldn't want to find out. I've loved Judy for eight years and Chris for almost six—I hope my life is never without them. They are what is important to me: them, who they are and who we are together.

9 & 10. JUDITH CARR

*B*eing a lesbian matches my feminist perspective, my energies are toward a better world for women—a woman-centered vision. I consider myself to be a radical woman, striving to have my life and activities in sync with my philosophy and politics. Being in touch with nature and the healing energies of herbs and composing music connects me with the rhythms of life and the goddess. I love the times on our land with lots of women working, cooking, talking and loving—collectivity at its best.

10. CHRIS DELAMATRE

I am a 27-year-old farmer and therapist. I "talk" to the corn, and help children and families grow. My work as a therapist focuses on enhancing children's self-esteem, and helping parents become more aware of the needs and rights of their children. I spend my "farmer" time caring for and playing with our animals, reading, watching the weeds grow, and relaxing in the pond. We provide temporary refuge for injured or abandoned young wild things and a home for rescued dogs, cats, sheep, chickens, ducks, etc. There are more than 100 animals here. The nurturing of our animals and land helps to provide a balance with the intensity of my work. This balance is what allows me to give my best to both things.

11. CINDY MILLER

I am 35 years old and a radical lesbian feminist. I have a Ph.D. in Psychology and teach Women's Studies and Psychology at the college level. I experienced a somewhat nontraditional child-hood, having grown up in a single-parent, mostly female, household. This, more than anything else that I can point to in my early life, left me open to all possibilities in life, including, and especially, the questioning of traditional dogma and lifestyles. Although as a young girl I dreamed about my storybook wedding, I rejected traditional marriage almost as soon as I could think for myself. I saw marriage as inherently oppressive and the notion that I would even want to spend the rest of my life with another person was beyond my imaginings. I was committed only to myself, my work, and feminist activism. All of this changed when I met and fell in love with Bernadette. As my relationship with Bernadette grew and we began talking about the future, I realized that a public affirmation and celebration of our relationship was important to me (it was only later, however, that I could call this public affirmation "marriage"). Our wedding was a beautiful personal and community celebration of lesbian existence. Although uncertainty always exists in a relationship, our marriage has allowed me to think more concretely and optimistically about our future together. It has allowed me to see commitment as enhancing, rather than stifling, in a relationship, in my relationship. It has made me think differently about myself, my life, and my needs. And as it turns out, it was a political action in the truest sense of feminism—it has empowered our community, which is still talking about "The Wedding!"

11. BERNADETTE RYAN

I am a 34-year-old radical lesbian feminist who grew up and was educated in the midwest, moved to upstate New York for surgical residency and moved to Houston in 1985. My becoming a lesbian and a feminist was a long process that occurred over the eight years I spent in college and medical school. Although the relationships that I had during my years in New York state were important to me, the majority of my energy was focused on my work. By the time I moved to Houston, I wanted a significant other with whom I could have a relationship that was as important in my life as my work. I met Cindy in August 1985 and our friendship developed into a sexual relationship over a few months. After about six months we were ready to move in together and over the succeeding months we gradually began hesitantly to talk of a future together. Neither of us had had to consider another in career moves before. We did not know how to respond to those who would not understand why we had made compromises in our careers. We were not sure we could explain it to ourselves. We needed public validation of our love, friendship and commitment. I am a recovered catholic and Cindy, a former episcopalian. We did not want a religious blessing but wanted to make a personal and political statement and receive community verification and support. Our major community in Houston is The Women's Group and that is where we chose to have our wedding. We would have liked to have had biological family present also but none of those that we felt safe in telling were able to make the trip. The ceremony was beautiful and the support from our friends wonderful. Our relationship has become a marriage and we can plan a joint future while retaining our individual identities.

12. DEL MARTIN AND PHYLLIS LYON

We became Lesbian activists by chance. When the Daughters of Bilitis was founded in 1955 we just wanted to meet other Lesbians. Then we got hooked by the Lesbian/Gay/Women's movements and haven't stopped since. We are proud of our accomplishments, together and singly, which have contributed to personal growth and social change.

Countless Lesbians have told us our book *Lesbian/Woman* helped them to "come out." Del's book *Battered Wives* has been called the catalyst for the national battered women's movement in the United States. Through Phyllis' work with the Council on Religion and the Homosexual, the National Sex Forum, and The Institute for Advanced Study of Human Sexuality, the field of sexology and sex education has become a bona fide profession. For us one challenge has led to

another. The current movement that has a great appeal for us is that of Old Lesbians (60 years old and up).

13 & 14. WASHINGTON, D.C. MOTHERS' GROUP

Our D.C. mothers' group was conceived in July 1982 as a "baby maybe" group. During these past five years, 25 women have participated in the group and nine children have joined our families. At present there are 10 active adult members with seven children—four girls and three boys. Currently each family has one child, but some of us are eagerly and actively trying to add a second. We've created our families through varied and imaginative routes. These include: adoption from the U.S. and abroad; artificial insemination through a sperm bank; intercourse with a friend; artificial insemination with an unknown donor, arranged by a friend; and artificial insemination with a known gay donor. Most of us decided to have children as part of a couple; some of us made the decision while single.

Many of us are trying to bring our feminism to our childrearing by selecting, for example, sex-neutral clothing, playthings, language and names. We are also very consciously creating new definitions of family by assuring that the non-biological or non-adoptive mother is seen by the child and the world as an equal mother. For example, most of us gave our children both mothers' last names; many of us have taught our children and the world to call us both "mommy"; and we have insisted that both mothers' extended families treat the child as theirs. We're all working very hard to give our children a positive feeling about being in lesbian families, whether that is a family of one mom, two moms, or a mother and co-mother. We are approaching motherhood very consciously, not only within our families but also within the lesbian community. This means, among other things, sharing information with other lesbians interested in motherhood, making a place in our children's lives for lesbians who want to be around children, and recognizing and trying to support lesbians who are not raising children. Motherhood brings us immense pleasure, but not without conflict. In addition to childrearing, our days are a constant juggling of other activities most important to us—political work, friendships, careers, love relationships, exercise, etc. Although all of these things cut into our time with our children, we've tried not to give them up completely. We know in the end these are the very elements that create strong, healthy families.

13 & 14. NANCY D. POLIKOFF

*B*ecause I am a mother, the assumption that I am heterosexual follows me everywhere. Therefore, being a mother has pushed me more than anything in my life to be an out lesbian, in order to actively resist that assumption of heterosexuality. I just started a new job teaching at American University School of Law, and it is the first time I've worked in an office where I am the only lesbian. This is because I was able to create the two major jobs I held before, one as a member of the Washington, D.C. Feminist Law Collective, and the other as a staff attorney at the Women's Legal Defense Fund. In my new job I try to say the word "lesbian" or "gay" every day in order to make lesbian and gay sexuality a public matter. I resist the idea that our sexuality is private; after all, heterosexuality isn't the least bit private.

Barbara and I raised Lainey together for three years. When we were in the process of breaking up I was devastated, but I had been through the break up of a major relationship years ago, and I knew I could live through it. This time I worried about how Lainey would be hurt. Although we all had a difficult couple of months, Barbara and I were unified in keeping Lainey's well-being a primary concern. We have been living apart for more than six months now, and Lainey goes back and forth easily between our two apartments and

knows that she still has both of her mothers, that we both love her and that we both take care of her. There are few role models for lesbian coparenting and fewer still for continuing to co-parent after the breakup of a relationship.

13. BARBARA HERBERT

*O*ut dyke doctor, does marches, demos, other urban events, loves work, good food, sex and conversation. Co-parent my daughter, great kid at age four, with a wonderful, generous, thoughtful dyke; nonetheless, I remain profoundly ambivalent about the politics of lesbian motherhood. After two decades of gay life, I have still not found a way to successfully construct family, community, work groups, love; the only available option is to keep trying. Work is central to my life. Being an out lesbian gives me energy, clarity, strength in doctoring (and helped get me a good residency, too). My professional fascination with disease is tempered by political understanding, a strong interest in public health, and by other dyke healers who push me and help me form my understanding of sickness and wellness. I love what I do although I hate the system that underlies my work. Having another lesbian doctor in my life to share the frustrations makes the continuing struggle easier. AIDS is a central reality in my life, personally, professionally, and politically. Our 20-year feminist fight for reproductive freedom and autonomy over our bodies is repeatedly challenged by this disease; it has never been more important to continue the struggle, particularly as it extends to the most vulnerable of our sisters. So I am especially pleased to be included in this picture of my daughter, her friends, and this group of lesbian mothers, all marching for free choice for all women.

13 & 14. MICHELE ZAVOS

*M*other, daughter, sister, lover. I am all of those. I am also a lawyer and run my own business. I came out in college, where it was easy and exciting to be a lesbian. It became harder. I can't even remember what my mother said to me when I came out to her, it was so painful. But now, Libby and I have been together almost 11 years; we have a two-year-old daughter, Addie, who brings wonder into our lives every day. We are close to our families of origin; they are extremely supportive of us and our choices. As I've gotten older some things have gotten murkier, others have become clearer. I find myself getting more radical as the outward trappings of my life become more traditional. Sometimes I think I want us to move to women's land and to raise Addie free of the influences of this patriarchal culture. As I look at what's happening in this country, I imagine what it was like to be Jewish or gay in Germany in 1930 and wonder what I should do politically and personally. Eight years ago I represented poor people in Georgia; today I represent men dying of AIDS. Six years ago I gave workshops on women in prison; now I speak to college classes on what it means to be gay. Sometimes I'm afraid, but I do what I think is right anyway.

13. LIBBY LEADER

*G*rowing up, it was a given that I would someday become a mother, but it never occurred to me that I would do it as a lesbian. So here I am at 36, raising our two-year-old daughter, Addie, with Michele Zavos, my lover of 10 ½ years. And I have to say that the two "accomplishments" that make me most proud and that are most central to my identity are my having helped to create an enduring love relationship and my having become a competent parent. True, I feel good about my job of four and one-half years—running the D.C.-area office of a small, woman-owned civil rights consulting firm.

And I find it tremendously rewarding when I'm called on to mediate a dispute or impasse between lesbians.

But what makes me proud is the way I'm living the personal parts of my life. I am proud that I'm out as a lesbian to everyone who plays a part in my life: not just to my friends and community, but to my entire family of origin, including my parents, my three sisters and their partners, my 90-year-old grandmother and my forty-some extended family members; to Michele's entire extended family of origin; to Addie's day-care teachers; to my bosses and co-workers. I am proud that I won't settle for less than acceptance of my lesbianism by the people in my life. And I'm proud of the choices Michele and I have made as parents; to try to raise Addie free of sex stereotyping, to create a family with two mothers who take equal responsibility and play equal roles as parents, and to convey our lesbian-feminist values to Addie by the very way we live our lives.

13. WENDY MELECHEN

*T*hree and a half years ago my lover, Lori, and I adopted a two-month-old child from El Salvador. For many people, adoption is something to be considered only as a last resort—something you move towards only when you can't get pregnant. For us, pregnancy became an option only when we thought we couldn't adopt. We are 30 and 31, we are both white and Jewish. We own a small print shop, which I manage. Lori has a Master's degree in special education. We both have a history of being politically active prior to becoming mothers—however, it is only during the past few months that we have again become active in progressive politics.

We feel we have a lifetime of work ahead of us— raising a boy, raising a child of a different race and culture, raising a child with two mommies as parents, and trying to do it all in a positive and responsible way. We believe it is very important to bring androgyny to child-rearing. We try to dress, talk to, talk about, and relate to Jordy in a way that cannot be linked to a specific gender. We have put a lot of energy into providing Jordan with role models, books, and environments that nurture and validate his birth culture in positive ways. Having adopted Jordan has changed our lives forever—we must constantly challenge and examine the choices and decisions we make for his life. We hope that as other lesbians adopt, and as many of our children come from abroad, that as a community we will engage in discussions concerning the politics of that choice. We love Jordy more than anything in the world and we hope that as a family we will be strong enough to face the challenges ahead.

14. DORIS INDYKE

As I get older, it strikes me that I am only now learning what it means to be in a committed relationship, and seeing, almost for the first time, how my path in life diverges from many friends and family. The decision whether or not to have children takes a lot of my thinking time. It helps to see so many wonderful and loving parents among my lesbian friends.

15. HORTENSE CONNER

I am 48 years old and the mother of five children, whose ages range from 32 to 16. There are four sons and one daughter. My mom, who is still alive, knows that I am gay and supports me in many ways. I feel that I am fortunate because I have the support of my family. At this time, I am in a loving and caring relationship with Pat. We have been living together for two and a half years. She has one son. I have two other grandchildren: Paul, who is seven, and Chris, who is two. The most important thing in my life at this time is my call to the ministry. Answering this call is important because it allows me to help people in a very positive way. I am proud to have completed college in 1983. I've known that I was a lesbian since I was

14; however, I didn't come out until I was 40. I've been an advocate for the homeless for a year. In order to relax, I read, write, sew, do leathercraft, ceramics, and latchhook. To be a lesbian is to be free. I don't have to pretend anymore.

16 & 17. MONA BACHMANN

After living in cities all my life, I recently came to the hills of western Montana. I'm living in a little trailer that I built. I am: Scorpio, Jew, 29 years old, writer, juggler, builder, lover, basketball player, fighter. My friends and family are real important to me, connections stretching between New York City, Seattle, Oregon and Montana. I've been a self-employed carpenter for the last 10 years. Besides learning how to build almost anything out of wood, in this work I've also learned responsibility. I try to stay aware of the reality behind the words "I choose."

17 & 18. BOO DAWSON

At 34, I have nothing to complain about as I'm getting everything I'm asking for. As a member of the butterfly clan (a Gemini), I have flitted and flirted my whole life through. But now as I discover recovery, love that grows, power that comes from slowing down, how to learn by other means than through mistakes, how to make an old dry sagebrush piece of land into a nest, how to make a living in rural western Montana, this butterfly has found a huge succulent flower for nourishment, and I don't flit much anymore. The Great Goddess provides for us here in the Bitterroot Valley. She has led me to believe that "our time's a comin'."

17. PAT GREYTAK

Most important in my life are the friends and lover I share it with, and the place where I experience it. They give me the support, love and inspiration to become aware of my desires, and accomplish my dreams. Their support and understanding have encouraged personal growth. Their energy has helped nurture my land and build my house; as I have done for them in this enticing Bitterroot Valley. It is here in western Montana that I've chosen to invest a majority of my time and energy. This environment enhances my spirit, for it offers an abundance of Mother Nature at her best, luring me with fresh water streams and magnetic mountain tops. But without my friends to share it with, it just wouldn't be the same.

17 & 18. KD DICKINSON

A 36-year-old self-employed carpenter, Gemini, Dyke, I live and work in the Bitterroot Valley surrounded by the Rocky Mountains in Stevensville, Montana. I built my house on land purchased with a friend of mine 10 years ago, whose house we also built. I love my life, my friends, my house, the land, my lover—who is also my work partner and best friend. The women in my life here are family to me and we spend a lot of time being together working, playing, growing, learning, being. Playing music, hiking, getting together with friends at the river or at one another's houses are some of the things I do in my free time here. Life is good.

17 & 18. MARY WILDEMAN

*M*y life is full of love, caring, and fun. I live on a magical hill looking over the Bitterroot Mountains. I live in this reality because of my blood family, and the women who share my life with me. I'm living in a log cabin that was constructed by the support and muscles of women along with my dream of "I can." This dream is a reality now. I carry the belief that anyone *can* do anything they put their minds and hearts to. Teaching the principle of "yes I can" is my next step. I'm almost finished with my teaching degree and I will be out in the workforce soon. My lesbianism has helped me to develop my inner strengths and realize the value of my weaknesses. I sit here thinking of all you women

I don't know, and never will, but knowing we are all a part of each other's lives. Thanks for being there.

19. TONI WHITE (MAYA WHITE SPARKS)

I am Toni White, also known as Toni Macaroni White Sparks, and i live in the foothills of the Blue Ridge Mountains in Virginia, U.S.A. I have no running water, no steady work (right now), and i feel like the richest womon in the world. The Earth is so beautiful. I have a family of wimmin near and far. And, when i'm not workin for money, i have time, time to be totally my Self (which is all ways expanding). I love to be part of daily home/family/ community situations. I love to travel. I love to be alone—to do crystal meditations, to draw, to write, to take pictures, to nap—to think *freely*.

Right now, my mind is full of ideas for a multi-cultural arts celebration for all peoples, here in Rappahannock County. And i'm prayin, prayin for the Mother of Us All, co-creating with Her a life for myself and for my family where we do our souls' true work and all our needs are taken care of. So mote it be. So it is.

20. LYNDA LOU EASE

*M*y roots and my heart are rural; i was born on august 11, 1945, in the panhandle of florida—the deep south. i identify myself as a radical separatist spiritual dyke poet traveler—and that doesn't come close to covering it. right now i clean houses and do all sorts of odd jobs for money but my real work—the work i passionately believe in—is within lesbian community, within lesbian relationships, and inside myself.

20. BECKIE LEE

*B*orn 9/12/53 in portland, oregon, where i grew up in a middle class, religious (christian science) family. i lived in oregon until i was 29, when i moved cross-country to florida. i've been "out"

as a lesbian since i was 17. since i was 25 i've had a beard. i am a bearded lesbian who sometimes lets the hair grow and sometimes not. i feel it's important for me as a radical lesbian to push the limits (both mine and others) as much as i possibly can.

20. SANDRA LAMBERT

The strongest visual images of disabled women I have had are those medical textbook ones of being naked and alone in front of a dark backdrop, your "deformity" highlighted, with a black rectangle across your eyes supposedly to protect your anonymity, but really to complete the dehumanization process. At WomanWrites, a Southern Lesbian writers conference, Beckie organized a workshop on body image and during it I spoke about the lack of images of disabled women. Afterwards Joan came up to me and suggested that she and I change that. In the photos we did together I am naked in an altered context— not alone, not anonymous, and beautiful.

21. JENNIE BOYD BULL

I pastor the Metropolitan Community Church (MCC) of Baltimore, an ecumenical Chrisitian church serving the lesbian and gay communities. We are an inclusive, healing community, making safe space for lesbians from many backgrounds to grow in selflove and in claiming our spirituality. I meditate and do Tai Chi for personal spiritual centering, and am daily grateful for my lover, Lila, and our home and three cats. I bake bread each week, including the communion bread for our worship. I'm also active with AIDS pastoral care through the AIDS Interfaith Network of Baltimore, and with the Baltimore City Commission for Women. But most of my time is spent in worshiping, teaching, and counseling. Sometimes I'm in the media—"She's a lesbian minister"—and I coordinate lesbian and gay community activities, such as our women's networking brunch, our

annual interfaith gay and lesbian Pride Day worship service, and our Holy Week Seder with Dignity (the Catholic gay group) and Adath Rayoot (the Jewish gay group). There are lots of gay and lesbian religious groups in Baltimore and we work together well. Lesbians into varying spiritual paths are also learning to trust each other's journeys and work together. I feel very much like MCC is a "bridge" community where transformation of tradition happens daily at all levels—it stretches my soul.

22. LINDA HOLTZMAN

I am a lesbian and I am a rabbi. These are words that could not have been spoken in public very many years ago. The fact that I can say the words and not be struck by lightning gives me real hope for the future. As a deeply committed feminist, I spend a lot of my life struggling with Jewish tradition. I believe that at the roots of Jewish tradition is not only patriarchy, but is also a women's culture, a women's tradition. The lives of our foremothers are valuable resources for us; it is difficult but also exciting to unearth the hidden treasures of previous generations of Jewish women. It has taken me most of my adult life to feel integrated as a Jewish professional and as a lesbian, but at 35, I'm feeling comfortable and proud of who I am. My work has been divided between the gay and lesbian Jewish community of Philadelphia and the Reconstructionist Rabbinical College of Philadelphia where I am the Director of Practical Rabbinics. Both are satisfying places to be; both help me to keep the personal-political-religious aspects of my life integrated, and to help others do the same.

My partner and I have a 16-month-old son. Watching Betsy give birth and sharing in Jordan's growing up have been profoundly joyous and glorious experiences for me. I hope that there is room both in the Jewish community and in the women's community for the life of this wonderful little boy to be celebrated.

23. BILLIE POTTS

My lesbianism is fundamental to my work and vision as an agent of change. In my life there are very few lines between paid work, political or women's community work, and what I do to relax. I am a 47-year-old lesbian feminist from a New York City Jewish working class background, author of *Witches Heal: Lesbian Herbal Self-Sufficiency*, *A New Women's Tarot*, *Small-Scale Goatkeeping*, and *Potworks: A First Book of Clay*. For more than thirty years, my "work" has been involved with transformative energies: earth and fire as a potter; earth, air, light, and water as a food and herb gardener-producer; and now with crystals and electro-magnetic energies as an ergonomist/activist researching and training on the health effects of video display terminals (VDTs) and other computer-mediated work. I am constantly delighted and excited to be a lesbian in this moment of time, for we are the envisioners/recreators of a non-patriarchal, non-coercive, transformed future through our diverse works, affectional and sexual energies, insights, and laughters.

24. KATHRYN L. EDWARDS, PH.D.

For most of my childhood I was intent on being a veterinarian. But like corn pollen in the wind, I, surprisingly, landed on the botanical side of science. It was the fact that "science" knew little about plants relative to animals and the unique physiological strategies of plants that captured my interest. At Kenyon College in Ohio I came out in a letter to the administration two years before my tenure decision. I am now tenured and that has freed me to be even more publicly open and more active. But being the only lesbian faculty member in an isolated community has taken a toll.

Being a scientist has been a love-hate struggle, a bridging of my world as a researcher and my world as a woman and lesbian. I love doing research, strategizing over methods, being a sleuth of sorts—the quest to understand the life/survival mechanisms of plants. But I hate the profession, the pettiness of collaboration, the power game, the grant game, the meetings where your voice is seldom heard and your body is viewed in subservient terms. I have compromised part of who I am in order to survive in the profession, and for that I am angry. But each year I am stronger and each year I make some changes, such as creating a network for women in the sciences, which enables us to learn about and share with each other. Committing myself to feminist action, women's studies, and biology has meant working essentially 12 months a year and being satisfied making moderate contributions to all. I love the country, the interaction between myself and nature/the earth, the unprocessed odors, the crisp night skies, and the feeling of self-sufficiency. But lesbian community and dyke action are in the cities. This is another bridge in my life.

25. PATTE MARTIN

Being a reproductive rights activist for many, many years has been and is still the most exciting and inspiring experience of my life. That I am a woman, a feminist, and a lesbian has permitted me to find wonderful sources of strength to persevere in the face of abominations, death threats, trials, and of course the ongoing need for superhuman reserves of compassion to care for the women who seek our services at the clinic. (I was once charged with and tried for criminal battery on an anti-abortionist. I received an acquittal. There have been two additional attempts by anti-abortionists to charge me with felonious assault. Currently I'm being sued for 3.9 million dollars by a man who was arrested for a bomb threat, but who later had the charges against him dropped.) One conclusion can be drawn about my life—it is never dull and boring. In recent times I've sought new horizons in my continuous pursuit of a calm private life, including studying with a spiritualist healer, and in women's medicine circles.

I've been progressively more "out of the closet" over the years. Now in interviews with potential clinic employees, I explain that "our staff consists of many women including women who live with men they aren't married to, nudists, vegetarians and lesbians. If you have any problems with any of this, you need to let me know, since I'm the boss, I'm one of the lesbians and I sign the paychecks." Interestingly, I've never had anyone turn tail and run from that preamble. Womanspace is thrilling, comfortable and comforting. The further I travel from the "closet," the more delightful my discoveries. My only wish is to find a powerful women's community and network in conservative Florida. Please let me know if you're coming this way. You're welcome.

26. ANA MALDONADO

*T*o me being a lesbian means being well-defined, centered, loved and supported as a woman who supports others individually and in their individuality. I particularly extend this to women whose empowerment in health care is vital for themselves and their families.

When I first came out as a lesbian in 1978 I had two small children, no professional education or skill (beyond that as an empirically trained midwife), and I felt very isolated and overwhelmed. Slowly I have evolved through my educational process and training as a Physician Assistant in Primary Care medicine and in my specialty of Women's Health Care and Midwifery to find myself in three different work environments in order to fulfill the different aspects of myself as a Latina and as a lesbian. I work at a farmworker clinic in Watsonville—Salud Para la Gente (Health for the People), at the Santa Cruz Women's Health Center providing lesbian health services, and in private practice as WomanCare/Midwifery Services providing alternative women's health care and homebirth services. For fun I live with my lover Jess, an aspiring Physician Assistant, and my daughter Sarah. I play racquetball, swim and run for recreation and endorphins, and lounge on the beach for relaxation. Community activities include being a Board member of the Santa Cruz AIDS Project and offering a lecture series on Lesbian Health Matters such as "Out of the Closet and Into the Exam Room," and "Lesbian Parenting."

27. ELEANOR LORD

*S*ince I retired from land surveying, I've worked to further feminist goals in Berkshire County, Massachusetts and have spent much of the last three years working to improve the life and health of the lesbian community there. I designed a questionnaire on lesbian lives and lesbians' attitudes about the community, interviewed 100 women, and published a report for the participants. In June 1987 I presented a paper about the evolution of this community to the Berkshire Conference on the History of Women at Wellesley College. I hope other women in other places will do similar kinds of studies, both to support our identities as lesbians and to affirm our communities as potential models for groups working for social change.

I'm in my fifties, came out in the early '70s, and am in a committed relationship. I feel good about myself because I am able to do what I want to do, have an interesting and nurturing lover, three terrific children and several close lesbian friends. I am lucky! I anticipate growing older in this community that values older women and even loves them! I get plenty of exercise maintaining Boulder Farm, hiking with friends and cheering on our softball team.

28. NITA O'BRIEN

*C*oming out seemed a natural part of my life, an expansion of loving my best friend when I was 28—ten years ago. Marty, my son, who is twelve now, grew up knowing and accepting who I was and the lesbians around him. The counseling (therapy) I do, especially the four and one-half years of working with sexual assault survivors and training volunteers to do crisis intervention, are what make me feel content and challenged. And working with wood in my spare time "smoothes" out frustrations... sanding wood until it's smooth as a woman's skin... soft yet strong and full of scent.

Over the ten years since I came out I have been rewarded over and over again by being active in both NOW and the Gay Hotline. Friendship and loving are both fragile and strong... we all still struggle to do this well. Nurturing people and helping them to nurture themselves and others is most important to me.

29, 31, & 104. DEE MOSBACHER, M.D., PH.D.

I'm a Clinical Fellow in Psychiatry at Harvard Medical School and work as the Chief Resident at Somerville Mental Health Clinic. There I co-ordinate the psychoeducational programs for families of patients with major mental illness. I'm also on the Board of the American Association of Physicians for Human Rights. I'm 38 years old and I started medical school when I was 30. Before that, in the early 1970s, I organized against the Vietnam War and for abortion rights. I taught gynecological self-help at a free clinic and worked for an auto mechanic. I also did construction work and wrote a play based on that experience. I have continued to write plays, and this year I won the national playwriting contest sponsored by the Long Island Lesbian Thespians, for my most recent play, *The Price*. I have a doctorate in Social Psychology from the Union Graduate School and now I'm on their Board of Trustees. While I was in medical school, I produced *Closets Are Health Hazards: Gay and Lesbian Physicians Come Out*, a videotape distributed by the American Medical Students Association, of which I was a national officer for two years. I'm currently involved in a research project on lesbians and alcohol and substance abuse.

I think that Nanette and I have been able to accomplish as much as we have because we have such a good relationship with mutual love, respect, and support for each other's work.

29, 30, & 104. NANETTE GARTRELL, M.D.

I am a Senior Associate in Psychiatry at Boston's Beth Israel Hospital. For the past seven years I have been teaching psychiatry to primary care residents. I recently completed a research project that revealed that a sizable minority of psychiatrists sexually abuse their clients. Our data challenges mental health professionals to address this problem and to provide more effective services to victim-survivors. I am currently co-principal investigator for a longitudinal study of lesbians who have children by alternative insemination. My private practice is almost exclusively lesbian. I think it's really important that lesbians are able to see a therapist who is comfortable being out and visible. Helping clients deal with their internalized homophobia is a major focus of my work. I've seen how self-esteem becomes progressively more impaired by living a closeted existence.

Dee and I have been together since 1975 and I feel incredibly lucky to have such a fulfilling relationship. I feel more in love every year. In 1985 we sponsored the Second National Lesbian Physicians Conference, and we have been involved in organizing lesbian psychiatrists nationally. I've been studying tap dancing since 1977 and it's my own favorite form of therapy.

32. ELEANOR N. SOTO

*B*oth personally and politically, I define myself as a Latina/Chicana, Lesbian Feminist. It is essential, to me, to be able to unite all the different parts of myself and to be able to express and represent the whole person in my work, paid and non-paid, and my personal life. Sometimes this has been very isolating and dangerous; other times it has felt like coming home—not always easy but at least safe to be out and sometimes to challenge the racist and homophobic assumptions that are everywhere. The battered women's movement has been such a place for me, not always easy but generally safe. Values such as self-empowerment and the rights of the individual have a place in our work. How else can we change a social system that believes it's alright to beat and control others?

I once had a dream in which I was trying to separate these two rivers, the Chicago and Illinois. Try as I may, they just kept running together. Waking up I realized that trying to differentiate the Chicana from the other parts of myself was just as useless. I'm presently 36 years old and work for the Family Violence Project in San Francisco. I'm originally from Los Angeles, California. In many ways, I've known I was a Lesbian all my life and an activist/organizer, and social worker.

33. ELVIRA WILLIAMS

I worked with a woman named Alice. She was 33 years old when killed by her batterer. Alice's struggle for freedom and her brutal murder made me realize I have a life. Her death brought me to life. So I'm learning how to live and not be a prisoner of my own fears or a prisoner of my own personal struggles or to remain a victim of my childhood, my disease of alcoholism, my being a victim of incest, my being a black woman, my being a lesbian, my being despised by people. Ya know what I mean? So, I'm going to live and I'm Gonna Talk. I want to encourage younger, older, and unborn lesbians to take pride and COME OUT.

34. RUTHIE CRONE

*W*hen Family House first opened 10 years ago there were many more "runaways"; kids looking for dreams coming true in Woodstock. Today we're facing an overwhelming phenomenon of the homeless. These kids are called "throwaways"— parents are dumping their kids. We give them counseling and support them in taking control of their lives. I firmly believe that the kids we see—in all their pain and hopelessness—are a reflection of the state of our society. Working in social services is good "patch-up" work, and extremely necessary, but ultimately the basic structure has to change. My passion is rooted in working towards transforming the capitalist system into a more supportive and life sustaining one, where self-determination is truly possible.

I grew up in Brownsville in Brooklyn, N.Y., and now I live in the Catskill Mountains. I choose to live in the country because when there is pain all around, I need to feel something alive and beautiful. The mountains feed my spirit, and I feed my woodstove in return! I'm 30 years old, and I've known I loved women since my last year in high school. I proceeded to "come out" in my freshman year of college. I feel that as lesbians we *must* be out in the world whenever possible because the personal is political and people will never get over their oppressive stereotypes if we don't bust their bubbles by concrete example. Sexuality is such a loaded issue for teenagers that it is often difficult to have them trust me when being "queer" is something they have such a hard time with. We, as lesbians, are building our network. I know for myself that the women who are my family are the force that fills my heart and helps me to work for change.

35 & 36. JOYCE HUNTER

*B*orn in New York City to a Black father and an Orthodox Jewish mother in 1939, I define myself as a Jewish person of color. I got my Master's in Social Work from Hunter College where I was president of Lesbians Rising as an undergraduate. For more than 10 years, I was one of a group that worked for passage of the Gay and Lesbian Rights Bill in the New York City Council. We finally won that fight in 1986. I'm a spokesperson for the Coalition for Lesbian and Gay Rights, a member of the New York City Commission on Human

Rights and of Governor Cuomo's Task Force on Lesbian and Gay Issues. I was the national co-coordinator for the 1979 March on Washington for Lesbian and Gay Rights and I'm a member of the executive committee for the 1987 March. I am now the Director of Social Services for the Hetrick/Martin Institute for the Protection of Lesbian and Gay Youth.

It took me a long time to feel good about being a lesbian. I grew up lonely and isolated. Nobody told me it was o.k. to be who I am. Today I have an opportunity to be there for young people, to help them feel good about who they are and to let them know they can have a good life in the future. I'm most proud of being a founding member of the Institute because it's going to help generations of young people to come. It's institutionalized, it's going to be here. When I get a chance, I love to listen to opera and jazz. I enjoy spending time with my two children, my grandchildren and my lover Jan.

37. MAUREEN F. SCHORR

I chose to be born Maureen Frances Schorr (after some delay at the drive-in movies) to James and Eileen Schorr, becoming by default the eldest and often wisest of their five children. After some education and wandering about I have settled in Baltimore where I share my life with Dr. Anne, who loves me and keeps me sane. I am now energetically employed as the Volunteer Coordinator at the Health Education Resource Organization of Baltimore, working with the volunteers who work with persons with AIDS. It is the perfect job for an imperfect idealist and I can not conceive of doing anything else right now. I am learning to love life and not to fear death. I prefer to think that I have chosen this life in anticipation of making a significant contribution to my own karma. I therefore 'ege and aver that there is rhyme to the reason of my life.

38. COLEVIA CARTER

*I*t is important to me as a Black woman and as a lesbian, in order to be whole and to survive, to build coalitions. It's important to understand that truly none of us are free until all of us are free. It is rare when people see me as a whole person. I want to help people realize what they miss when they are constricted by prejudice. As Harriet Tubman once said "The underground railroad does not run on a track, rather it is a knowing face, or particular place that leads to freedom." This kind of knowing makes me feel safe from harm. I want to get to that place with as many people as I can.

39. ANNA MARIE RECHICHI

*B*eginning at the age of 22 and for the last 24 years I have lived my life as a lesbian. Having participated in the Women's Community for the past 10 years I have been actively involved in different projects and events sponsored by the Cleveland Women's Community. To watch the growth of the Lesbian Community during this time has been both encouraging and exciting for me. Being in the Community gave me the support to have an "I can do" attitude and be willing to take risks at changing careers. At 38 years of age, after 17 years of food service management, I began my career as a welder.

I was born in Cleveland, Ohio in August 1941. My parents are both Italian. I was brought up as a Catholic and attended Catholic Elementary School. In high school I was very athletic and after graduation I was involved in the Cleveland Women's Track and Field Team as a shot-putter, discus and javelin thrower. I also won awards in shot-putting. Today I continue to be involved in sports by playing women's volleyball and baseball. Much of my enjoyment is in gardening and many outdoor activities. Relaxing, to me, is driving to the lake with my lover and dogs, having dinner, and watching the sun set. Knowing that I am a

Lesbian, accepting it and finding happiness in it, gives me peace of mind and spirit and strength to be for other women.

40. PAT SKEETS MASON

I am a 34-year-old lesbian of color who is constantly striving to center myself in the light of self-knowledge and universal love so that I may walk through the worldly maze of self-doubt and cultural oppression/suppression. HEAR ME, SEE ME, TOUCH ME, KNOW ME—for I am *one* in the ALL of IT!!

40. SUNNY NEAL

I am Two-Suns, legally called Sunny Neal. I am a Native American Indian woman in my 55th year. I am proud of my independence and freedom to choose how I want to be, who I am. *I am a survivor* and I have struggled for years to be independent. My lover of almost five years supports me in this and joined me in St. Petersburg to share the comforts of our wonderful lesbian community. Web (Women's Energy Bank) is the center of the community for me. I am a phone volunteer for The Line: a Lesbian and Gay information and referral service. The Line gave me information about St. Pete's Lesbian community that helped me survive when I moved here. I am a mermaid, gypsy, witch and hermit lesbian at times. My mother is my model and inspiration and my sister in blood has always accepted and applauded these aspects of me. My four grown children are glad I chose to be everything that I am. Although I have a degree in Mental Health, which helps me on The Line, I work in Physical Therapy. I especially enjoy working with paraplegics and quadriplegics.

41. MARY SCHULTZ

*P*eople are so scared of change. So scared of being different and so they conform. I want people to know I am not a part of the system. I am different. I am an individual.

42. SHANNON MORSE

*M*y job at the lumber mill is that of heavy machine operator. I drive fork lifts, straddle buggies and operate various other lumber mill machinery. My sophomore year of college in 1978, Thanksgiving weekend, consummated the beginning of a four and one-half year relationship which set the style of my life from then til now. Though I am not "out" at work, I have a unique communications system. I leave brief messages inside the boxcars that I load in hopes that they will reach other members of the "community" across the country.

In my spare time I like gardening and riding my horse. On the social side, I enjoy sports of all seasons and participate in the city recreation programs of basketball, softball and soccer. In the winter I capitalize on the snowy Montana slopes to do a little skiing. I used to feel that being a lesbian was something that I had to hide or justify. Over the years I have found that being a lesbian is only something that contributes to me being me. I no longer see my lifestyle as something of an obstacle but more as a challenge that helps me be the best person I can be.

43. ABIGAIL JOHNSON

*A*s a small girl I was in the farm fields each summer and realized I was different from my peers—a lover of land and a lover of women. I was to become a gentle woman farmer, but being a woman I denied my farm desires, obtained a B.S. in Medical Technology to support myself financially, and found a woman to love and live with as a partner in progress for the rest of my days. Discovering this was not enough for me, I returned to Horticulture School and upon graduating purchased The Christmas Tree Farm. I have never known such inner peace and harmony as I did working my land, developing a deep love and respect for Mother Nature. Becoming one with the farm I somehow managed to lose my friend and my lover of nine years. I have sold my farm and am beginning to reclaim myself. The gentle woman farmer still remains and I am developing a perennial herb farm in North Georgia.

44. LESLIE BURGESS

*F*or me each year since my 30th has felt like a profound gift because for a long time I really believed I wouldn't live to be 30. And here I am! I'm alive and opening to an incredible journey in life and love. I feel like a multi-faceted crystal, each surface different, reflecting a different now and then, each an important part of the whole. I catch light, I absorb it, give it back, often gently, sometimes harshly. I am a lesbian, loving womyn, loving myself. I am a former prostitute and an important part of me coming into myself is talking about that part of my life, normalizing it. I am a poet, a counselor, and I'm active in the domestic violence movement, especially as a prostitutes' rights advocate. I have survived much violence and am moving beyond surviving to fulfilling myself by being me, living me as fully as I can at each given moment and voicing my choices politically, spiritually, musically, and noisily.

45. KELLEY READY

*A*bout ten years ago I dropped out of college and began to look for an alternative to what I had expected my life to be as a middle-class suburban girl from an Irish Catholic background. I decided I wanted to learn to be a printer, a non-traditional trade that I hoped would give me access to communication and allow me to contribute materially to the people's struggle. By the time I joined the Red Sun Press Collective in Boston five

years later, I had developed my skills as an offset press operator enough to be able to make that kind of contribution through the collective's donations to groups working for political, economic and social change. Having resolved the question of what to do with my life (for this time period, at least) I soon found myself facing the question of my sexuality and I came out as a lesbian a year later. Of course that process untapped new areas of myself to explore, particularly the effect my family's alcoholism had had on me. I continue that journey as well as searching for ways to integrate aspects of myself, the writer, the activist, the internationalist, that have yet to be more fully realized in my life.

46. KIT QUAN

I immigrated with my family from Hong Kong to San Francisco in 1969, at the age of eight. My mother has worked as a seamstress, a linen folder, and currently as a file clerk. I believe that claiming one's own language(s), culture(s), and history (ethnic, class), having access to education and job training, and speaking up are crucial to the empowerment of women of color and working class women whose thoughts and experiences are often unheard or misunderstood. As a working class Asian lesbian who learned English as a second language and who came out and worked in the feminist and lesbian movements while still a teenager, I've had to wrestle with a shitload of racist, classist, and ageist assumptions and political standards. That's why I like going to action-packed kung fu films in C-town and hanging out at my favorite bakery to watch old Chinese women eating bows and drinking coffee and talking like they own the place. (C-town = Chinatown, bows = Chinese street buns or meat-filled buns, pronounced like "bow" in "bow wow.")

47. TACIE DEJANIKUS

*B*ack to the beginning. In 1971 I was 20 and decided to join the radical feminist newspaper *oob* (*off our backs*). At my first meeting I sat in red nylon hot pants and matching top, not understanding a word. The meeting seemed to last forever and as I got up to leave early a collective member asked sarcastically if I would return. I did and stayed for 14 years. Those years as a member of the *oob* collective were my activist awakening. Already influenced by the civil rights and anti-Vietnam war movements and a summer in Appalachia, I listened intently to this new radical feminist politics, which borrowed ideas from these movements and invented new ones—scary and wonderful—like lesbian feminism and collectivity. Working there was a satisfying and stimulating blend of the practical, the professional and the visionary. The politics spoke to an unarticulated childhood uneasiness with arbitrary authority, race and class distinctions and limitations placed on girls and women. After a few years on the paper, I came out. By the mid-70s there was a lesbian assumption at *oob*; an assumption that the sexual boundaries between women were artificial and that anti-lesbianism was illogical. I came to feel the naturalness of lesbianism, not as a sexual preference, but as something that flourishes when women remove themselves from the domination of male culture and its heterosexual presumption.

Since leaving *oob* I have been involved in a variety of feminist work such as Lesbian International Visibility (LIV), the D.C. Lesbian Committee to Free Sharon Kowalski, and a lesbian reading group. Now I'm working to make the 1987 National March for Lesbian and Gay Rights a success. What sustains me through the ups and downs of my political work is my lover of five years, Angela, my original family, my friends and my belief that it's better than watching TV.

DEDICATION, 48, 49 & 50. AUDRE LORDE

*T*hose of us who stand outside the circle of this society's definition of acceptable women; those of us who have been forged in the crucibles of difference—those of us who are poor, who are lesbians, who are Black, who are older—know that *survival is not an academic skill*. It is learning how to stand alone, unpopular and sometimes reviled, and how to make common cause with others identified as outside the structures in order to define and seek a world in which we can all flourish. It is learning how to take our differences and make them strengths. *For the master's tools will never dismantle the master's house.* They may allow us temporarily to beat him at his own game, but they will never enable us to bring about genuine change. And this fact is only threatening to those women who still define the master's house as their only source of support. [From "The Master's Tools Will Never Dismantle the Master's House," in *Sister Outsider*, The Crossing Press. © 1984 by Audre Lorde.]

51. CLAUDIA HINOJOSA

I was born in the 1950s in the largest city of the world, Mexico City, where politics is an everyday part of life. I became involved in feminism through a study group begun in 1977. We then founded Grupo Lambda de Liberación Homosexual—one of the first such groups in Mexico—where I served as staff and public spokesperson for several years. I have worked as a radio and TV journalist as well as collaborated closely with *FEM*, the Mexican feminist journal, which is more than a decade old. In recent years I have traveled extensively as the organizer for a Mexican women's theater group, Compañía Divas, and have been active as a feminist in the UN Decade for Women and at international lesbian events sponsored by ILIS (International Lesbian Information Service). Currently I am writing about my experiences and reflections as a Latin American lesbian feminist.

51. CHARLOTTE BUNCH

*B*orn in 1944, I grew up in a small town in New Mexico with little political awareness but a strong sense of what was fair. During the 1960s, this transformed me into a full-time organizer and then propelled me to feminism in 1968 when I helped to found Washington D.C. Women's Liberation. In 1971, I came out and joined with a group that started The Furies—a lesbian feminist collective and newspaper. I spent the 70s engaged in many feminist activities in the U.S. and as an editor of *Quest: A Feminist Quarterly*. During the 1980s I have focused on issues of global feminism and how to connect these to the work of local activists. My latest book, *Passionate Politics: Feminist Theory in Action, 1968–1986*, tells it all better. I am currently the Laurie New Jersey Chair in Women's Studies at Douglass College at Rutgers University.

52. MAY SARTON

*A*t 75 I am happy about my life and happy that I came out when it was hard to do in 1965 with the novel *Mrs. Stevens Hears the Mermaids Singing*. It is now extensively used in Women's Studies in the colleges. It was my tenth novel as I was and am determined to be known as a good writer who happens to be a lesbian. I have written seventeen novels, five journals, three books of memoirs, twelve books of poems. The audiences these last years when I read poems have been wonderful: standing room only everywhere from The Smithsonian in Washington, D.C. to Arts and Letters in San Francisco. I live alone with my Himalayan cat, Pierrot, and Grizzle, a tiny miniature dachshund who was given to me after my beloved sheltie died. I garden and see friends all summer but try to concentrate on writing in the winter. That is hard to do because of the avalanches of mail that pour in here every day, but I no longer answer every letter as I used to do.

That is no longer possible since a stroke last year. *After the Stroke*, a journal, will come out in early 1988. It's a great life but a very demanding one.

53, 54 & 55. ADRIENNE RICH

I have been for thirteen years a very public and visible lesbian. I have felt my identity as a feminist threatening to some, welcome to others; but my identity as a lesbian is something many people would prefer not to know about. Invisibility is a dangerous and painful condition, and lesbians are not the only people to know it. When those who have power to name and to socially construct reality choose not to see you or greet you, whether you're dark-skinned, old, disabled, female, Jewish, or speak with a different accent or dialect than theirs, it is as if you looked into a mirror and saw nothing. Yet you know you exist and others like you, that this is a game with mirrors. It takes some strength of soul—and not just individual strength, but collective understanding—to resist this void, this nonbeing into which you are thrust, and to stand up, demanding to be seen and heard. It is important to me to remember that in the nineteenth century, women—all women—were forbidden by law to speak in public meetings. Society depended on their muteness. But some, and then more and more, refused to be mute and spoke up. Without them we would not even be here today. [Adapted from a talk given at the Scripps College Conference, Claremont, California, 1984, entitled "Invisibility in Academe." It appears in *Blood, Bread, and Poetry*, © 1986 by Adrienne Rich. Reprinted by the permission of the author and W.W. Norton, Inc.]

55. MARY FARMER

I knew that I was a lesbian in my early teens but did not arrive at a place of loving myself as a lesbian until I was in my twenties. It was in the context of my new community, the D.C. radical lesbian community, that I began to appreciate and love myself and to learn the basic political lessons that still shape my life and work. The foundation of those lessons was, simply put, "the personal is political." At age 38, that philosophy continues to guide me in my personal relationships and in my work as a feminist bookstore owner.

56. CHERYL CLARKE

Since May of 1973 I've lived as a lesbian. I don't believe I could live without being a lesbian. I was born in Washington, D.C., in 1947 to working-class parents who believed their daughters should be independent. I've been an educator since 1969. The most important activity of my life is working with women to change the quality of our lives. I am the author of *Narratives: Poems in the Tradition of Black Women* (1982) and *Living as a Lesbian* (1986), and a member of the *Conditions* magazine editorial collective since 1981. Writing is the way I fight. I am a member of the Board of Directors of New York Women Against Rape and hope to be a part of the worldwide struggle to end violence against women in our lifetimes.

57. ELANA DYKEWOMON

I love my life as a lesbian. I've loved women since I fell in love with my nursery school bus driver when I was three. But I nearly died trying to establish a lesbian self, pre-movement. What gives me enormous strength and pleasure now is being one of many, creating the lesbian world I need in order to live. I worked hard/was lucky, *Riverfinger Women* was published when I was 24, and provided the only "real" money I ever made as writer—which enabled me to write *They Will Know Me by My Teeth* in 1976. In the meantime, I distributed films with the Women's Film Coop in Northampton, worked in the Valley Women's Center and in the Socialist/Feminist Movement before becoming a Lesbian Separatist during that intense burst of dyke energy in the mid-70s.

In 1978, burned but not exactly burned-out, I moved to the coast of Oregon, joining-up, lovingly, with Zelda Waletzky, with whom I lived until 1986. Zelda and I started Diaspora Distribution, to get lesbian works out to women-only audiences. In Oregon I learned patience, printing, and what it means to be a Jew outside of big urban centers. I gathered and hand printed *Fragments from Lesbos* in 1981. Wanting to re-enter daily political lesbian community life, I moved to Oakland in 1983, printed signs for a department store for three years, joined the Jewish Lesbian Writers Group, worked on fat and disability politics, found many compañeras. These days I live alone, down the street from Zelda, next door to my companion Susan Jill, try to get by, work on *Sinister Wisdom*, and do my own writing. I believe that "the revolution" exists within us, in our lesbian capacity to keep reinventing a loving world.

55, 58, 59 & 64. MINNIE BRUCE PRATT

Born in 1946 in Selma, Alabama, I live now in Washington, D.C., three blocks up the street from my lover of six years, Joan E. Biren. I came out as a lesbian in 1975 when I had been married for nine years and had two small boys. I came out because: one woman talked to me about women's liberation and told me she was a lesbian; other women kissed in front of me; I heard and read feminist theory, and poetry; I fell in love with a woman who had the rolling gait of a sailor and wore silvery shirts and a gold pocket watch; I looked into my future as a wife, a mother, a working woman, and saw an arid stretch of time, the deadly repetition of what had always been; I knew that to live as a lesbian would be to invent something new, more passionate, more interesting.

Since then I have earned my living as a teacher at different colleges; nowadays I invariably come out as a lesbian to my students some time between the first and third week of classes. For five years I was a member of the editorial collective of *Feminary: A Lesbian Feminist Journal for the*

South. I have written two books of poetry, *The Sound of One Fork* and *We Say We Love Each Other*, and co-authored, with Elly Bulkin and Barbara Smith, *Yours in Struggle: Three Feminist Perspectives on Anti-Semitism and Racism.* I am presently writing poems about my children, who I lost custody of, who are grown now, and are my friends. For now, in addition to teaching women's studies, my main work is writing. I write essays to understand the net of oppressions thrown over my life and the lives of others. I write poetry to keep my sanity, to get justice, to get joy, to get myself out of the past, to get word by word into a place where I haven't yet been and which I haven't yet foreseen.

60 & 61. JUDITH SCHWARZ

*B*orn in Virginia, I came out in 1963 in San Francisco while working at the Technicolor photo-finishing plant with about fifty other Lesbians. My most exciting work to date has been the archival research that resulted in *Radical Feminists of Heterodoxy: Greenwich Village 1912–1940,* and the joy of working as co-coordinator of the Lesbian Herstory Archives and Lesbian Herstory Educational Foundation. As a woman born with Cerebral Palsy, I am excited by the possibilities of new technology for disabled people, as well as the possibilities through optical scanning and computer indexing for easier access to women's history. I sometimes fantasize about how we can get all 650 Lesbian subject category files and 1200 periodical series onto three optical disks, and find every single word among all that paper.

I love mysteries, finding little-known women in our past, visual images, cats, people with a sense of humor, independent and caring women, and getting out of the city as much as possible.

60. DEBORAH EDEL

I didn't realize in the mid-1960s when accepting a job shortly after college that I would be establishing a lifetime career as an educational psychologist concerned with the learning disabilities of children and adults. I didn't realize in the early 1970s when I fell in love with a woman and came out that in recognizing my Lesbian self I would restructure the way I understood my own history. I didn't realize in the mid-1970s that how I loved women and how I felt was called butch and that in this second naming of myself I would have yet a fuller sense of myself as part of a Lesbian subculture with a rich cultural history. I didn't realize in the mid-1970s when along with other women I started the Lesbian Herstory Archives that what I was helping to create would go beyond the bounds of a simple undertaking to become a central force in my life and an institution in the Lesbian community. I didn't realize that the papers I would file, the letters I would write, the slideshows I would give, and the researchers I would help would nourish and strengthen me as fully as they have. I didn't realize that I would be making a lifelong commitment to help build a cultural center that as it continues to grow continues to question, to challenge and to change ideas as it gathers all our Lesbian history.

I now realize that each change in my life changes the larger picture and that with each shift comes increasing self-inheritance. I look forward to future changes while living strongly in the present.

62. CLAIRE OLIVIA MOED

*M*y heart is a fierce locomotive and it takes me many places. I'm a slut for love. I've got to be honest. This holds true for both men and women. And I love to kiss. I'd like to say for the record that I have never kissed anyone else but my girlfriend of three and one-half years, J. L. W., with the exception of the following: all my friends, about two-thirds of the women of the W.O.W. Cafe, Weesie in front of her straight friends, Joke P., a flying bear, my Lezzie parents Deb Edel and Joan Nestle, and any ex-lover I am currently speaking to. Oh yeah, and Terry in the bathroom of the Blue and Gold Bar but that's only because Peggy and Lynn dared us to go in there and kiss and then they locked us in. And when I kiss I love to leave a lipstick mark where everyone can see it. I consider it living art. J. L. W., however, doesn't view my lipstick in this light and this leads to many interesting romps around the house. I don't come out because I think it's politically important. I come out because I'm a lousy liar when it comes to love.

62. JOAN NESTLE

I am very lucky to have lived through and learned from three crucial histories: the queer fifties, the activist sixties and the lesbian-feminist seventies. None of these legacies are outdated, and their gifts of insight and of strength have shaped the two major commitments of my life: helping to found the Lesbian Herstory Archives and 21 years of teaching in the SEEK (Search for Elevated and Enlightened Knowledge) program at Queens College. The SEEK program originated in the 1960s street anger of Black and Puerto Rican young people who wanted a chance at a higher education in the City University system. The program was only supposed to last for 10 years, but the vigilance of students and teachers has kept this radical educational dream alive.

The battles still rage; the need for joy is, perhaps, even greater. With a kiss for my friends and a raised fist for the government, I am ready for the nineties.

63. MARIAN STERN

*B*orn and raised in New York City, I came to Binghamton to go to school. I thought it was too "small town" for me, and left for Boston as soon as I graduated. I spent eight years there, working at various jobs, establishing and running a business, and getting a graduate degree, before I decided to return to Binghamton last year. Although I occasionally miss the movies, restaurants and pace of the "big" city, I'm learning to appreciate what a small town can offer, and specifically, what Binghamton can offer lesbians. Herizon (213 State St., if you're ever in town) has provided, since 1975, the basis for organizing and uniting the community. The chance to be creative, to be responsible for ourselves and our events, and to learn new skills are all encouraged here. I enjoy being Treasurer (even counting the pennies!) and working in an organization. This involvement has helped give me the strength to come out to my family, and to feel secure in, and proud of, our community.

63. FAITH ROGOW

I'm a Jewish dyke who spends a lot of time trying to make those two parts of my life work together. I frequently have a guitar in my hands which I use to compose music for Jewish women's rituals, teach Jewish music, and play rock-n-roll for lesbian audiences. I draw my inspiration from B'not Esh (a radical Jewish women's group), Herizon (the women's community of Binghamton, NY) and my lover, Del. I expect to finish my PhD in women's and Jewish history in the near future, which means gluing myself to the computer for the next few months, but I'd really rather be singing, playing basketball, and hugging my honey.

64. JO HARTSOE

I am a 40-year-old lesbian chef who lives in Atlanta, Georgia with my lover of nearly 13 years in a house we bought together eight years ago. I moved to Atlanta from Michigan in 1969 shortly after graduating from college, coming out, and buying my first car (in that order). The car lasted 17 years and almost 200,000 miles and would probably still be going strong if I hadn't been seduced by GM's promises of low interest rates last fall. I have played on the same softball team, the Amazons, for the past nine seasons, and have been active for more than 12 years in the Atlanta Lesbian Feminist Alliance (ALFA), one of the longest-lived lesbian-feminist organizations in the U.S. Stability, continuity and longevity are very important to me and it is these characteristics that I work to help my lesbian community achieve.

65. ELEANOR SMITH

The main strands in my life over time have been being raised in a large middle-class Mennonite family by farm-raised parents; being disabled by polio at age three; becoming a lesbian (glimmer at 16, sweetheart at 20, political realizations at 30); and being fascinated by communal living arrangements and living in several. Born in 1943, I've been employed at clerical work, counseling and teaching. Now, after many years of physical stability, my dominant reality in 1987 is that my body is giving out in new ways. My goals are to survive, help make revolution, and have fun doing it. I worry that I'll just manage the first. My lover and I are looking for group living creations.

65. DENNIE DOUCHER

Being a 35-year-old woman, I feel extremely positive, creative, motivated, and happy. I am successfully pursuing and balancing several priorities: a relationship, school, career changes, and time for myself. I attribute my success to a basic positive belief in myself and my metaphysical growth and to all the emotional support I receive from my friends and from a loving relationship that allows me to be me. The women's community in Atlanta provides a wonderful resource for networking, supporting each other, loving, and sharing our dreams. I feel very fortunate to be a part of this community!

65. BLUEBIRD

Bluebird is 44 years old and has been a Lesbian for 10 years. At this time she is focusing on mental patients' rights and is working nationally and locally to develop self-help alternatives. Between working as a nurse and with the Mental Patient Movement she gets little time to herself but still manages to go to occasional women's events.

66. TIANA ARRUDA

Brasilian, 44 years old, I have spent half of my life in Rio de Janeiro and the other half in the U.S. I remember falling in love with women since I was 7 years old—my second grade teacher was my first big crush. I've had a rich and rewarding life full of friendships and work that I have enjoyed in liberation and political struggles. A founder of the Women's Building of the Bay Area, I have worked in feminist collectives since 1977: Mujeres en Lucha/Lesbian Latinas, *Feminary*, San Francisco Women's Centers, and the last six years at Old Wives Tales.

67. CAROL KARLMANN

I fell in love with my baby-sitter when I was three years old and I've been crazy about women ever since. I had always wanted to work in the women's community and in 1980 my lover Joie and I had the opportunity to buy Womencrafts, a lesbian/feminist shop. Every day we celebrate being lesbians with all the wonderful women who come to our shop. It's been a real dream come true.

67. JOIE DEALL

I'm a 51-year-old Lesbian who was a late bloomer. I came out in 1963, at the age of 28, just as "Butch-Fem" roles were going out of style. I've been a stone Butch, a butch, a Dyke separatist and now a loving and loved Lesbian woman. Carol and I have been lovers for about nine years and keep growing and learning together. "We haven't got it easy, but we've got it!"

68. MARGUERITE KOTWITZ

*S*oon after coming out in 1968, I became active in the fledgling gay movement. I operated a gay switchboard and referral service out of my home in Palo Alto, California, and participated in a gay speakers' forum. Later I helped start an employees' union at Stanford University that provided the nucleus for the union now representing all Stanford employees. While at Stanford I worked on and managed distribution for one of the first lesbian newspapers in the Bay Area, *Mother*, later renamed *Proud Woman*.

I left Stanford in 1971, compelled by a need to combine my artwork and my politics into what has become my life's work—being a storyteller in clay. It's gratifying to know that my matriarchal pottery, under the name Amazon Earthworks, is being spread around the world by many kindred souls. My dream is that archaeologists will one day come upon my work and it will provide a positive image of strong womyn for all to see—a lasting statement that "We Are Everywhere."

70. AMIE LAIRD

*T*here is a part of yourself that is uncovered when working a womyn's music festival that can never honestly be denied. It is that part that identifies and strengthens the core of what it means to be female. I had heard the word "lesbian" for the first time only two months before that festival. I was just coming out—my strength was in my innocence. Since that time, I've gained an awareness that can not be shaken from me. This society, this patriarchy, its institutions have prefabricated an identity for us as women, in which nothing is fair and very little is true. But I refuse to deny myself the pleasures of creating my own identity

as a woman. That is why I am a lesbian. I will not participate in any system where women are not allowed to live honestly.

I am an artist; a sculptress. The cognition of women in this field is in an ill state. But my work is my sanity; it's an attempt to distill out a truth and establish an inner identity. My existence is very unpredictable (being a Scorpio, an artist and lesbian). My relationship with my lover is the most solid and grounding thing in my life. She is my reality. I could not live as honestly as I have without her or without the greater lesbian community. All I really want to do is to spark an awareness, through my work and my being. I am a warrior fanning the fire.

70. J. FINCH

*A*fter 13 years of marriage, I came out as a lesbian at the age of 33. Looking back at my adolescence with this "new" information, I was fully able to understand myself as a young womon. I lived on a rural homestead for 12 years, the last five by myself. When I lived isolated in the rural area bordering the Michigan music festival land, I considered the festival as my way of remaining sane because it offered access to other lesbians. The festival has always been a place to renew bonds of love and friendship, as well as to replenish my lesbian energy.

I returned to school at the age of 38 to fulfill my dreams of being a veterinarian. I'll always continue my work with battered wimmin, the Michigan music festival, dancing, and learning the names of wildflowers I see on my nature walks. Being a lesbian has meant "coming home" and awakening my sense of spirituality. It has also meant finishing the process of learning to love myself, so that now I can embark on my lifetime commitment with my partner knowing I am truly capable of loving another fully.

71 & 72. ALIX DOBKIN

*W*hen I came out as a Lesbian in 1972 it felt just like coming Home. Since then my primary focus has been that of building a sweet, supportive and energizing environment for myself and my family, that is, the community of women in which I now thrive. For the past 15 of my 47 years Lesbian Feminism has been a challenge, a joy and an education beyond imagination. It has been a privilege to help construct the Woman-Identified Culture that sustains and enriches me, and that will continue to provide for future generations of women.

72. JULIE DOBKIN

I moved to San Francisco in 1981 to study massage and to leave my ex and my best friend, who had become lovers. We worked through a lot and they followed me out here. Now we're a close family, for which I'm especially grateful, as I've been mostly single since I came out in 1980. For more than 10 years before, I'd been bi-sexual. At 38, I feel very lucky to have found the life and work I have, being a masseuse and manager at Osento, a woman-only bathhouse in San Francisco. Participating in the healing arts is extremely satisfying as is helping Osento be the special place that it is. The more there is richness and beauty in my life, the more I'd like to express that. I also want to continue and grow in my support of native people's struggles for our mother earth.

My parents were and are progressive and enlightened people who taught us about the world in a way that helps us to understand and appreciate other people's oppressions as well as my own as a jewish lesbian (although sometimes a jewish lesbian in S.F. can forget for a minute). My family is a large part of my heart-life. Being an aunt is one of my greatest joys. About twice a year I visit my Pop and our whole *mishpucha* (extended family) in New York City. Working at the Michigan Womyn's Music Festival charges my

batteries for the whole year. I chose to become a lesbian because I need to be around women who put women first, and now it doesn't seem to be a choice anymore. As difficult as it is to feel truly connected with others in this world, I find more of a chance for understanding with women in general, and lesbians in particular.

73. MAXINE FELDMAN

I am a Jewish Lesbian who was born in Brooklyn in 1944 under the sign of Capricorn. All this means to me is that I am rich in my culture and pushy and proud. I've been a dyke all my life and came into my own in 1969 with the rebirth of the Lesbian and Gay Community. In California I co-founded the first Gay Activist Alliance on a junior college campus. The best accomplishment for me was putting out the first lesbian record, "Angry Atthis." To think about being part of the viable lesbian music industry, festivals, tours and concerts is one of my greatest pleasures. That I have worked hard as an activist, performer, and humorist for the past 18 years and almost made a living at it is a fantasy become reality. I ran my own coffee house, Oasis, in Boston for three years to help new performers get started and to give the ones who have been around as long as myself a place to experiment with new material. I feel my life as a lesbian has been truly blessed. Sure I've had some horror shows and plenty of battle scars, but I've gotten to travel all over, meet dykes everywhere, make new friends and share my hopes, dreams and future visions with them.

Today I'm taking very good care of Maxine. I am a compulsive overeater, a drug addict, and alcoholic. That I am now abstinent, sober and clean is the best gift I ever gave to this Jewish dyke. I'm now more concerned with the light in me than having the light on me. I'm on a new road with a lover who not only shares my addictions but my love of Judaism. I can look back and feel proud of my participation in our lesbian community. To see growth and change in myself and others is a gift not to be taken lightly. I love being a lesbian, I love being able to be myself anywhere, and most important I have learned to really love myself. Can't wait to be a part of what's next.

74. HAZELWITCH PRODUCTIONS

*H*azelwitch Productions consists of six volunteer producers with experience ranging from one to 12 years, assisted by dozens of other volunteers. Our goal is to produce high-quality events (women's music, drama, comedy, workshops, and films) that will empower individual lesbians and feminists in our community, and to provide the broader community with a nurturing space to enjoy women-identified culture with us. We also assist local groups (such as the women's center, NOW, peace groups, New Age groups) who want to learn to produce. Hazelwitch began producing in 1981, continuing a heritage of women's production companies in Houston that goes back to 1975.

74. GAIL ELDRIDGE

I am a survivor—of incest, chemical dependency, heterosexual marriage, my son's adolescence, anti-semitism, cancer, and an early woman's collective. I strive to act rather than react, to live rather than exist, to embrace change rather than resist—often with humor, sometimes with pain, always with interest. Putting my energy into women's culture is an empowering experience; my efforts are always magnified and transformed by the creative interchange of all involved.

74. SHERRY COLLIER

A festival-goer of many years, I embrace the opportunity to share the culture of womyn and enjoy this lovely planet together. I'm in the graphic arts trade by profession (finding it a beneficial skill for community work). I love our Earth Mother, seeking every occasion to explore Her beauty

and save Her from destruction. The lesbian community, with all its support and strife, love and power, is food for my soul, and I encourage others to work for our harmony. Blessed be!

74. JANICE A. REED

*F*or more than ten years I have been teaching young women and men skills in thinking and in communicating, tools to use in choosing responsibly and in living together peacefully. From each one I have taught, I have learned. I find my own direction that of becoming more honest and more loving. As a woman and as a lesbian, I notice myself expressing greater and greater self-love and building a stronger self-image; one that reflects woman's strength and goodness, her importance and her value. My choice to be lesbian has taken away nothing from others or from my love of all others. It is a choice that allows me greater breadth and depth in validating myself and those with whom I live.

74. CHERRY WOLF

*T*he aspects of my life that I value the most are honesty and creativity. Being self-employed has given me the freedom and independence to realize these qualities. At the moment, I operate two businesses—a carpentry/home repair business called Womanwork and a D.J. service called Soundscapes, Unlimited. Living honestly for me also involves being drug and alcohol free. This enables me to be in touch with my true feelings and experiences, and helps my growth as a person.

Being active in the lesbian/women's community has been an important part of my life for the last eight years. I focus on promoting and enhancing women's culture. I have been a member of Hazelwitch Productions for six years, and also co-host a three-hour women's radio program on KPFT, our local Pacifica station in Houston, Texas.

My life has been full of music. Sharing this part of me will always be my special contribution to the community and my family of friends.

74 & 76. POKEY ANDERSON

*F*or my first 22 years, I was certain I knew no lesbians. Finally, in 1972, two friends shattered the conspiracy of silence: "Pokey," said one, "we are lesbians." I came out a year later, and life was never quite the same after. Over the years, I have participated in lesbian-feminist concert productions, politics, publishing and broadcasting. The groups' names could easily make alphabet soup: IWY, HGPC, NOW, NGLTF, GRNL, PBT, OOPs, GLSH, WILD, HW, KPFT. I've worked with lesbian separatists and togetherists, with gay men in three-piece suits and those in feather boas. I have come to believe that our most powerful tool is truth—the diverse truths of our lives, shared. I have drawn much strength from the bravery and talent of the many women who have come before me. But what keeps me going is watching the truth, spoken from one heart to another, transform those who come after me.

75. LAURIE FUCHS

I'm a Jewish lesbian in my mid-30s. Like many women who work full-time in women's music and culture, my work is a big chunk of my life. In 1976 (one year after coming out, with all that "newly come out" energy), I started Ladyslipper, with a vision of uncovering, collecting in one place, and making available to other interested folks, a comprehensive body of musical work recorded by women. That has become closer to reality than anyone expected! The Ladyslipper Catalog, from which individuals, stores, schools and libraries may read about and purchase recordings, now contains more than 2000 titles. I'm glad that in the beginning I gave no consideration to how much work this might entail, or how big Ladyslipper as an organization might become, or how much

would be required in terms of business savvy, capital, financial risk, and other details! I feel proud to be part of an effort that supports the versatility and beauty of the musical accomplishments of women. And I'm thrilled that much of this is finally being archived by libraries who acquire large portions of the catalog. I personally love our feminist, lesbian, instrumental and international offerings. Other aspects of my work that give me satisfaction are putting out quality recordings as a small record label, doing graphics, and friendships with other women involved in this women's music and culture network.

To help keep my life in balance, I live on 13 acres, 26 miles from my job, with my lover of seven years, two Siberian Huskies, one kitty (all female), two stuffed lesbian lions named Pleasant and Agreeable... and an ever-changing front-yard view of blue herons, egrets, ducks, turtles and other wild creatures. Watching them, and hearing the waterfall fall, places it all in some necessary perspective.

77. KATE CLINTON

*F*or eight years before I began acting funny full-time, I was a high school English teacher. That hones your skills. If you can keep a class of kids in remedial English interested during 8th period on a Friday afternoon in the spring, you can do anything. I love making people laugh. My work as a fumerist, feminist humorist, is two-fold—fuming at those things that oppress women and celebrating our lives as a way to end that oppression. Since my work is toward ending the oppression of women, it looks like I'll have a job for a few more years.

78 & 79. BODEN SANDSTROM

A New York state 1950s super achiever, I grew up trying hard to live up to my potential, but I always felt insecure and confused—being a woman then was always second best. I loved music (French horn) and horseback riding most of all. I probably would have become a conductor, but I had no role models so instead I became a librarian—nice but unfulfilled. I grew as much as possible in left wing politics, but was still insecure. Being with women in feminism started my energy and I became a complete person when I became a lesbian in the 1970s. Being with lesbians gave me the support and strength to get back to music and showed me the way to being a sound engineer, which is my art. I started Woman Sound in 1975 with Casse Culver, and it later became City Sound Productions. City Sound now does many major shows and concerts in D.C. and is one of the most well known and respected companies in the area. This year I was honored to be in *Mix Magazine* in an article on women sound engineers.

In my work I've always been out, which has only helped me gain clients. In order to fulfill one's innermost capabilities, I believe one must be a whole person and must never hide.

80. CASSELBERRY–DUPREÉ

*E*volutionary, fun, profound, free, strong, ethical, spiritual, universal, vivacious, philosophical—oral tradition woven together tapestries of sound.

81 & 84. STORMÉ DELARVERIÉ

*S*tormé DeLarverié is featured in a new film by Michelle Parkerson, *Stormé: The Lady of the Jewel Box*. This is Michelle's description of Stormé: "She's 66 years old and doing well as a bodyguard in New York City. She's full of show biz lore and a lot of streetwise knowledge. Her father was white, her mother was Black and she grew up in New Orleans in the 20s. Stormé was a male impersonator with the Jewel Box Revue in the 1950s and 1960s. She was the company's emcee and only woman. It was a lavish show on the level of the Folies Bergère. Fabulous costumes, wonderful set design, original music, comedy. It was the first successful touring show of female impersonators in American history. It was composed of white,

Black, Hispanic and Native American performers when segregation was still the word. Just imagine taking a touring company of female impersonators by car across the country, through the South. Being stopped on highways by state troopers because they were a mixed group. And then they find out the person driving the convertible is, in fact, a woman dressed as a man and in the car are Blacks and whites. It was way out!"

82, 83 & 84. MICHELLE PARKERSON

*G*enerations of Black women did what they had to do to make it possible for me to do what I do best. Communication is what I'm after: film, writing, performance and, ultimately, the public forum. What matters is, in some form or fashion, to move, disturb, affect people to struggle for change. I am 34. At 19, I discovered my love and lust for women. Since then, I have nurtured the passion. As a Black Lesbian, I am equally proud of my gayness and my African American heritage. I am blessed to have the enduring support of my family, my lover and an extended family of gay women and men. I will take care of my blessings in the face of rampant racism, sexism and homophobia, in the shadow of AIDS. Political commitment fuels my work, informs my dealings in the world. In 1977 I came out. In 1986, I became co-chair of the National Coalition of Black Lesbians and Gays. In that decade, my understanding of what being a Lesbian is all about has expanded. Beyond butch/femme roles, beyond radical separatism, women who love women have a larger sense of the female Self manifest in every man, woman and child. We find emotional and metaphysical power in bonding with women.

Other than that, I'm just trying to make it from day to day.

85. KAREN THOMPSON

It's ironic that people now consider me to be a lesbian feminist activist. Yet, before the accident in which Sharon was severely disabled, I didn't really understand what any of that meant. I also didn't understand about sexism, racism, ableism, militarism, ageism, classism, or homophobia. I didn't understand that they are all interconnected or even begin to question who they benefited. I didn't understand that if I didn't stand up for someone's rights today, then tomorrow Sharon's and mine might be stripped away. I have come to realize how our system oppresses anyone who is different. Our choices are to remain helpless and powerless or turn that energy into a positive outlet by taking action. Through the pain that Sharon and I have experienced, I am hopeful that others will learn how to protect themselves and will become active in the many struggles for human rights.

86. URVASHI VAID

For me there is no separation between political action and daily life. I work in a wide range of movements because as an Indian woman, an immigrant, a lesbian and a leftist, my identity is not single-issue. As a lawyer I have worked for prisoners' rights and gay and lesbian civil rights. Currently, I am responsible for public education and media relations for the National Gay and Lesbian Task Force.

87. JENIFER FIRESTONE AND SUE HYDE

Jenifer Firestone is a social worker, jock, political activist, homemaker, and relational visionary. Jenifer tours with the *Ten Percent Revue*, a musical celebration of life in the queer lane. Sue Hyde is a transplanted Midwestern political activist and cook. She works for the National Gay and Lesbian Task Force organizing for sodomy law reform in the 25 states that still criminalize gay and lesbian sexuality.

To move out into the world from the safe harbor of a lover's arms, to provide that safety even when it means a move away. That's what we're about. Struggling to go beyond established models that cramp and distort our ambitions for family, community and intimacy with women who are important to us. We recognize that our individual destinies are distinct from but as important as the one we share together. We hope the world is not the same place in our wakes as it was before we sailed through it. We ourselves, in strict adherence to the laws of the universe, have lost no energy and transformed each other, down to our last atoms. We take as our watchwords vision and ecstasy.

88. NAN D. HUNTER

Nan D. Hunter grew up in a small town in North Carolina and now, much to her amazement, lives in Greenwich Village.

88. ABBY R. RUBENFELD

Since January 1983, I have been Legal Director of Lambda Legal Defense and Education Fund, the oldest and largest lesbian/gay rights legal organization in the country. Before that I was in private practice in Nashville, Tennessee for several years. I am presently the Chair of the American Bar Association's Committee on the Rights of Gay people, a subgroup of the Section on Individual Rights and Responsibilities. I am the coordinator of the National Lesbian/Gay Civil Rights Roundtable, which brings together lesbian and gay litigators and political leaders from all over the country to strategize on sodomy law reform, AIDS issues, and lesbian/gay rights generally. It is important to me to be able to be open about my lesbianism in all aspects of my life, and I am honored to be able to work full-time on behalf of our rights. In the face of the devastation of AIDS, it is comforting to know that our movement continues and that we have the power to keep going.

In my "spare" time, I play rugby, which I love. I have been in a wonderful relationship with Meryl C. Friedman, the co-founder of the Gay Teachers Association, for three and one-half years, although my work intensity constantly threatens even her gentle, persistent understanding and support. I have a dog, Buckwheat, who is very important to me. I consider myself a Southerner and love the South. I love my work.

89. DEBORAH JONES

Among other things I am a sculptor, mask maker, teacher and performer. I am single, forty-seven years old, and have been lesbian since high school, which has given me a valuable perspective on the world. My most difficult achievement and cherished goal is being me, that is, expressing and accepting all aspects of myself. For me to acknowledge some of my less admirable traits is like going over the fence at the Seneca Army Depot only much scarier. The truly personal is always political.

90. BRENDA CRUMLEY

Currently, I am a Staff Sergeant with the Ohio Air National Guard working in Law Enforcement and Security Police. I believe in working with the current system toward a more egalitarian state and I think change is possible in this country. Now I'm also a teaching assistant at Ohio State University going for my Master's degree in sociology. In between that and time on the base, I'm an apprentice in a lesbian carpentry business. I like to work with my hands, but the most rewarding work I've ever done was the three years I worked with children with disabilities in a residential facility. I like camping outdoors, riding my motorcycle, playing piano and taking care of my pets.

I'm in recovery from alcohol and drug addiction. December 1984 is my sobriety date and in 1985 I was willing to admit I was gay and not bisexual. Alcohol and drugs are a large problem in the gay community. We can't claim our own power while being addicted. I'm twenty-four years old and joined the Guard in 1984. I've extended my service to September 1991 but I might go on active duty so I can qualify for money to finish my education and a Veterans' Administration loan to buy a house. It was a difficult decision for me to state openly that I am a lesbian because of the military. But I decided that nothing they could do would change who I am or what I am. I know that I do have a support system behind me. And if I'm willing to say who I am, maybe other lesbians will be willing to say who they are. There is strength in unity. True strength comes, not from physical force, but from being able to feel what you feel and honor how you feel about yourself.

91 & 92. JEAN GROSSHOLTZ

My life is wonderful, exciting and rich with friends, ideas and fun. I am 58 years old, a revolutionary, a lesbian, a political activist, a teacher, and pitcher on the premier women's softball team of Western Massachusetts, The Hot Flashes. I have been struggling for peace and justice since I was 12 years old and I do not intend to die until we get it. I have traveled extensively on the Indian subcontinent and in Southeast Asia, and have written books and articles about Asian politics. I have met many women working for peace and justice, learning to resist injustice in themselves and their lives, and making alliances with other women. Knowing these women in the United States and abroad, I know we will figure out how to save ourselves, the planet, and the people of the world from the mad men who control it.

I have been a lesbian all my life. I love women and have been loved by some wondrous women. And I am both envious and proud of the young women I teach who fall in and out of love, dance and sing and carry on with women right here on this campus. I like to think that I had something to do with that and I like to know that the fear and pain of living in the closet is on the way to extinction. I have been teaching politics for 25 years and I am proud that many of my students are political activists on the front lines. But I do not think that the political, economic or educational institutions of this country will ever work for women or justice. I think that anything decent in this country was won in the streets by people unwilling to accept injustice. That's where we all need to be.

93. RENEE C. HANOVER

*R*etired from work but not from life—I'm a political radical, activist, old, Jewish, (grand)mother, lesbian lawyer. My life has been productive and helpful to others, especially those oppressed by the status quo. A poverty background has been the most meaningful influence in my life. Political and community activity is meaningless unless those most oppressed give guidance and leadership. After helping to organize Local 65 in New York City, I went to Chiago as a member of the Communist Party underground in the 1940s. In the 1950s I fought McCarthyism and initiated the first "wade-in" against racial segregation on Chicago beaches. In the 1960s, I helped to start the Gay Liberation Front, joined the Women's Liberation Movement, and was the first out lesbian attorney in the country to represent lesbian and gay clients and issues in Chicago and from the District of Columbia to California. I'm glad I have never been a fence-sitter and have been involved in the progressive movements that have touched my life. My positive influence on others and their pride in me gives me comfort.

94. LESLIE CAGAN

*D*uring more than 20 years of full-time political activism in the justice and peace movement, I have grown to appreciate the difficulty of building coalitions, as well as the urgent need for such alliances. Many of my energies have gone into mass mobilizations and protest activities. While the internal dynamics of the coalitions that organize these events are usually difficult (at best), there is nothing that quite matches the feeling of tens and hundreds of thousands of people marching in the streets, Being at the core of such activities has been energizing and challenging, and being an out lesbian always adds another dimension. The level of homophobia and sexism in the peace and justice movement is certainly less than it was 15 years ago, although it remains alarmingly high.

Through the years I have heard complaints of burn-out, a concept that is alien to me. For sure, I get tired and even discouraged from time to time. But a few weeks in the sun usually re-fires me. The real source of my continued energy comes from knowing that throughout this nation and around the world there are women and men struggling for their most basic rights, for a world truly with justice and at peace. Whenever we find ourselves in struggle—for money for AIDS, for an end to U.S. intervention, against racist violence, for full reproductive freedom for all women—there is hope. Whenever we come together in large numbers—respecting our differences while finding our unity—there is power. Whenever we bring our full selves into common effort with others, we see a future.

95. BARBARA DEMING

*B*arbara Deming was born in 1917 in New York City and died in 1984 in Florida. Throughout her life, from the civil rights and anti-war movements of the 1960s to the feminist and lesbian movements of the 1980s, Barbara's commitment was to struggle against violence wherever she found it, in a way that was not itself violent. Barbara wrote: "Every human being deserves respect. We assert the respect due ourselves, when it is denied, through noncooperation; we assert the respect due all others, through our refusal to be violent. But how can we communicate the power there is in acting out truth, if we give the impression of not daring to be truthful to ourselves—about our own deep feelings; not daring to respect them? ...Back in my twenties (which was in the 1930s) I was keeping a journal, and I wrote in the journal, 'I am a lesbian; I must face this truth.' Then rereading my journal a few days later, I thought, 'Gosh, I shouldn't have that down here in black and white. Someone might read it.' So I took my scissors and cut out that sentence and tossed it in the wastepaper basket. Perhaps half an hour later, as I was moving around the room, I glanced down and there, glaring up at me most conspicuously from the wastepaper basket, was this cut-out sentence. And I remember that it hit me: you can't throw truths away. If you try to throw them away, you get into worse trouble than the trouble you were trying to escape." [Excerpts from "On Anger" in *We Are All Part of One Another*, Jane Meyerding, editor, and *Reweaving the Web of Life*, Pam McAllister, editor. See also *Prisons That Could Not Hold* by Barbara Deming.]

95. BLUE LUNDEN

I'm 51 years old and live in community with three other lesbians in the Florida Keys. I've been a lesbian all my life. I left home and joined the resistance in the gay bars of New Orleans when I was 16. Being a butch, I was frequently arrested for "wearing the clothes of the opposite sex." I now recognize this as my earliest act of civil disobedience.

I spent 25 years in New York City raising a daughter, getting sober, becoming an activist and doing community building. I came to the Florida Keys to live closer to the earth so I might develop my spiritual life, and most of all, because Barbara

Deming was here and she was a crone, a guru, a shaman, a witch, a priestess, a saint. Being with her evoked the best parts of me that I was trying to become. When she died almost three years ago, I was reeling with grief, felt I'd lost not only her dear presence but the way to that best self I was learning to become. She said, "I won't lose you when I die and I won't leave you when I die," and I know it's so. Her spirit is strong in me—"we are all part of one another"—and my Croning is scheduled for September.

96. MARY C. MORGAN

*B*efore becoming a judge, I was a family law specialist. In the late 1970s, I successfully defended lesbian mother Jeanne Jullion's right to have custody of her son. Now my partner Roberta Achtenberg, who is the directing attorney of the Lesbian Rights Project, and I have a two-year-old child.

In 1981, I was the first open lesbian appointed to the bench. I am now the presiding judge of the Municipal Court in San Francisco. I also teach at San Francisco's Judicial College in a continuing education program for lawyers. The subject of homosexuality usually doesn't come up in these classes, but I'm well known as a lesbian and I feel it is important for me to have visibility in the judiciary. It breaks down people's stereotypes to know there are people just like them who are lesbian. But when considering lesbian and gay rights, we must protect those of us who are the most vulnerable, not just those who can assimilate and pass. I want people to know I'm a lesbian, but I can't stand it when the only thing they know is that I'm a lesbian. For fun, I like to scuba dive.

97. DALE MCCORMICK

*A*t 40 years old, I love my life, and feel incredibly fortunate to have political activism, a supportive gay and straight community surrounding me, a healthy and satisfying relationship with the woman I love, a job where I am free to be myself (usually!?) and about the most wonderful cat in the world. Of course, it wasn't easy and it hasn't always been this way. I always knew that I was lesbian, but didn't come out until I was 18 when I slept with my best friend. A forced psychiatric visit or two later, several years of silence between me and my family, and years of inner turmoil led me to come to grips with who I am and to be proud of myself. I am a carpenter by trade, was one of the first women to earn a journeyman's card in this country, and have had my own construction business. My books on carpentry and home repair (including *Against the Grain*) have helped empower hundreds of women.

Politically, I have moved from working in the peace movement during the 1960s to being active in Democratic politics as an "out" lesbian in this rural state. When I decided to run for delegate to the Democratic National Convention and say the "L" and the "G" words in my campaign literature, a lot of people told me I was crazy, but I won! The thing I am most proud of is the Maine Lesbian and Gay Political Alliance (MLGPA). We started as a tiny organization fueled largely by my campaign and the tragic death of a gay man in Bangor, Maine. About 20 gay men and lesbians have made the MLGPA one of the most effective and respected political organizations in the state. My dream is to be elected to the state legislature; actually, my lover and I often fantasize about "job-sharing" the position of Governor. As soon as we finish building our new house, we'll get started on it.

98. GWENN CRAIG

I became involved in the Lesbian and Gay Movement during the tumultuous times that saw Anita Bryant's anti-gay campaign making headlines and the first gay rights ordinance go down to defeat in Dade County, Florida. I'd dabbled in the late '60s student movement, especially getting Black Studies courses at my Catholic women's college in Chicago. And I had grown up in Atlanta

during the heyday of the civil rights movement. But the clincher was coming to San Francisco, too late for the hippie movement, but just in time to meet Harvey Milk, become his campaign volunteer and then his friend, and be inspired by his simple message: come out, learn to love one another, and learn to use our political voices, form coalitions and gain power to make change.

I was a "late bloomer," only coming out in 1975 when I was 24. By 1977, I was being quoted in newspaper articles and featured on television as a "gay leader"; by 1978 I was running the "No on 6" campaign (along with Bill Kraus) to fight the witchhunt against lesbian and gay school workers; in 1979 I was elected citywide to a local Democratic party position, having run as an open lesbian; in 1980 I was an elected delegate to my first Democratic National Convention; from 1981 until 1983 I was president of the leading gay political group in San Francisco; and by 1984 I was co-chair of a national lesbian and gay political organization. Today, I get to merge my political commitment and interests with my work life, as grants director at Vanguard Public Foundation, a progressive funder of grassroots groups doing community organizing to bring about social change on all fronts. I still am active with the Harvey Milk Lesbian and Gay Democratic Club and I've been on the board of the Lesbian Rights Project for nearly a decade. What a decade it's been. And in 1968, I had thought I'd be a music major and embark on a singing career. Now my 17-year-old daughter wants to major in performing arts at UCLA and become a star on the musical stage. Who knows?

99. KATHLEEN NICHOLS

*T*here are two "lesbian out front" activities of which I am most proud. I was the first open lesbian elected to public office in Wisconsin. I was also the chairperson of the Governor's Council on Lesbian and Gay Issues for four years. This special executive body focused on making certain that our state's gay rights law was obeyed and on convincing the gay and lesbian citizens of Wisconsin that we might use the unique civil rights protections we have. I am 35, first generation Irish-American, a classical lapsed Catholic and originally a working-class girl with the vocabulary of a pedant. I was a "lipstick lesbian" after it stopped being "femme," but a long time before it ceased to be a treasonable offense. I have been an activist for 15 years and have held political office for almost six. Aside from lesbian and gay issues, I concentrate my political energy on services for people who are disabled or chemically dependent. My lover, Cristina Martinez, grew up in Chicago and as a result has an instinctual aversion to politics. But she loves me anyway.

99. TAMMY S.G. BALDWIN

*L*ooking back over my first term in public office, I am most grateful to those before me who made it easier for me to hold office as an openly gay woman. I was 24 years old when I won a seat on the Dane County Board of Supervisors. Three months later I was appointed to fill a vacancy on the Madison City Council. As a local elected official, I have concentrated my energies on human services and civil rights issues. I juggle my political life with my studies at the University of Wisconsin Law School, and eventually hope to be employed full-time in the political arena.

I've always felt that strong women role models have played an important part in the development of my sense of pride and confidence as a lesbian and a feminist. My grandmother Doris, my mother Pam, and the dynamic women I met during my four years at Smith College have all provided inspiration and support. In my spare time I can usually be found playing volleyball, pinochle, or spending time with my cat Katie.

99. KAREN CLARK

*D*aughter of tenant farmers in Rock County, Minnesota, I earned my college degree in nursing and moved to South Minneapolis in

1967. Twenty years later, I'm serving my fourth term in the Minnesota House of Representatives representing a core city district—something I'd never have predicted. I grew my politics in the anti-war and civil rights movements of the 1960s, and the feminist and lesbian/gay movements of the 1970s, and honed them into a neighborhood-based platform of economic and social justice that was the basis for my first election in 1980. Some of my major legislative work has been in affordable child care and housing, human rights and workers' rights issues, and in linking these to national issues of peace and justice by working on economic conversion and Central America issues.

Friends and family are more important to me now than ever, and seeking a balanced, holistic life is my primary challenge. I'd love to give up my claim to being the *only* open lesbian currently elected to a state legislature. I hope that more open lesbian and gay people will seek public office in the future and I stand ready to encourage and support them.

100 & 101. VIRGINIA "GINNY" APUZZO

I am the Deputy Executive Director of the New York State Consumer Protection Board, Governor Cuomo's Liaison to the Lesbian and Gay Community, and Vice Chair of the Governor's AIDS Advisory Council.

I think ours is an extremely courageous community and I am proud to be a part of it. The courage of the women and men I meet is an abiding source of strength. It is the source of the passion in my life and my work. Ours is a courage that has come from having known fear and tasted freedom. The taste of that freedom must continue to fire our passion for possibility. The greater our possibilities, the greater the cost of our pursuit.

102. JOYCE NEWSTAT

I am a 29-year-old loud, proud, pushy Jewish dyke. I came out when I was 20 years old as the product of an introduction to feminism class. Since then, my major challenge has been to incorporate political life into my personal life. My lover, friends and family keep me strong. They have taught me integrity and the importance of being a visible lesbian. Mostly, my best friend and lover, Katherine, keeps me inspired.

102. KATHERINE ALFIERI

I am a 26-year-old Italian Lesbian Feminist. I came out in March of 1983—met Joyce three weeks later and we have been inseparable ever since. The strength of our relationship and commitment to having children provide me with a constant source of strength in the midst of the legal world I am about to enter. As an attorney, I will work in the public interest to advocate for those whose voices have not yet been heard.

59 & 105. JEB (JOAN E. BIREN)

*T*here are too few lesbians from the past whose names we can call and even fewer whose images we can conjure up in our mind's eye. I have tried here to honor a small number of the many of us who are making a way as lesbians today. In part, this is so that future generations will have a fuller knowledge of those who came before them. It is also for us to have a more complete visual record of ourselves in the present. In this look at contemporary lesbian life in the U.S., there is obviously much that is missing. Perhaps you would like to see more lesbians in business suits or more lesbians making love. I am willing to work very hard to make an image that I think we need to have, but I can't always find what I am looking for. So if you are a lesbian and if you feel that you are not reflected in these pages, think about having me with my camera at your workplace or in your bedroom.

2025 Update: I make fewer new images these days. I am advocating for lesbian and queer photography to embrace all of us. If you want to let me know who you think is missing or underrepresented in media today, you can write to me at: jebmedia@hotmail.com. I would also like to hear what you think about this book.

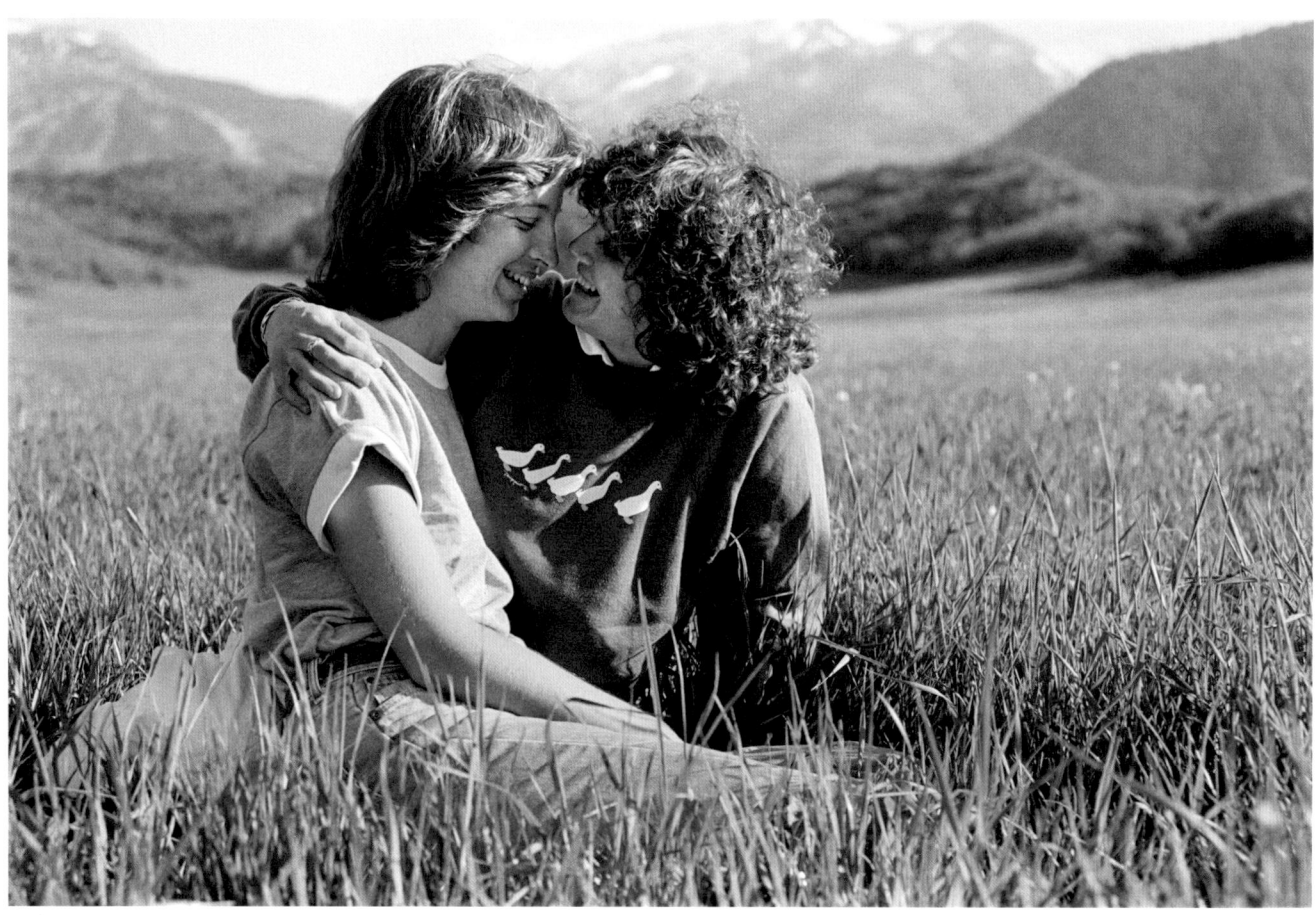

104

104. Dr. Nanette Gartrell and Dr. Dee Mosbacher share a tender moment together vacationing in Snowmass, Colorado, 1984.

Afterword

I have been looking at Lesbians since this book was originally published in 1987. A mad, muddy nine-year-old watching Lesbians roam through craft fairs, braided tails swaying back and forth on the bridge of their backs, arm in arm with leather jackets tightly locking in. Me, silently meditating on where I would fit, feeling time shift, framed by structured glasses and sensible shoes. Lesbians teaching the rituals of sport to the squeak of waxed gym floors, and checking my ID with t-shirt sleeves and dark blue jeans that had matching folds. I have been watching Lesbians from building worlds together to tearing them apart. I have been watching them make their way around visibility and invisibility. In moments of community, complication, and divide. I have been watching myself in the mirror, finding my own place, digging in, and hiding behind it.

This work. An archive of Lesbians being, in joy. Being in love. Being in labor. Being in light and dark. The pure contrast of blacks and whites calls upon times of struggle, defeat, and triumph. But also the gray of in-between. When our hearts are big but fragmented. When our love is tender and our bodies grow. When the human forms in this book are a breath of the air before I was visible. The ones who guided me through and into being "out front." The ones who stood on the stage. Who showed up to work, and who showed up for the future.

This book is a light to rekindle in 2025. I look straight at it. And then when I close my eyes, their bodies collage around me like a deep embrace. The kisses and whispers and simple smiles that gently interweave into my own. The hymns of intersectionality that resonate through my every pore. The book is full of people I know and don't know, and who represent others born since. New ones who dance in the disco all night long and chant until their voices break, and who sit at the river and watch one lonely leaf float past. The ones who work until two beads of sweat roll down to their side and into the top of their jeans, and the ones who have paint on their fingers while they drive to the beach. This book is freedom from judgment or criticism of what is or isn't. Photos that hold a moment that is nothing but true. No comment section. Just living is power.

In 2021, the re-release of JEB's *Eye to Eye* brought us back to a celebration of being seen. That gaze of "before," cemented in compositions that allowed us all to breathe with each turn of the page or tap on the screen. Those moments that could have been lost to the future, but gratefully, JEB was there with a camera. And in the twenty-first century, the dyke technology timeline was full of flashbacks. For a brief moment, as we were entranced with the consistent rhythm of the scroll, we briefly found ourselves in pause, drifting off to when the quiet was quieter and bodies were bodies without comment. We grabbed onto the notion that the physicality of a film camera and the intention of looking at Lesbians could transform us. Through postures bent from falling into phones and protests turned into infographics, we looked to each other once again, and for those moments, we shared that feeling of our chests lifting, looking up and out.

Now JEB comes back when we need more perspective, the rhythm of remembering. One book is just one, but two is a pulse. The re-release of *Making A Way* gives us new life with the further notion that we aren't going and haven't gone. We can and will go. Anywhere. With anyone. I recommend sitting outside with your copy. One breath per image and sharing a moment with the bodies who shaped the space you get to sit in right now. Who opened a world to me, where I could get on stage and be seen, with all the Lesbians collaged around me like a deep embrace. Working toward a world in which it is enough just to be.

JD Samson
2024

INDEX

The numbers below refer to both the statements in the "Speak Out" section and to the photographs in the book, which are numbered consecutively. The "Speak Out" section statements are in the order in which the women are listed in the captions.

INDEX

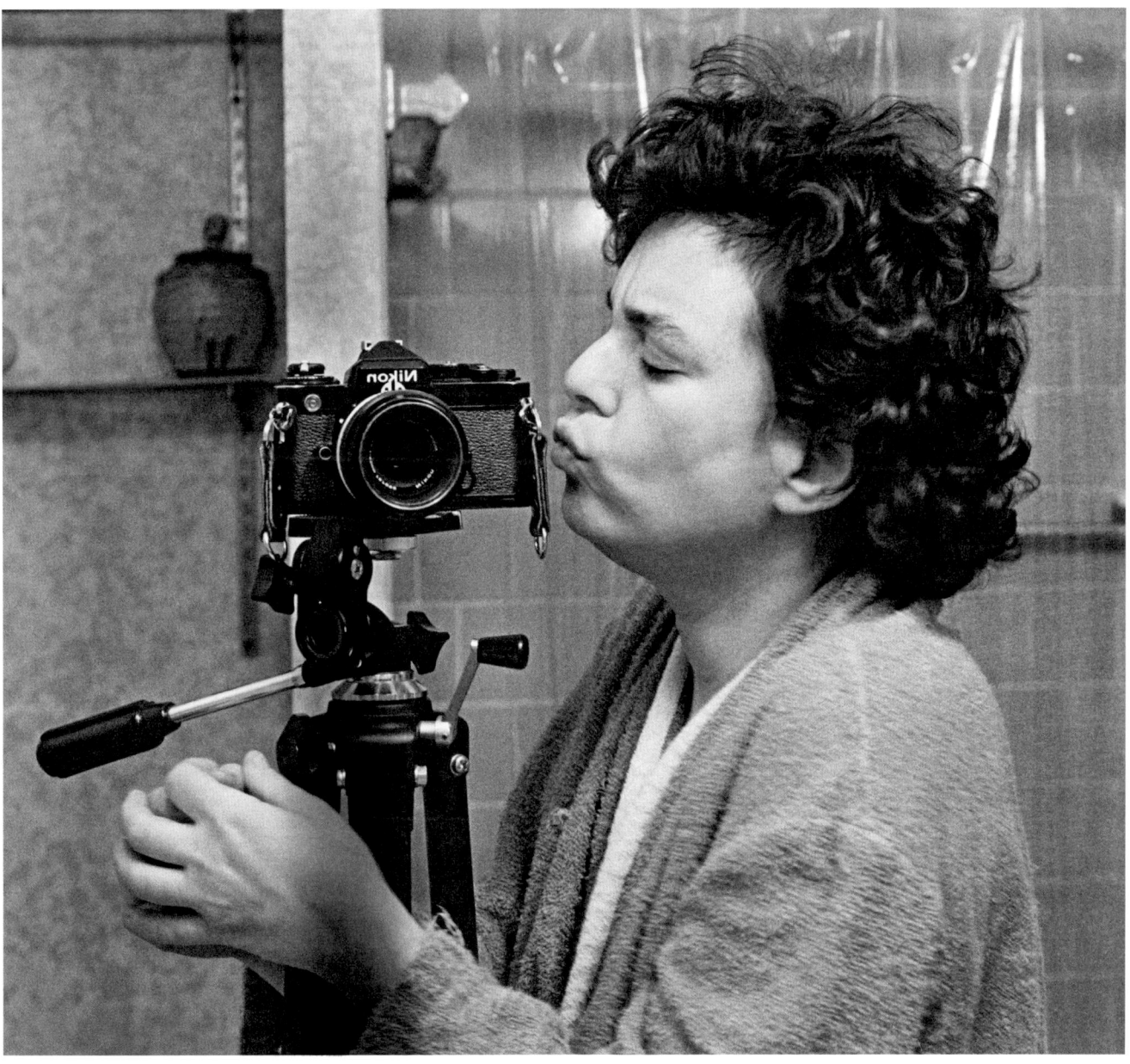

105

105. I love photographing lesbians.
Self-portrait kissing my camera
in the bathroom of my home in
Washington, D.C., 1981.